D1025317

# Deregulating the Public Service

*Can Government Be Improved?*

John J. DiIulio, Jr.
*Editor*

The Brookings Institution
*Washington, D.C.*

UNIVERSITY LIBRARY
Lethbridge, Alberta

*Copyright © 1994 by*

THE BROOKINGS INSTITUTION

*1775 Massachusetts Avenue, N.W., Washington, D.C. 20036*

*All rights reserved*

*Library of Congress Cataloging-in-Publication Data*

Deregulating the public service : can government be improved /
[edited by] John J. DiIulio, Jr.
    p. cm.
    Includes bibliographical references and index.
    ISBN 0-8157-1854-3 (cl)  —  ISBN 0-8157-1853-5 (pa)
    1. Civil service reform—United States. 2. Public administration—United States.
3. Bureaucracy—United States. 4. Decentralization in government—United States.
5. Administrative agencies—United States—Management.  I. DiIulio, John J., Jr.
  JK692.D47    1994
  350.4'0973—dc20                                    93-40348
                                                      CIP

9 8 7 6 5 4 3 2 1

The paper in this publication meets the minimum requirements of the American National
Standard for Information Sciences—Permanence of Paper for Printed Library Materials,
ANSI Z39.48-1984

# ₿ THE BROOKINGS INSTITUTION

The Brookings Institution is an independent organization devoted to nonpartisan research, education, and publication in economics, government, foreign policy, and the social sciences generally. Its principal purposes are to aid in the development of sound public policies and to promote public understanding of issues of national importance.

The Institution was founded on December 8, 1927, to merge the activities of the Institute for Government Research, founded in 1916, the Institute of Economics, founded in 1922, and the Robert Brookings Graduate School of Economics and Government, founded in 1924.

The Board of Trustees is responsible for the general administration of the Institution, while the immediate direction of the policies, program, and staff is vested in the President, assisted by an advisory committee of the officers and staff. The by-laws of the Institution state: "It is the function of the Trustees to make possible the conduct of scientific research, and publication, under the most favorable conditions, and to safeguard the independence of the research staff in the pursuit of their studies and in the publication of the results of such studies. It is not a part of their function to determine, control, or influence the conduct of particular investigations or the conclusions reached."

The President bears final responsibility for the decision to publish a manuscript as a Brookings book. In reaching his judgment on the competence, accuracy, and objectivity of each study, the President is advised by the director of the appropriate research program and weighs the views of a panel of expert outside readers who report to him in confidence on the quality of the work. Publication of a work signifies that it is deemed a competent treatment worthy of public consideration but does not imply endorsement of conclusions or recommendations.

The Institution maintains its position of neutrality on issues of public policy in order to safeguard the intellectual freedom of the staff. Hence interpretations or conclusions in Brookings publications should be understood to be solely those of the authors and should not be attributed to the Institution, to its trustees, officers, or other staff members, or to the organizations that support its research.

*Board of Trustees*

John C. Whitehead
*Chairman*

Leonard Abraham
Ronald J. Arnault
Elizabeth E. Bailey
Rex J. Bates
A. W. Clausen
John L. Clendenin
Kenneth W. Dam
D. Ronald Daniel
Walter Y. Elisha

Stephen Friedman
William H. Gray III
Teresa Heinz
F. Warren Hellman
Samuel Hellman
James A. Johnson
Thomas W. Jones
Vernon E. Jordan, Jr.
James A. Joseph
Nannerl O. Keohane
Martin J. Koldyke

Thomas G. Labrecque
Donald F. McHenry
Bruce K. MacLaury
Constance Berry Newman
Maconda Brown O'Connor
Samuel Pisar
David Rockefeller, Jr.
Howard D. Samuel
Ralph S. Saul
Robert H. Smith
John D. Zeglis
Ezra K. Zilkha

*Honorary Trustees*

Vincent M. Barnett, Jr.
Barton M. Biggs
Louis W. Cabot
Edward W. Carter
Frank T. Cary
William T. Coleman, Jr.
Lloyd N. Cutler
Bruce B. Dayton
Douglas Dillon
Charles W. Duncan, Jr.
Robert F. Erburu

Robert D. Haas
Andrew Heiskell
Roger W. Heyns
Roy M. Huffington
James T. Lynn
William McC. Martin, Jr.
Robert S. McNamara
Mary Patterson McPherson
Arjay Miller
Donald S. Perkins

J. Woodward Redmond
Charles W. Robinson
James D. Robinson III
Robert V. Roosa
B. Francis Saul II
Henry B. Schacht
Gerard C. Smith
Robert Brookings Smith
Morris Tanenbaum
James D. Wolfensohn

# Foreword

REFORMING THE PUBLIC SERVICE and making government more responsive and efficient has in the past decade become a topic of continuing interest. This interest culminated in reports by three national commissions: the National Commission on the Public Service, led by Paul A. Volcker, former chairman of the Federal Reserve System, in 1989; the National Commission on the State and Local Public Service, led by William F. Winter, former governor of Mississippi, in 1993; and the National Performance Review, led by Vice President Al Gore in 1993.

These reports called for deregulating the public service by reducing the number and complexity of personnel and procurement regulations under which most federal, state, and local government bureaucracies operate. In this book John J. DiIulio, Jr., and the other contributors examine the problems and prospects of public service deregulation at each level of government, across levels of government, and within particular service sectors. Deregulating the public service, they emphasize, is no magic cure for the long-standing ills of government administration in the United States. But it does represent the best available strategy for improving government performance and renewing public trust in our nation's federal, state, and local civil service systems and administrative practices.

For much of its history the Brookings Institution has been a leader in expanding knowledge about public management. With this volume and other recent books on public administration, it is proud to continue this tradition.

John J. DiIulio, Jr., is professor of politics and public affairs at Princeton University and nonresident senior fellow at Brookings. He and the contributors would like to thank Thomas Mann, director of Brookings Governmental Studies program, for supervising the project. Jim Schneider edited the manuscript; Alison Rimsky, David Bearce, and Laura Kelly verified its factual content; Cynthia Terrels provided word processing assistance; Susan Woollen prepared it for typesetting; and Julia Petrakis compiled the index.

Funding for this project was provided by The Lynde and Harry Bradley Foundation.

The views expressed here are those of the authors and should not be ascribed to the trustees, officers, or staff members of the Brookings Institution.

BRUCE K. MAC LAURY
*President*

*Washington, D.C.*
*December 1993*

# Contents

# Introduction: Democracy and Public Service

## Paul A. Volcker and William F. Winter

AS THE CHAIRPERSONS of two recent national commissions assessing America's public service, we are keenly aware of the need to make government at all levels more responsive, accountable, and cost-effective. The question, however, is what, if anything, can be done to achieve this elusive goal?

In 1989 the National Commission on the Public Service, popularly known as the Volcker commission, issued its report, *Leadership for America: Rebuilding the Public Service.* Focusing on the federal service, its recommendations ranged from providing more competitive pay, which would better reflect conditions in the marketplace, to making greater efforts to decentralize personnel management, which would allow agency heads the flexibility they need. Running through all the proposals was a common thread: much more attention must be paid to nurturing the pride and competence of men and women willing to devote themselves to careers in public service. And one important element of that approach was to reverse the trend toward using more and more political appointees who typically stay in government for only two or three years (and often have equally short time horizons in their policy and administrative decisions).

Several of the commission's recommendations have received favorable action. To take one limited example, the call for a more flexible civil service administration was answered in legislation that made it possible to pay federal employees who work in high-cost or labor-short areas of the country more than employees of the same personnel grade who work in less costly or less competitive areas. Also, a general realignment of salaries for senior civil service personnel went a long way toward rewarding public managers for assuming greater responsibility.

But for every small step forward, obstacles to additional progress remain. The Bush administration proved unable to restrain the proliferation of political appointees, and the early evidence with respect to the new administration is no better. Faced with the necessity of reducing the national deficit, the Clinton administration has chosen to freeze pay and limit future salary increases, undercutting the earlier pay reforms. Clearly, the National Performance Review, headed by Vice President Gore, faces challenges as enormous as those encountered by the Commission on Organization of the Executive Branch of the Government (the second Hoover commission, 1953–55).[1]

The National Commission on the State and Local Public Service, widely referred to as the Winter commission, picked up where the Volcker commission left off. Its 1993 report, *Hard Truths/Tough Choices: An Agenda for State and Local Reform*, found that the public service problems identified by the Volcker commission were even more rife in state and local governments: workers demoralized by the politicization of the bureaucracy, a loss of public trust, and a decade's worth of bureaucrat bashing; severe fiscal constraints; inadequate compensation; strained labor-management relations; outmoded personnel practices; and outdated management information systems. The challenge is to meet these problems as they present themselves in fifty very different states and tens of thousands of local jurisdictions.

Thus, while our experiences in chairing national commissions on the public service have made us more conscious of the need for meaningful reform, they have done even more to make us mindful of the political, fiscal, and social obstacles to reform. Experience teaches that citizens' and legislators' interest in the problems of the public service is generally short-lived, and action to remedy the problems is often short-circuited by the next election, the next media-declared crisis in government, or the next swing in public mood. And sometimes the momentum behind public service reform has been lost in the midst of efforts to grapple with other pressing public policy challenges.

Today there is no more profound challenge than the financial weakness of state and local governments and the need to reduce the federal deficit. We yield to no one in our concern that these challenges be met. At the same time, however, we believe it is crucial that policymakers at all levels of government avoid seeking small or symbolic savings by across-the-board cuts in "the bureaucracy" at the expense of lasting reforms sorely needed to motivate public workers, attract the best available talent, and make the government work more efficiently.

The Volcker and Winter commissions were by no means the first to focus attention on the myriad problems of the nation's public service. At the federal level, for example, the first and second Hoover commissions (1947–49 and 1953–55) were preceded by the Keep commission (1905–09), the President's Commission on Economy and Efficiency (1910–13), the Joint Committee on Reorganization (1921–24), and the President's Committee on Administrative Management (1936–37), known widely as the Brownlow commission. The two Hoover commissions were followed by the study commissions on executive reorganization (1953–68), the Ash council (1969–71), the Carter reorganization effort (1977–79), the Grace commission (1982–84), and the ongoing National Performance Review. In addition, the twentieth-century archives of state and local governments contain thousands of reports on administrative reform. Thus many if not most of the problems addressed in the Volcker and Winter commission reports were discussed or forecast decades ago.

The Brookings Institution has been the source of some of the most prescient works on public service reform. In 1957, two years after the release of the report of the second Hoover commission, Brookings published *Executives for Government: Central Issues of Federal Personnel Administration*. And in 1964 it published *The Image of the Federal Service*, which emphasized the need to make careers in public service far more attractive and identified recruitment, training, and personnel practices that, then as now, frustrated efforts to achieve excellence in government.[2]

We are very pleased, therefore, that Brookings has resumed this tradition with the present volume. Although there are some things in it that either one or both of us might disagree with, and although the subject of public service reform naturally invites different emphases, we strongly support the theses in this book. The diverse and distinguished scholars, practitioners, and journalists whom John DiIulio has brought together on this important project lend wisdom and weight to the cause of public service reform.

In particular, we want to highlight three emphases of this volume that, in our judgment, refine, focus, and extend the work of the Volcker and Winter commissions: improving the administration of government, deregulating the public service, and educating the public.

## Improving the Administration
## of Government

As every schoolchild knows (or used to know), the Progressive reformers of the 1880s through the 1920s changed the face of American government. It was they who attacked political patronage and launched civil service systems. As Gerald Garvey and John DiIulio remind us in chapter 2, it was the Progressives who based the public service on the bedrock of merit selection, tenure, and position classification. And it was their faith in the possibility of good government that attracted thousands of highly talented, public-spirited citizens into careers in government.

But the government constituted by the Progressives, in its concern about ensuring honesty and fairness, came to be too inflexible to be fully effective, particularly as the work of government expanded and complexities multiplied. In response to political, technological, and other changes, civil service systems have evolved in ways that often frustrate the Progressive ideals of efficiency, honesty, and confidence in government. The nation needs, therefore, to improve the administration of government so that it can realize these ideals. The civil service systems must be changed in ways that make it easier to achieve democratically enacted public purposes with available human and financial resources.

Accordingly, we are sympathetic to the reform impulses that have animated the popular and useful call to "reinvent" government.[3] We recognize that almost any attention focused on the problems of the public service and how to fix them is probably to the good. But the notion that somehow government can be reinvented should not be taken literally. As many of those experienced in the study and practice of public administration have observed, the problems of improving government service cannot be dissolved by catchy reform slogans or administrative bromides.[4]

Government does need to learn good business practice in everything from its accounting to its procurement procedures. But public administration neither is nor ought to become just another form of business administration. As was pointed out in another Brookings study, some of what appears as government red tape is the by-product of democratically enacted health, ethics, and civil rights laws that most Americans favor: "one person's 'red tape' may be another's treasured procedural safeguard."[5]

Likewise, while government needs its entrepreneurs, in the sense of people with vision, initiative, and energy, the hallmark of the successful businessman is a single-minded emphasis on the bottom line of dollar profits. As the Progressives understood, public servants must be dedicated to the public interest, and the public interest may require balancing a number of competing interests, none of which is easily measured. In practice that mission will require that some critical number of our ablest citizens devote a considerable portion of their lives to service within government, forgoing the pursuit of maximizing income and sacrificing privacy to respond to the challenge of shaping public policy. Public administration cannot be improved without them.

## Deregulating the Public Service

Not even the most public-spirited government workers can succeed if they are hemmed in on all sides by rules, regulations, and procedures that make it virtually impossible to perform well. The most talented, dedicated, well-compensated, well-trained, and well-led civil servants cannot serve the public well if they are subject to perverse personnel practices that punish innovation, promote mediocrity, and proscribe flexibility.

The Volcker commission highlighted the need to clear away the rules, regulations, and procedures that enervate the performance of public servants. For example, it recommended that the federal Office of Personnel Management deregulate the hiring process by giving departments and agencies broad, but still circumscribed, authority to set their own rules and, by experimenting with on-the-spot hiring of both undergraduate and graduate students, to minimize paperwork and delay.

Likewise, the Winter commission identified problems that stem from the overregulation of state and local public servants: time-consuming but worthless paperwork requirements, rules dictating that multiple levels of approval be secured for routine decisions, jobs dedicated solely to monitoring the work of others. Civil service systems, the commission found, have become lifelines of overregulation: thousands of separate classifications or job titles; overreliance on written examinations that are outdated and irrelevant to the jobs at hand; automatic, seniority-based pay increases that reward workers for pushing paper in conformity to established procedures, not for performing well or working more efficiently. The Winter commission echoed the Volcker commission's call to deregulate the public service via such actions as introducing more flexible hiring and promotion policies, reducing the number of job classifications to no more than fifty, abandoning ineffective pay-for-performance systems, and adopting a single-signature policy on small procurement purchases.

The Clinton administration's National Performance Review has also recommended deregulating federal personnel and procurement rules to make government work better and cost less. Excerpts from sections of the National Performance Review report, the Winter commission report, and the Volcker commission report that recommend deregulation appear in the appendix.

Unfortunately, the phrase "deregulating the public service" invites possible confusion. To be clear, we are not talking about reducing government regulations on airlines, trucking, and other private industries, important as that debate is. Rather, we are talking about pruning overgrown government personnel regulations that make it exceedingly difficult to attract talented people into public service careers and trimming work and procurement regulations that discourage public servants from exercising initiative, assuming responsibility, and experimenting in the interests of better service delivery and greater cost-effectiveness.

As John DiIulio and the other contributors to this volume make clear, the idea of deregulating the public service needs to be studied and tested. But as they also make clear, there is already sufficient reason to conclude that detailed regulation of public employees is not compatible with productivity, high morale, and innovation. Of course, as a 1963 report of the American Academy of Political and Social Science stated, "there is no universal program that can possibly cure the staffing ills of all public-service jurisdictions."[6] But deregulating the public service while maintaining appropriate avenues of accountability is almost certain to improve the administration of the nation's federal, state, and local governments.

## Educating the Public

What we appreciate most about this volume is that it represents a first-rate effort to educate the public about the need to improve government administration and the difficulty of doing so. John

DiIulio and the other contributors acknowledge the exploratory, open-ended nature of their analyses and recommendations. In a scholarly spirit they approach deregulating the public service as a necessary but insufficient condition for improving its administration. They recognize that different levels of government, different jurisdictions, different service sectors, and, ultimately, different departments, agencies, and the people within them may be more or less ready for deregulation. Their tone is appropriately hopeful but skeptical, confident but qualified.

Of one thing we are positive: effective public service is essential to our democracy. Yet, the American people are not getting the quality of service to which they are entitled and upon which confidence in government rests. The need for reform cannot be overstated. This volume contributes mightily to the necessary public discussion of the future of our public service. We would be pleased if it generated renewed critical interest in the issues and problems identified by our commissions.

## Notes

1. John J. DiIulio, Jr., Gerald Garvey, and Donald F. Kettl, *Improving Government Performance: An Owner's Manual* (Brookings, 1993), p. 8.

2. Paul T. David and Ross Pollock, *Executives for Government: Central Issues of Federal Personnel Administration* (Brookings, 1957); and Franklin P. Kilpatrick, *The Image of the Federal Service* (Brookings, 1964).

3. David Osborne and Ted Gaebler, *Reinventing Government: How the Entrepreneurial Spirit is Transforming the Public Sector* (Addison-Wesley, 1992).

4. John Larkin, "Reinventors Urged to Proceed with Caution," *PA Times*, vol. 16 (February 1, 1993), pp. 1, 7; Charles T. Goodsell, "Reinvent Government or Rediscover It?" *Public Administration Review*, vol. 53 (January–February 1993), pp. 85–87; and DiIulio, Garvey, and Kettl, *Improving Government Performance*, especially chaps. 1–4.

5. Herbert Kaufman, *Red Tape: Its Origins, Uses, and Abuses* (Brookings, 1977), p. 4.

6. John W. Macy, Jr., "How Should We Implement a Program to Obtain an Adequate Public Service?" in Stephen B. Sweeney and James C. Charlesworth, eds., *Achieving Excellence in Public Service* (Philadelphia: American Academy of Political and Social Science, 1963), p. 63.

# 1 ||| What Is Deregulating The Public Service?

## John J. DiIulio, Jr.

THE NATION'S federal, state, and local public service is in deep trouble. Many government agencies cannot attract and retain first-rate executives, managers, and line staff. Most do not operate in a way that inspires public confidence. In reaction, some observers say "privatize everything," others deny that serious problems exist, and still others chant "run government like a business." All three responses are misguided. The real challenge is to articulate and implement an effective strategy for improving government administration, and soon. So far, this challenge has gone unmet.

The underlying problem of public administration in the United States is probably not that most public servants exercise too much discretion on the job but that most exercise too little. In 1988 Constance Horner, director of the federal Office of Personnel Management, called for "deregulating" the public service to achieve more flexibility.

The size of the government work force could be substantially reduced if public managers had more flexibility in making basic personnel and purchasing decisions, and if lower paperwork requirements freed them to focus more on the services they are supposed to provide. [There are] tens of thousands of pages of regulations restricting their every move.

Federal managers have little discretion to use pay to reward and retain good employees. . . . Status on the basis of seniority is the dominant ethos of civil service administration. . . . It would be much better if senior managers could get their appropriated budgets and decide how many people to hire, at what pay levels, to get the job done.[1]

In 1989 James Q. Wilson concluded his book on government bu-reaucracy by seconding Horner's motion. For government agencies to attract good workers and perform better, Wilson argued, the government must be deregulated: "detailed regulation, even of public employees, rarely is compatible with energy, pride in work-manship, and the exercise of initiative. . . . Most people do not like working in an environment in which every action is second-guessed, every initiative is viewed with suspicion, and every contro-versial decision denounced as malfeasance."[2] Similarly, Steven Kel-man traced the roots of government's procurement problems to rule-bound procurement officers. "The problem with the current system is that public officials cannot use common sense and good judgment in ways that would promote better vendor perfor-mance. . . . The system should be significantly deregulated to allow public officials greater discretion."[3]

Essentially, deregulating the public service means changing per-sonnel and procurement procedures in ways that enlarge the discre-tion of government employees. This book explores the proposition that deregulation would make careers in government more reward-ing and efficiency in government administration more possible. It represents an open-ended effort to describe, analyze, and evaluate the idea of deregulating the public service and to place it in the context of other contemporary approaches to public service reform.

As Paul A. Volcker and William F. Winter comment in their introduction to this volume, proposals to deregulate the public service figured prominently in the 1989 report of the National Com-mission on the Public Service (the Volcker commission) and the 1993 report of the National Commission on the State and Local Public Service (the Winter commission). The proposals were moti-vated by systematic as well as anecdotal evidence that the efficiency of the public service has been slowly choked by restrictive person-nel, job, and procurement regulations. And the cost in talented public servants lost may be even greater. In a survey conducted for the Volcker commission, college honor society students were asked to rank what they valued most in a job. They responded (1) chal-lenging work, (2) personal growth, (3) pleasant working condi-tions, (4) good social relations, (5) job autonomy, (6) service to society, (7) job security, (8) professional recognition, (9) opportu-nity for advancement, (10) pay and other financial rewards, (11) prestige.[4] Given these rankings, it came as no surprise to the members of the commission that careers in the public service had become unattractive not only to the best and brightest, but also to the average well-meaning citizens who already worked in government.

Members of the Winter commission were overwhelmed with information, including the testimony of state and local public officials from across the country that the public service has become entangled in a thicket of overgrown regulations. To cite just one example, in over half the states the number of separate government job classifications has mushroomed to fifteen hundred or more. Rather than breeding management flexibility and administrative efficiency, they have become technical and legal obstacles to anything other than bureaucratic business as usual.

Thus both the Volcker and Winter commissions embraced deregulation of the public service, not as a certain cure for the diverse, complex, and long-standing administrative ills of the nation's government agencies but as one necessary if insufficient condition for curing these ills—if, indeed, they can be cured at all. As Volcker and Winter comment in their preface, deregulating the public service may be necessary because not even the "most talented, dedicated, well-compensated, well-trained, and well-led civil servants can serve the public well if they are subject to perverse personnel practices that punish innovation and promote mediocrity."

The question mark in this volume's subtitle—*Can Government Be Improved?*—is real, not rhetorical. The contributing authors do not believe it is yet possible to specify the general political, legal, budgetary, or other conditions under which deregulation is most likely to occur. Nor are they entirely confident that deregulating the public service would begin to solve the many serious problems of government administration identified in the reports of the Volcker and Winter commissions and their many blue-ribboned predecessors. But if deregulation is not a sure bet, it is the nation's best available chance to improve administration in ways that matter to public employees and citizens. And although deregulation may work better at some levels of government and in some public service sectors than in others, it is probably as close as we are likely to come to a universal strategy for inducing and permitting public servants to work in ways that yield the greatest possible return on the public's human and financial investments in government.

Compared with many of the more popular contemporary approaches to the problems of government administration, deregulation is bound to seem narrow, tentative, overly mindful of existing political constraints, and, dare I add, academic. But as most of the contributors to this book see it, deregulating the public service is an interesting and potentially important approach to reform that needs to be debated, not deified, and studied, not sold.

Thus most of the contributors focus on the inner workings of public agencies. They train their attention on the question of what, if anything, can be done within and across public bureaucracies to improve administration. They recognize that Byzantine difficulties await any effort to make basic changes in civil service systems. Preoccupied with the task at hand, they have relatively little to say about the current crop of ambitious but unproven proposals to "empower" citizens or citizen-customers as direct participants in day-to-day government administration. They are also ambivalent about the effectiveness of such touted techniques as total quality management and skeptical about their relevance to much of what goes on within the public sector.

Moreover, the contributors are unblinking when it comes to the ethical and practical trade-offs that deregulating the public service could entail—for example, the likelihood that vesting public employees with greater discretion could engender more instances in which public offices are perverted into instruments for achieving private gain. Finally, they treat deregulation in a genuinely empirical spirit, that is, as a reform idea that remains open to refutation by argument, observation, or (best of all) experiment.

Thus, apart from occasional rhetorical flourishes or heuristics, this volume does not offer the catchy maxims or canonical certainties about how to improve government administration that have done so much to fuel popular reform movements, past and present. Instead, the arguments for deregulation in these pages are tempered by a frank recognition of limited knowledge about what administrative practices and conditions actually matter to government performance, how these variables relate one to another, and how best they can be measured over time. Far too little is known about the relationship between process and performance in the public sector to frame an all-purpose theory of what works in reforming public service. Also, respect for the rudiments of applied social science methodology does not permit broad generalization from a handful, or even a small truckload, of what may well be unrepresentative examples.

Given these limitations, this volume is intended to explore proposals for deregulating the public service, not to implore policymakers or administrators to adopt them. At least as the contributors interpret it, the weight of the evidence favors new and large-scale experiments with deregulation, and thus policy changes that would facilitate them. But that interpretation rests on a number of assumptions that are themselves open to debate.

One assumption occurs in chapter 2, in which Gerald J. Garvey and I argue that the civil service system bequeathed to us by the reformers of the Progressive Era contained, if not the seeds of its own destruction, then surely the seeds of its own overregulation. Eager to build an expert, professional public service that would be insulated from political pressures, the Progressives anchored the system in the principles of merit, tenure, and job classification. The reformers were committed to efficiency in government, but they loathed corruption more than they loved efficiency. As a result, they shaped the rules for administering American public bureaucracy in ways that were bound to foster rather than impede the proliferation of personnel, job, and procurement regulations. Unions for public employees, a development largely unforeseen by the Progressives, also had the unintended evolutionary consequence of making civil service systems more rule bound. And the onslaught of overregulation was further driven by the rise of divided government, restrictive changes in administrative and ethics laws, and the phenomenon of judicial rulemaking.

But a historical exploration of the origins and growth of public service overregulation should not preclude hope that deregulation is possible. There is nothing inevitable about the way the American public service has evolved, and recognition of the enervating consequences of overregulation is only a generation old. Besides, the obverse of bureaucrat bashing is the willingness of at least some public leaders to consider whether the fault for much poor government administration lies not in our bureaucrats but in the systems within which they are forced to operate.

In chapter 3 James Q. Wilson makes a case for deregulating the public service and weighs the prospects for reform in relation to those for other government bureaucracies, including public schools. In their influential writings on school reform, John E. Chubb and Terry M. Moe argued that, all things being equal, less bureaucratic, more team-oriented forms of school organization lead to improved student performance on standardized tests.[5] But public schools, they contended, are rarely organized in the ways that invite success. Organizationally the schools are captives of perverse political environments that make meaningful reforms virtually impossible; hence their case for school choice. Wilson accepts Chubb and Moe's analysis but points out that at least some public schools do perform well. He discusses the features they have in common and explores the conditions under which deregulating public schools might work. His analysis offers some reason to be cautiously optimistic about the prospects for improving schools by deregulating them.

In the end, however, Wilson is anything but Pollyannish: deregulating public schools, police departments, and other government bureaucracies is as difficult as it is desirable. For those to whom deregulating the public service is a Big Answer to the Big Question of how America can unleash the creative talents of its public servants, he offers this caution: "public management is not an arena in which to find Big Answers; it is a world of settled institutions designed to allow imperfect people to use flawed procedures to cope with insoluble problems."

But there are those who seem to believe that regulation can rid the public service of "imperfect people." Since Watergate, all levels of government have witnessed a proliferation of public service ethics laws. Typically, the language of these laws presupposes that public officials—elected or appointed, job candidates or careerists, cabinet level or entry level—are closer to being felons than public-spirited citizens. Thus the minutest traces of any conflicts of interest are often enough to disqualify otherwise outstanding applicants. Wrongdoing by officials is to be prevented by detailed financial reporting requirements. Public employees who shirk duty, subvert policy, and steal government property are to be detected and punished, but those who perform well or routinely go beyond the call of duty are neither recognized nor rewarded. In short, many government ethics laws are morally hollow and practically useless instruments of what Paul C. Light has termed "compliance accountability," that is, "efforts to assure conformity with carefully drawn rules and regulations" that emphasize correcting problems after they occur and depend on "the deterrence value of visible punishment."[6]

In chapter 4 John P. Burke explores the ethics of deregulating the public service. The keystone of present federal ethics regulation is the Ethics in Government Act of 1978. This law, and the many state and local laws adopted in its wake, embodies an "exclusively regulatory definition of ethics" that may well be "self-defeating, generating negativity, if not cynicism, antagonism, and an adversarial reaction, among those whose conduct [it seeks] to elevate."

But although the legalistic regulation of public ethics has largely failed, deregulation is not thereby bound to succeed. Deregulating the public service, Burke emphasizes, would necessitate a broader understanding of ethics in government, especially on the part of public officials themselves: "ethics as personal honesty and integrity, ethics as fairness toward others, ethics as respect for others, and ethics as a commitment to diligence and excellence in performing one's work." His conclusion is more sanguine than not: "a public sector that is trusted by its citizenry . . . is likely to be a public sector even more committed to the effective delivery of those goods and services that a democratic citizenry rightfully expects of it."

In chapter 5 Constance Horner broadly surveys the prospects for deregulating the federal civil service by assessing the political factors that have conditioned past reform efforts. Speaking as one who has herself attempted to foster deregulation within the federal service, her conclusion is mixed. The political climate for deregulating, she contends, has never been better, but formidable political, legal, and intellectual obstacles to reform remain.

Some of those obstacles can be surmounted. In chapter 6 Steven Kelman examines the federal procurement system. In his 1989 book Kelman argued that the discretion of federal procurement officers had been regulated so tightly that they were barred from letting their knowledge of past vendor performance influence contracting decisions and were often forced to let contracts to vendors whom they knew would not perform well. The regulations inflated costs and diminished the quality of services. But, he contends, the federal procurement system is not beyond benefiting from deregulation. In fact, he explains how his book actually sparked a review of procurement practices within some federal agencies and concludes that deregulating the federal procurement system is both possible and desirable.

In chapter 7 Neal R. Peirce, focusing on Florida and Philadelphia, explores the prospects for deregulating the state and local public service. In recent years Florida has been the scene of some of the boldest state-level experimentation with public service reform. And Philadelphia has done what big cities are supposedly unable to do—begin to get its fiscal house in order by negotiating major changes in contracts with powerful municipal unions.

Without any pretense to having conducted a systematic survey, Peirce contends that deregulating state and local public service is possible. Although today's self-interested leaders of public employee unions have become the chief protectors of the civil service systems founded by yesteryear's good-government Progressives, in Florida and Philadelphia the unions did not constitute insurmountable barriers to reform. Peirce concludes that deregulating public service is fine as far as it goes, but it does not go far enough. Instead, it should be one component of a broader effort to overhaul government service delivery systems, motivate public employees, and involve citizens more fully in government decisionmaking.

In chapter 8 Richard P. Nathan, who launched and directed the work of the Winter commission, focuses on the need for leadership within the state and local public service. If the public service is to be deregulated, he argues, it must have leaders who recognize the need for reforms and are determined enough to see the reforms through. In fact, deregulation "to surmount and tone down civil service rigidities and collective bargaining rules" can actually aid strong executives. And because leadership within the public service can be learned, he offers some simple but powerful lessons for those who want to learn. Nathan thus reaches beyond the reports of the Winter and the Volcker commissions to the 1937 report of the Brownlow committee, which stated flatly that only "false friends of democracy" wavered at the need for strong executive leadership. Without strong executive leadership, neither deregulation nor other approaches to reforming the public service can succeed.

In chapter 9 Donald F. Kettl assesses the potential effects of deregulation on the boundaries of government, the interfaces between various agencies, jurisdictions, and levels of government that affect public service. In the past few decades "the boundaries across which government, its programs, and its officials must work have become far more numerous and infinitely more complicated," so that government performance and responsiveness have been severely compromised. The reality of life within the public service is "multiple programs, multiple agencies, multiple levels of government, and complex public-private partnerships" that challenge even the most integrated reform efforts.

Deregulating the public service has many advantages as a strategy for improving the performance of those who work at the boundaries of government, as well as obvious merit for those who work in shrinking domains where direct administration by a single agency is still the norm. But neither deregulation nor other recent reform ideas adequately appreciate the complexities of contemporary government administration. What is needed, Kettl argues, is a new generation of public administrators who are expert "boundary spanners," public employees capable of bridging different programs, agencies, government levels, and public-private arrangements, and who are comfortable reaching out to citizens and bureaucrats at each stage of the administrative process.

In chapter 10 Mark H. Moore examines deregulation as a necessary ingredient in the administrative success of so-called community-based policing. Since the end of World War II most big-city police departments have been hierarchical, paramilitary organizations rather than groups of participative management teams that cut across ranks or functional specialties. Most departments have not emphasized the need for officers to climb out of their patrol cars and seek direct, personal, and regular communication with the people who live in the places that they police.

But in the past decade, Moore and others have persuaded a new generation of police administrators and policymakers that community-based policing makes good sense. Dozens of jurisdictions have now experimented with some form of it. A broad political consensus favors the concept. And there is increasing evidence that it not only reduces citizens' fear of crime but reduces crime itself.

Yet no jurisdiction, not even those big-city departments where it has been tried, has made much headway in institutionalizing community-based policing as the administrative standard. If, as Moore suggests, the reason may have much to do with restrictive personnel regulations and other rules that continue to govern most police agencies, deregulating the public service may be a key to effective implementation of community-based policing initiatives.

In chapter 11 Mark Alan Hughes maps the post–World War II evolution of regulations that have done much to derail the performance of public mass transit bureaucracies. The story culminates in

the 300-page 1991 Intermodal Surface Transportation Efficiency
Act. To the hundreds of detailed regulations under which mass
transit agencies and their workers must labor, it added scores more
intended to create, in the language of the bill, "a national intermodal transportation system that is economically efficient, environmentally sound, provides a foundation for the nation to compete in
the global economy, and will move people and goods in an energy-
efficient manner." But as Hughes contends, the practical effect of
the act is to further hamper the ability of mass transit agencies to
manage themselves in a reasonable and reasonably cost-effective
way. He uses the telling case of the Southeastern Pennsylvania
Transportation Authority to illustrate the need and potential for
deregulating the public service where the rubber meets the road.

In chapter 12 Melvin J. Dubnick considers the theoretical underpinnings of deregulation proposals. The theories that motivate deregulating the public service, reinventing government, and minimal
state or privatization reform efforts share significant similarities and
differences. All three posit that, under most conditions, structures
that are less bureaucratic are superior to more bureaucratic ones. All
three theories are, in effect, efforts to "dethrone King Bureaucracy,"
to overthrow the paradigm of public administration that has with-
stood so many previous reform efforts. Although deregulating the
public service has a somewhat stronger theoretical foundation than
the other two approaches, Dubnick concludes by calling attention
to the many untested conceptual and empirical assumptions that
underwrite all three approaches.

The idea of deregulating the public service is largely untested.
But the contributors to this volume agree that exploratory efforts to
deregulate the public service are in the public interest. As this book
goes to press, the report of the Clinton administration's National
Performance Review has been released and is facing scrutiny in
Congress and the media. Already, the report has been criticized for
failing to address the proliferation of political appointees, dealing
only superficially with legislative micromanagement, and overstat-
ing the potential for saving money by shrinking the size of a federal
civilian work force that has remained flat since 1950 while government spending has soared, and that has shrunk steadily relative to
the number of state and local government employees. It is to be
hoped that these and other criticisms, fair and foul, do not taint the
report's proposals for deregulating federal personnel and procure-

ment practices. At a minimum, experiments with deregulation launched by the review should be given a chance to work and undergo careful evaluations. Deregulating the public service is not reinventing government, but all the contributors to this volume believe that it is a sensible, timely, and potentially effective strategy for improving the way government agencies do what they do.

## Notes

1. Constance Horner, "Beyond Mr. Gradgrind: The Case for Deregulating the Public Sector," *Policy Review*, no. 44 (Spring 1988), pp. 34–35.

2. James Q. Wilson, *Bureaucracy: What Government Agencies Do and Why They Do It* (Basic Books, 1989), p. 369.

3. Steven Kelman, *Procurement and Public Management: The Fear of Discretion and the Quality of Government Performance* (Washington: AEI Press, 1990), p. 1.

4. National Commission on the Public Service, *Leadership for America: Rebuilding the Public Service—Task Force Reports to the National Commission on Public Service* (Washington, 1989), p. 108.

5. John E. Chubb and Terry M. Moe, *Politics, Markets, and America's Schools* (Brookings, 1990); and "Politics, Markets, and the Organization of Schools," *American Political Science Review*, vol. 82 (December 1988), pp. 1065–87.

6. Paul C. Light, *Monitoring Government: Inspectors General and the Search for Accountability* (Brookings, 1993), p. 3.

# 2 ||| Sources of Public Service Overregulation

Gerald J. Garvey and John J. DiIulio, Jr.

IN 1958 Paul Van Riper concluded his history of the U.S. civil service system by calling for a "representative bureaucracy," an administrative structure "in which there is a minimal distinction between the bureaucrats as a group and their administrative behavior and practices on the one hand, and the community or societal membership and its administrative behavior, practices, and expectations of government on the other."[1] It is an appealing idea, and a familiar one, recalling as it does Woodrow Wilson's vision more than a century ago of a civil service that would broadly reflect a democratic citizenry.[2]

Ours *is* and always has been a representative public bureaucracy in terms of the political ideals, loyalties, and values that its members share not only with one another but with citizens generally. Surely few Americans fear the emergence of what Wilson termed a "semi-corporate body [of officials] with sympathies divorced from that of a progressive, free-spirited people."[3] Alas, however, what is *not* representative about our public sector—and what seems to be getting less and less representative every day—are the constraints under which civil servants work. No other group of Americans must deal day in, day out with the kind of rule-bound workplace civil servants confront. Overregulation saps their morale and efficiency, in the end making self-fulfilling prophesies of the invidious judgments commonly made about appointive officials' lack of energy and imagination.[4]

In this chapter we survey the evolution of the federal civil service and the internal features and external forces that have converted structures the Progressives conceived in an imagery of efficiency into hidebound, unresponsive old-line agencies.[5] What follows is neither a comprehensive history nor a full critique but a preview of the case for loosening personnel regulations and operating restrictions in a government that has itself become overregulated. In a period when deregulation has become a watchword in the private sector, achieving a truly representative bureaucracy calls for deregulation of the government as well.

## The Evolution of the Federal Civil Service

Today's civil service systems originated in the civil service reform, "good government," and "scientific management" movements of the Progressive Era. For George William Curtis, Carl Schurz, and other political reformers after the Civil War, the evils of the spoils system and the degradation of filling public jobs by political patronage were defining moral issues, much as slavery had been in the antebellum period.[6] But if clean government was the reformers' primary goal in the late nineteenth century, efficient government was an important secondary aim, and one believed to be strongly complementary to the first.[7]

The reformers' vision lured thousands of idealists into service in a rapidly expanding public bureaucracy, one citizens would revere for its efficiency and innovativeness as well as its rectitude. Efficiency in the civil service first of all required that civil servants be experts. Because government had become more complex, Woodrow Wilson wrote in 1887, "a technically schooled civil service will presently have become indispensable."[8] To staff the administrative state, the reformers therefore sought to recruit people prepared by formal education or relevant practical experience for the technical duties of governance.[9] According to the reformers' expectations, the expertise of the individual appointees plus efficient design of the bureaus in which they would work should produce—again, in Wilson's words—"a corps of civil servants prepared by a special schooling and drilled, after appointment, into a perfected organization, with appropriate hierarchy and characteristic discipline."[10]

This emphasis on recruiting workers of rectitude and expertise implied stricter employment guidelines. Mid-nineteenth-century government personnel practices—President Andrew Jackson's "spoils" system—had permitted easy admission to the public service, allowed easy dismissal of an appointee for causes having nothing to do with his technical competence, and afforded a maximum of flexibility in a superior's authority to match duties with abilities. Workers easily moved in and out, up and down, within the table of government employment.

The 1883 Pendleton Act changed all that, providing for the appointment of career officials on the basis of merit.[11] Once appointed, the civil servant would enjoy the promise of steady government work and the right not to be fired except for cause. To the principles of merit and tenure, the reformers in due course added that of job classification, under which personnel experts would "scientifically" assign responsibilities to units, match skills to assigned responsibilities, and systematically link workers' salary scales with their skills.[12] The Classification Act of 1923 provided for grades to be established within each government service category and required uniform compensation for occupants of the same grade within the same service.[13] The "equal pay for equal work" standard became official, as did the "rank in the job" principle (as opposed to the "rank in the person" more common in European systems). In 1949 Congress extended job classification to all civilian federal employees except those specifically excluded. The Classification Act of 1949 also centralized classification authority in the Civil Service Commission and replaced the top three classification categories (which had been set up by the 1923 act) with the unified general schedule of eighteen grades, each with its internal promotional steps carrying increased pay with increased seniority in the grade.[14]

The 1978 Civil Service Reform Act completed the statutory structure of the federal career service that exists today.[15] It retitled the Civil Service Commission the Federal Office of Personnel Management (theoretically putting OPM on a par with the Office of Management and Budget in the Executive Office of the President) and provided for increased flexibility in appointing and promoting personnel. The act also created the senior executive service, intended as an elite cadre of generalists in public management who could fill the critical job slots intermediate in rank between the president's political appointees at the pinnacle of the federal bureaucracy and the rest of the career service in the administrative, professional, and technical jobs.[16]

## Standing the Progressives' System on Its Head

The Progressives eradicated the widespread use of public office for private gain. But they did so at a high cost, for their reforms made possible the emergence of overly rigid, bureaucratized personnel systems that can frustrate productive workers, protect unproductive ones, and—perhaps worse—seem incapable of distinguishing one from the other and rewarding effective performers according to their desserts. Doubts accumulated about the efficacy of public personnel administration American-style, and the image of the service deteriorated.

In 1964 Franklin P. Kilpatrick, Milton C. Cummings, Jr., and M. Kent Jennings conducted a cross-sectional survey of more than 5,000 Americans and concluded, "guaranteed security of job, income, and retirement dominates the image people have of what federal employment has to offer." The attitude that the federal service was unexciting and hidebound was "dangerously out of phase with the occupational values and attitudes of those groups in society for whom its present and projected personnel needs are greatest, and for whom competition from the private sphere and other levels of government will be most severe."[17] The authors called for a new personnel philosophy, one that would in effect stand the Progressives' approach on its head.

> The traditional philosophy demands that reasons be given for treating any employee or group of employees differently from any others. The time has come to put the shoe on the other foot. We need a new approach which demands that reasons be given for *not* according any employee or group of employees the kind of special, differential treatment both uniquely suited to their needs and uniquely designed to enhance their quality, creativity, productivity, and sense of worth as individuals.[18]

The argument of the present volume extends these conclusions. The public service as constituted a century ago needs to be reconstituted in ways that reduce overregulation and induce higher productivity from the government work force.

## The Sources of Overregulation

Overregulation in the public bureaucracy may be considered, in part at least, the result of an excessive reaction to a nineteenth-century regime of underregulation. To a far greater degree than is the case today, the architects of civil service relied on internalized moral restraints as a decisive check on abuses of administrative discretion. Believing in an ethic of service that reduced the need for extensive external regulation, the Progressives were willing to delegate broad discretionary authority to appointive officials. They expected that the public bureaucracy would indeed be representative in the sense of the term used by later scholars. Woodrow Wilson, for example, envisioned a civil service "so intimately connected with the popular thought, by means of elections and constant public counsel, as to find arbitrariness or class spirit quite out of the question."[19] Certain dogmas of professionalism and expertise prevalent at the time also help explain why the Progressives seem in retrospect to have been relatively unfearful of abusive exercises of delegated authority.

The final decades of the nineteenth century witnessed the establishment of many of America's leading professional associations.[20] Professionalism implied greater attention to the value of academic credentials, more rigorous intellectual and professional standards, and an emphasis on the ethos of a discipline as well as on its technical lore. In the public service system as set up by the Progressive reformers, civil servants—at least in the higher grades—would come from the ranks of the nation's professionals. Gifford Pinchot and Frederick Newell, to name only two of the best-known appointive officials of the period, were, with their highly educated, upper-middle-class, technocratic backgrounds, representative of many top Progressive bureaucrats. In theory at least, it would have been contrary to their training, personal preferences, and even professional ethics to substitute policies of their own for goals specified by their political superiors (although Pinchot's much publicized dispute with Interior Secretary Richard Ballinger showed that any theory of bureaucratic humility can be pushed only so far).

The scientific managers carried the implications of this line of thought to its limit. Frederick Winslow Taylor urged careful analysis of production processes. Shoveling coal—a favorite example of his—required a definite sequence of bendings, liftings, and turnings. Once the constituent elements had been identified, precise procedures for the easiest, speediest execution could be formulated and taught to workers.[21] Frank Gilbreth, a leading exponent of Taylor's ideas, popularized belief in the one best way to complete any task.[22] As Dwight Waldo summarized, "Just as there is one best way to shovel coal there is one best way to organize or conduct an administrative activity. Since both 'best ways' rest on facts they are, of course, true and not proper subjects for differences of opinion."[23]

The proof that administrators were experts, which after all was the basic assumption of the civil service, would lie in their knowledge of the best way. And knowledge of the best way would leave them with no choice but to use it. Thus appointive officials would feel intellectually and even morally obliged to apply standard accounting procedures, best engineering practice, or whatever other best way of tackling problems represented the state of the art in their field.

The theory of expertise supported the reformers' willingness to write laws that would today be regarded as unacceptably general and vague. Progressive Era legislators typically used open-ended statutory charters to delegate discretionary powers to the experts, whom they trusted to produce proper decisions in specific cases. The usual regulatory statute, for example, contained terms hardly more specific than "public convenience and necessity" or "just and reasonable" (two of the standard formulations in the federal laws that set up the Interstate Commerce Commission, the Federal Personnel Council, and other early independent agencies). Legislative practice is very different today, and for reasons that originate, at least in part, in the lawmakers' desire to hamper the once "unhampered discretion" (Wilson's term) of those who must execute the laws. Why the change, and how exactly has it contributed to a new set of problems—of an overregulated government—in the effort to solve old ones?

To begin with, the Progressives' vision of depoliticized public administration bears little resemblance to today's bureaucratic process. Appointive officials, especially at the more senior ranks (the very ranks at which the norms of professionalism and hence neutrality were expected to operate in the most rigorous way) participate, often actively, in making public policy. The prevailing model of the administrative process also has them actively and sometimes self-interestedly involved in interest brokering and adjustment.

Perhaps not surprisingly, the doctrinal as well as the actual shift toward a broader conception of the administrative function, of senior officials as policy advisers and interest brokers, occurred during the extraordinary theoretical ferment and institutional adaptation of the 1930s. The Progressive architects of what Stephen Skowronek has called the New American State had hoped to create a politically neutral space segregated from partisan dealmaking and patronage dispensation.[24] During the New Deal years the guiding theory of the federal bureaucracy moved away from the Progressives' ideal toward a new doctrine that senior appointive officials should be agents of the presidential administration in power. *Because* of their expertise, they owed political superiors their best judgment on issues of policy as well as on matters of implementation.[25] This new doctrine could hardly have helped but raise questions about how much authority elected officials might legitimately delegate to appointive functionaries.[26]

Under the impetus of New Deal thinking and institutional development, the federal administrative bureaucracy became increasingly important in American society at the same time that its political neutrality became increasingly suspect both in theory and on the basis of experience. The New Deal outlook demanded an intensified search for doctrines and mechanisms by which those making political decisions would try to maintain control. These changes in administrative theory and practice, combined with the advent in the late 1940s of divided government as a persistent feature of American governance and the growing sense of inadequate performance or nonperformance in office by members of "a bloated bureaucracy," help explain the continuing effort (especially by Congress, but also by the federal courts) to impose controls on a growing, politically suspect public bureaucracy.

The new attitude toward the higher civil service made the old politics-administration dichotomy as untenable in theory as empirical studies were proving it to be undescriptive of actual practice. In the mid-1930s E. Pendleton Herring introduced the idea that administrative agencies are forums in which interest groups compete for political preferment.[27] In one form or another his interest-adjustment model has become the common view of the subject.

In 1966 Grant McConnell gave classic expression to a view that had been gathering strength and accumulating evidence for years: the broad discretionary charters of many of the Progressive Era regulatory agencies actually accomplished the opposite of what their framers had intended. The Progressives vastly overstated the proclivity of expertise to eliminate personal discretion. The vaguely worded statutes that had set up the agencies left room for great freedom in decisionmaking. Given the enormous financial stakes inherent in decisions affecting the regulated parts of the U.S. economy, it was natural for representatives of special interests to try to influence them. Expertise could not by itself proof administrative conduct against pressure from private interests, nor could professionalism and scientism ensure that administrators would choose the "one best way"—assuming it could be discerned to begin with—in the intensely, inescapably political environment of modern big government.[28]

## The Means of Overregulation

Given the doctrinal background and experience of a New American State that had apparently passed into middle age, it seems all but inevitable that external controls of increasing scope and severity would be imposed to supplement the internal ethic of public service as a check on administrative discretion. The most important of these controls has been legislative micromanagement—the close involvement of Congress in everyday agency affairs. To this must be added those overlays of rules that derive from more or less direct political causes (tensions between the branches in a post–New Deal Era of divided government), the heightened ethical sensibilities of post–Watergate America, the burgeoning importance of "administrative law," the continuing and often demanding judicial scrutiny of administrative actions, and from an agency's internal practices. Finally, the unions for public employees have themselves added to the civil servant's burden.

### Legislative Micromanagement

Motivated in part by a desire to close the Progressive Era open charters of discretionary authority, Congress has taken to passing laws remarkable for their length, specificity, and mandatory provisions. The 1970 Clean Air Act and its major amendments (1977, 1990), the 1970 Occupational Safety and Health Act, the 1974 Employees Retirement Income Security Act, the 1976 Federal Land Policy and Management Act, and the 1978 Natural Gas Policy Act all demonstrate elected officials' ability to legislate in minute detail on matters of great technical complexity when they decide to reclaim vague discretionary powers from bureaucrats.[29] These statutes are not untypical of contemporary legislation chartering or empowering administrative agencies. The result has been a congressionally imposed regime of rules, both substantive and procedural, that cramps appointive officials' freedom of action.

### Divided Government

Since the late 1940s the nation has witnessed a protracted tug-of-war between a legislature increasingly dominated by one party and a presidency under the control of the other.[30] Under the regime of divided government, intensified efforts to oversee and control the bureaucracy were natural political developments, given a civil service of doubtful political neutrality. The 1938 Hatch Act was perhaps the first fruit that the new suspicion of bureaucracy engendered in Congress.[31] More and more supposedly objective checks were imposed to keep track of who gets promoted when and in which agencies.

Some observers have challenged the widespread view that divided control undermines government's capacity to deal with public problems and leads to policy stalemate or gridlock.[32] But whatever its effect on policy formulation and adoption, divided government has had far-reaching effects on policy implementation and public administration. On the one side the White House has concentrated decisionmaking authority in the hands of presidents and their expanded legions of political appointees. On the other side Congress and congressional committees have subjected the decisions of administrative agencies to legislative micromanagement. Elected leaders and top staff in each branch have treated the bureaucracy as if it were "in the camp of the enemy."[33]

Thus, whatever divided government has or has not meant to national policymaking capacities, and whatever difference a return to unified party government may make in legislative-executive relations, one abiding legacy—overregulation of government agencies and workers—has been profound and perverse. Divided government has lived on in the rules that hamstring what public administrators can do and how well they can do it. Ways of dealing with the bureaucracy learned by elected and appointed leaders in both branches during the era of divided government must be unlearned for there to be much hope of stemming the tide of overregulation and making other reforms that could improve government performance.

*Ethics Laws*

As they had during the reformist agitation a century earlier, ethical concerns came to the fore in the American politics of the early 1970s, precipitated by the Watergate scandal of 1972–73, the much publicized dismissal of whistleblower Edward Fitzgerald for reporting irregularities in Defense Department procurement practices, and other scandals.[34] Most significant among the legislative responses was the Ethics in Government Act of 1978, which severely restricted the range of jobs civil servants might accept after leaving federal employment, toughened financial disclosure rules, tightened the rules governing public officials' acceptance of gifts, and generally clarified the regulations governing public employment.[35] Then in a series of laws passed in the late 1970s Congress mandated that all executive departments except Treasury and Justice have inspectors general to investigate reports of waste, fraud, or abuse.[36] The structure of investigative procedures and ethics requirements reinforced the rule-bound atmosphere of the public service.

*Administrative Laws*

In 1946 Congress passed the Administrative Procedures Act, which represented a compromise between two competing traditions: the administrative tradition, reflecting the Progressives' sense that a complex industrial society needs expert regulation of a kind that legislatures, courts, and political parties cannot adequately provide, and the rule-of-law tradition seeking to strengthen legal controls on administrative expertise.[37] Under the Administrative Procedures Act and kindred statutes, the controls entail often cumbersome legalistic rituals (modeled, ultimately, on court proceedings) for many areas of administrative decisionmaking.[38] The process ultimately leads to the pervasive exposure of official actions to detailed review by the courts.[39]

*Judicial Rulemaking*

That judges must not only occasionally save citizens from themselves through judicial review of popular legislation but also save them from their bureaucrats through judicial oversight of administrative actions has remained a vital conceit in American political thought. The impulse to government activism during the Great Society years—the spate of new laws and the additional administrative burden of execution—reactivated the judges' supererogatory disposition, creating yet another source of regulations for public officials to deal with.

A marked increase in administrative decisionmaking started in the late 1960s, much of it associated with the continuing growth in welfare-related programs (aid to families with dependent children, food stamps, and the so-called new property jurisprudence these programs stimulated).[40] The surge in consumer protection, environmental controls, and occupational health and safety regulation also contributed to the administrative burden.[41] An increase in judicial reviews followed, and in the 1970s a vast and complex body of administrative law developed to limit exercises of administrative power that were "arbitrary, capricious, an abuse of discretion, or otherwise not in accordance with the law."[42]

Since the mid-1970s the courts have retreated from detailed specification of procedures.[43] Federal judges, especially with the increased numbers of judicial conservatives appointed by Presidents Reagan and Bush, have also displayed a greater willingness to defer to administrative expertise in matters of substance. But a tradition of judicial watchfulness looms over the administrative process that may allow an easy return to the practices of earlier days should judges deem it necessary to recommence regulating that process.

### Bureaucratic Genesis

Although we have thus far emphasized external factors that have shaped the overregulated federal workplace, some organizational and procedural requirements seem to propagate internally. Federal administration is burdened with thousands of organizational and procedural rules resulting from a process of organizational self-germination and nurturance peculiar to bureaucracy.

Bureaucracies are well known for generating behavioral codes, established practices, and standard operating procedures.[44] Some are agency housekeeping measures or traffic rules intended to maintain the organization's internal flow of work. Few ever rise to a level justifying attention in legislative inquests or court reviews of administrative proceedings. Yet cumulatively (and especially when considered in conjunction with externally imposed regulations) they lay a heavy weight on the selection, assignment, and promotion of personnel, the procurement process, and the delivery of government services to private citizens.

The defensive instincts of bureaucrats, their desire to make what have been called "declarations of innocence," may represent one important source of these self-generated, or at least self-reinforced, rules.[45] As governance becomes increasingly complex and the crossplay of interests more dynamic, the harried public official yearns for refuge from hostile litigators, importunate lobbyists, and investigators from Congress and from the home department's inspector general. The official retreats to some rule to cover for his or her official acts. "I was only following regulations" becomes the protest of the risk-averse and yet another explanation for the official timidity or lassitude that many bureaucracy watchers identify as characteristic of agency operations.

### Public Sector Unionism

Unionism in the public sector has been, if not itself a powerful engine of overregulation, at least a force resisting efforts to simplify and streamline public personnel administration systems. In 1961 President Kennedy issued executive order 10988, which authorized the formation of collective bargaining units without restriction among federal civil servants.[46] But because Congress determines civil servants' salary scales, the improvement in working conditions and the protection of the classification system have been the real benefits won by collective bargaining.[47] Civil service tenure is a bulwark against budget-driven reductions in force; so are the protected, compartmentalized position descriptions of the federal classification system, in which pay, like rank, is in the job and sometimes quite independent of the performance of the person.[48] The public employee unions supported bumping provisions that make it difficult to reduce public sector work forces except at the often unacceptable cost of eliminating younger workers who might be the more desirable performers but also have the least seniority.

## What Is To Be Done?

For too long it has been difficult to attract well-motivated people into the public service. Virtually since the passage of the Pendleton

Act there have been wage and benefit disparities between the public sector and the private sector, especially at the executive and upper management levels.[49] Most government employees have never received the sort of first-rate professional training common in the corporate world. But notwithstanding the disparity and contrary to the easy explanations offered by bureaucrat bashers, the essential problem has never been that most government employees are lazy and incompetent.[50] Let all else that ostensibly ails the public service be fixed—let solutions be found to strengthen the federal recruitment process, raise public employees' pay, develop leadership and executive management skills, and even somehow allay the morale problems among civil servants that result from bureaucrat bashing—the most dedicated and imaginative government employees would still fail under the peculiar frustrations of the overregulated public workplace.

It is almost always possible to find a reason somewhere for a given bit of red tape.[51] But it is the overall atmosphere of rule-driven restriction that engenders resentment, discouragement, and indifference among civil servants. Given the controls in our government agencies that so often penalize initiative, can we be surprised if bureaucrats do not always work as efficiently as they might? The effect is exactly what Alexis de Tocqueville foresaw in 1840: "a network of small complicated rules, minute and uniform, through which the most original minds and the most energetic characters cannot penetrate. . . . [S]uch a power does not destroy, but it prevents existence; it does not tyrannize, but it compresses, enervates, extinguishes, and stupefies."[52]

There are several widely discussed prescriptions for the nation's overregulated government. Privatize it, some say; modernize it or entrepreneurialize it, say others. Each solution has attracted thoughtful and influential adherents. But each has its shortcomings. None adequately deals with the psychology of a public service that has become timid and rule bound. Nor do the privatization, modernization, or entrepreneurial approaches focus on the problem of bureaucratic genesis (except, sometimes, to assume it away).

*Privatization and Modernization*

The theory of privatization contends that a disequilibrium has developed in the balance between services provided by public bureaucracies and those provided by the market.[53] Privatization attempts to correct the alleged imbalance by increasing the proportion of private sector transactions (including contracts between government and private firms) relative to the proportion of those that result from bureaucratic decisionmaking.

In the 1980s, advocates of privatization produced evidence that the transfer of certain government functions to for-profit firms could save money and improve performance.[54] But the case has proved weaker—or anyway less universally applicable—than it first appeared. Privatization efforts, initially confined to contracts for collecting trash or managing central heating systems, gradually reached toward managerially and morally complicated functions such as running prisons.[55] The privatizers argued for taking on more and more functions traditionally thought to be inherent in the idea of the sovereignty of the public and, in a democratic state, necessarily subject to political control. But the conviction has grown that legitimate, important reasons remain to keep public agencies in control and make them as efficient as private firms.

The political obstacles to privatization, including the opposition of public unions, and legal limits (perhaps most importantly the welter of rules covering government contracting and procurement procedures), also proved more formidable than had been expected.[56] For example, privatization has often been a code word for contracting out. But contracting out government work either carries bureaucratic costs of its own or threatens political embarrassment, even criminal dereliction, if added layers of bureaucratic supervision are not created.[57] Even the longest privatization frontier evidently needs much government and many public servants behind it. How the government that remains and the officials who staff it are to be regulated thus remains an important issue under any foreseeable progression of the impulse to privatize.

Some opponents of privatization argue that the cure for inefficiency in civil service administration is to modernize it, to do essentially what the Progressives tried to do but to do it right—simplify job classification policies and procedures, introduce effective performance appraisal and reward programs, install computerized management information systems, and redouble efforts to professionalize government agencies, especially at senior levels. The modernizer, however, finds restrictions at every turn. The very personnel rules and work regulations that have made the reforms necessary have also made it hard for neo-Progressives' initiatives to succeed. And public employee unions have used these same regulations to weaken or block many modernizing reforms.

### Entrepreneurialism: Reinventing Government?

Between the privatizers and the modernizers are the advocates of a more entrepreneurial public service. Proponents of this approach, which the more sanguine liken to a reinvention of government, prescribe businesslike reforms wrought by politicians who will clear the pathways of change for results-oriented administrators and mission-driven workers.[58] The entrepreneurial approach has often worked, but it needs skillful leaders who share a vision of change. Where such leaders are absent, as they so often are, or where they run out of steam or leave the position, as they so often do, what may remain is a handful of tales recounting evanescent success, some management proverbs ("steer, not row"), and a public service about as unproductive as it was when the excitement began.

The entrepreneurialists assume that government administration is merely straitjacketed business administration. From the Progressive Era onward, reformer after reformer has proclaimed that public servants just need to run their agencies "more like business." But the consensus of careful observers, let alone of practitioners, is that this is impractical and a perversion of responsibility. As Graham Allison has concluded, "the notion that there is any significant body of private management practices and skills that can be transferred directly to public management tasks in a way that produces significant improvements is wrong"[59]

### Deregulating the Government

More privatization, accelerated modernization, and greater entrepreneurialism may indeed have some value for civil service reform. But no "solution" to the problem of an inefficient bureaucracy that fails to focus on the constraints within which public servants labor can get to the crux of the problem. This realization points toward a possible fourth approach to reform: deregulating the public service by reducing or eliminating personnel rules and work regulations that sap public employees' productivity and make careers in public service unattractive to talented, energetic potential candidates.

Deregulation is a reform idea that probably cuts closest to the heart of our public service inefficiencies. The principles of hiring on merit, employment tenure, and job classification tilted public service toward overregulation, and bureaucratic genesis, public sector collective bargaining, and other developments of the past half-century have pushed it ever farther in that direction. The time has come for a tilt the other way. The aim must be to find the critical balance, not only between private sector and public sector organization, but between the checks on bureaucratic discretion and the opportunities to promote excellence and initiative in bureaucratic performance. The United States needs to recognize the costs of paperwork in an overregulated bureaucracy, of securing multiple approvals even for routine decisions, of government jobs dedicated solely to monitoring what is done by incumbents of other government jobs.

In 1988 Constance Horner, former director of the federal Office of Personnel Management, stated the case for civil service deregulation:

The size of the government work force could be substantially reduced if public managers had more flexibility in making basic personnel and purchasing decisions, and if lower paperwork requirements freed them to focus more on the services they are supposed to provide. [There are] tens of thousands of pages of regulations restricting their every move.

Federal managers have little discretion to use pay to reward and retain good employees. As a rule, superior performance goes unrewarded with better pay. Nor does promotion come more swiftly to workers who show superior commitment and talent. Status on the basis of seniority is the dominant ethos of civil service administration. . . . It would be much better if senior managers could get their appropriated budgets and decide how many people to hire, at what pay levels, to get the job done.[60]

Horner's call for deregulation should not be confused with the selective withdrawal of public supervision of the airline, banking, natural gas production, trucking, or other private industries, or even with the move from command-and-control to market-based regulation in environmental affairs. Nor do Horner or any of the other contributors to this volume imply that substantial efforts to simplify and streamline federal personnel procedures are not already well under way.[61] But more progress in the same direction is needed.

The reconstitution of the public service should begin with a renewed appreciation of the ethic of service that the Progressives espoused, a suggestion consistent with that of John Burke in chapter 4. Reconstitution should broaden the autonomy that public managers enjoy so as to promote an organizational culture of performance rather than of security. It should also, when appropriate, support increased reliance on contracting out and selective privatization of additional public functions.[62] It should encourage the development of leadership skills at all levels of public service. But most imperatively, it should combine these initiatives with a loosening of the classification straitjacket.

Privatization, modernization, and entrepreneurialism have been studied extensively. However, there has yet to appear a serious exploration of the benefits and disadvantages of deregulating the civil service. How might this reform strategy be applied in practice, and with what potential benefits at each level of government (federal, state, and local), in the various administrative sectors (transportation, criminal justice, and so forth), and in different functional areas (personnel selection, procurement processes)? This volume represents a preliminary effort to answer these questions.

## Notes

1. Paul P. Van Riper, *History of the United States Civil Service* (Evanston, Ill.: Row, Peterson, 1958), p. 552. The term itself seems to have been taken from John Donald Kingsley's *Representative Bureaucracy: An Interpretation of the British Civil Service* (Yellow Springs, Ohio: Antioch Press, 1944).

2. Woodrow Wilson, "The Study of Administration," *Political Science Quarterly*, vol. 2 (June 1887), pp. 197–222, reprinted in *Political Science Quarterly*, vol. 56 (December 1941), pp. 500–01.

3. Ibid., p. 500.

4. *Appointive* in the following pages may apply to high-level nonelected officials, such as presidential appointees; to formally appointed civil servants in the career schedules, GS-9s and so forth; or in some contexts to both categories.

5. Despite variations in the details of their programs, the Progressives agreed on certain broad policy aims for reforming state and municipal public administra-

tion as well as the federal public service. The civil service structures that evolved therefore generally resembled one another and continue to do so.

6. William E. Nelson, *The Roots of American Bureaucracy, 1830–1900* (Harvard University Press, 1982), pp. 120–22.

7. As Woodrow Wilson wrote, "We are now rectifying methods of appointment; we must go on to adjust executive functions more fitly and to prescribe better methods of executive organization and action. Civil service reform is thus but a moral preparation for what is to follow. It is clearing the moral atmosphere of official life by establishing the sanctity of public office as public trust, and, by making the service unpartisan, it is opening the way for making it businesslike" ("Study of Administration," p. 494). Frederick C. Mosher has observed that the association of public personnel administration and morality was "the theme of the nineteenth century reformers." *Democracy and the Public Service* (Oxford University Press, 1968), p. 70.

8. Wilson, "Study of Administration," p. 500.

9. See McConnell, *Private Power and American Democracy* (Knopf, 1966), p. 43; Samuel P. Hays, *Conservation and the Gospel of Efficiency: The Progressive Conservation Movement, 1890–1920* (Athaneum, 1955, 1975), especially the preface; and Bruce A. Ackerman and William T. Hassler, *Clean Coal/Dirty Air: Or How the Clean Air Act Became a Multibillion-Dollar Bail-Out for High Sulfur Coal Producers and What Should Be Done about It* (Yale University Press, 1981), chap. 1.

10. Wilson, "Study of Administration," p. 500.

11. 22 Stat. 403.

12. A contemporary textbook, one of the first to treat personnel administration as a special body of expert knowledge, pronounced, "the job is the molecule of industry; and what molecular study has done for physics and chemistry, job study with the aid of every possible instrument of precision can begin to do for industry"—which certainly captures the spirit of both scientific management and job classification. Ordway Tead and Henry C. Metcalf, *Personnel Administration: Its Principles and Practice* (McGraw-Hill, 1920), p. 255, quoted in Jay M. Shafritz, *Position Classification: A Behavioral Analysis for the Public Service* (Praeger, 1973), p. 108.

Federal statutes from as far back as 1853, 1854, and 1855 had established rudimentary job classification schemes by requiring executive department heads to grade their clerks. The statutes also set the salaries of all assignees to each grade. Van Riper, *History of the United States Civil Service*, p. 54. Later, municipal and state governments began to experiment with classification formulas. In 1912 Chicago, and shortly thereafter the state of Illinois, instituted the first municipal and state classification systems, with other jurisdictions rapidly following suit. Shafritz, *Position Classification*, p. 16.

13. March 4, 1923, 42 Stat. 1488.

14. October 28, 1949, 63 Stat. 1488.

15. P.L. 95-454 (October 13, 1978), 92 Stat. 1111.

16. See Mark W. Huddleston, "The Senior Executive Service: Problems and Prospects for Reform," in Carolyn Ban and Norma M. Riccucci, eds., *Public Personnel Management: Current Concerns—Future Challenges* (Longman, 1991), pp. 175–89.

17. Franklin P. Kilpatrick, Milton C. Cummings, Jr., and M. Kent Jennings, *The Image of the Federal Service* (Brookings, 1964), pp. 244–45.

18. Kilpatrick, Cummings, and Jennings, *Image*, pp. 269–70. To similar effect, see Frederick C. Mosher, "The Public Service in the Temporary Society," in Dwight Waldo, ed., *Public Administration in a Time of Turbulence* (Scranton, Pa.: Chandler, 1971).

19. Wilson "Study of Administration," p. 501. The congressional debates over the Pendleton bill had ended with the rejection of a plan for the admission of civil service appointees only at entry levels. Hence the Pendleton Act allowed entry from private employment to any level in the civil service hierarchy—another contrast with most European systems, which emphasize promotion from within a largely closed cadre of public sector professionals. Lateral entry opened the American federal civil service for two-way traffic, contributing to Wilson's vision of a civil service as, in effect, a representative sample of American society.

20. David F. Noble, *America by Design: Science, Technology, and the Rise of Corporate Capitalism* (Knopf, 1977) pp. 36–40.

21. Frederick Winslow Taylor, *The Principles of Scientific Management* (Norton, 1967 [1911]), pp. 43–47, 137–38.

22. Samuel Haber, *Efficiency and Uplift: Scientific Management in the Progressive Era, 1890–1920* (University of Chicago Press, 1964), chap. 3.

23. Dwight Waldo, *The Administrative State: A Study of the Political Theory of American Public Administration* (Holmes and Meier, 1984), pp. 57–58.

24. Stephen Skowronek, *Building a New American State: The Expansion of National Administrative Capacities, 1877–1920* (Cambridge University Press, 1982). Fredrick C. Mosher characterized the years 1883–1906 as an era that aspired to "government by the good," which then gave way to a period (1906–37) that aspired to "government by the efficient." The original ethical theory, with its ideal of service and denigration of the taint of politics, was never rejected but was elaborated by the evangelists of efficiency, the scientific managers. *Democracy and the Public Service* (Oxford University Press, 1968), pp. 64–79.

25. Patricia W. Ingraham and David H. Rosenbloom, "Political Foundations of the American Federal Service: Rebuilding a Crumbling Base," *Public Administration Review*, vol. 50 (March–April 1990), pp. 213–14.

26. And of course the National Industrial Recovery Act compounded the affront to traditional American doctrines of public law—specifically, antitrust doctrines—by authorizing bureaucrats to enter into cartel agreements with representatives of private industry. See Theda Skocpol and Kenneth Finegold, "State Capacity and Economic Intervention in the Early New Deal," *Political Science Quarterly*, vol. 97 (Summer 1982), pp. 255–78.

27. Edward Pendleton Herring, *Public Administration and the Public Interest* (McGraw-Hill, 1936), pt. 3.

28. Grant McConnell, *Private Power and American Democracy* (Knopf, 1966), pp. 49–50.

29. For the Clean Air Act see P.L. 91-604 (December 31, 1970), 84 Stat. 1676; P.L. 97-375 (December 21, 1982), 96 Stat. 1820; and P.L. 101-594 (November 15, 1991), 104 Stat. 2399. The Occupational Safety and Health Act is P.L. 91-596 (December 29, 1970), 84 Stat. 1590; the Employees Retirement Income Security Act, P.L. 93-406 (September 2, 1974), 88 Stat. 829; the Federal Land Policy and Management Act, P.L. 94-597 (October 21, 1976), 80 Stat. 2744; and the Natural Gas Policy Act, P.L. 95-621 (November 9, 1978), 92 Stat. 3350.

30. Typically, there has been a Democratic Congress and a Republican-controlled presidency, but of course for a few years in the late 1940s and early 1950s, Congress was Republican and the presidency Democratic. Divided government must itself be placed within the overall constitutional framework of separated powers. Jerre Williams has commented that separation of powers inhibits action in regulatory agencies. Much of the typical agency's energy is dissipated in absorbing the tensions generated in the competition of the branches. This also applies across the old-line bureaucracy. The various commissions and bureaus must carry out "the broad, general, and usually disputed delegations of power from the Congress," and they must simultaneously "satisfy the executive branch of the government on its budgetary and legislative proposals and satisfy the courts as to the scope of [their] activities and the fidelity with which they are carried out." Jerre Williams, "Cornerstones of American Administrative Law," in Donald D. Barry and Howard Whitcomb, eds., *The Legal Foundations of Public Administration*, 2d ed. (St. Paul: West Publishers, 1987), p. 34. See also, especially on the Reagan years, James P. Pfiffer, "Political Appointees and Career Executives: The Democracy-Bureaucracy Nexus in the Third Century," *Public Administration Review*, vol. 47 (January–February, 1987), pp. 57–65.

31. August 3, 1938, 53 Stat. 1157. See Robert Roberts, "The Public Integrity Quagmire," in Ban and Riccucci, eds., *Public Personnel Management*, pp. 145–47.

32. Morris P. Fiorina, *Divided Government* (Macmillan, 1992); and David R. Mayhew, *Divided We Govern: Party Control, Lawmaking, and Investigations, 1946–1990* (Yale University Press, 1991).

33. Francis E. Rourke, "American Bureaucracy in a Changing Political Setting," *Journal of Public Administration Research and Theory*, vol. 1 (April 1991), p. 116.

34. See Ralph Nader, Peter J. Petkas, and Kate Blackwell, *Whistle Blowing: The Report of the Conference on Professional Responsibility* (Grossman, 1972), pp. 39–54.

35. P.L. 95-521 (October 26, 1978), 92 Stat. 1824.

36. Inspector Generals Act of 1978, 92 Stat. 1101. See also William T. Gormley, Jr., *Taming the Bureaucracy: Muscles, Prayers and Other Strategies* (Princeton University Press, 1989), pp. 122–24.

37. June 11, 1946, 60 Stat. 237. Jerry L. Mashaw and David L. Harfst refer to this compromise as a synthesis taking place in the context of the struggle between what they call the Madisonian and the New Deal philosophies of public administration. See *The Struggle for Auto Safety* (Harvard University Press, 1990), p. 22.

38.  See Gerald Garvey, *Facing the Bureaucracy: Living and Dying in a Public Agency* (San Francisco: Jossey-Bass, 1993), p. 193 and sources cited there.

The APA applies to an agency's procedures only as a residual, so that if another statute specifically prescribes a procedure for a particular agency, the APA does not apply. See Martin Shapiro, *Who Guards the Guardians?: Judicial Control of Administration* (University of Georgia Press, 1988), pp. 39–40. One result of this arrangement is to make the act less of a universal law covering the whole of the federal administrative process. But a corollary is that it increases the number of applicable laws, making administrative framework a crazy quilt.

39.  The relatively strict version of the rule-of-law principle is usually traced to the influence of Lord Alfred V. Dicey. He and his disciples on both sides of the Atlantic foresaw a rapidly expanding body of "law" emanating from the officials who would staff the rulemaking agencies of the administrative state. He left room for considerable discretion in the exercise of administrative duties, but as his contemporary Oliver Wendell Holmes, Jr., once observed, any idea tends toward the limit of its logic. The Diceyian idea was to confine administrative action through close scrutiny by judges sitting in the ordinary courts. Alfred V. Dicey, *Introduction to the Study of the Law of the Constitution*, 10th ed. (St. Martin's, 1961 [1885]), especially p. 202. The doctrine explicitly prohibited the exercise of "wide discretionary authority" by ministerial officials, a teaching that obviously left some room for interpretation. For decades the dominant interpretation was a strict one, narrowing the latitude allowed to bureaucrats as severely as the cases would allow.

40.  See generally Charles Reich, "The New Property," *Yale Law Journal*, vol. 73 (1964), pp. 733–87; see also Paul Verkuil, "The Emerging Concept of Administrative Procedure," *Columbia Law Review*, vol. 78 (March 1978), pp. 258 and 296–300 on the new regulation and pp. 318–19 on hybrid rulemaking.

41.  Consumer Product Safety Act, P.L. 92-573 (October 27, 1972), 86 Stat. 1207; National Environmental Policy Act (establishing the EPA), P.L. 91-190 (January 1, 1968), 83 Stat. 852; and Occupational Safety and Health Act, P.L. 91-596 (December 29, 1970), 84 Stat. 1590.

42.  The words are from the APA, 60 Stat. 237, Sec. 10 (e)(1). In *Goldberg* v. *Kelly*, 397 U.S. 254 (1970), the Supreme Court added significantly to the number, cost, and fairness requirements of many administrative proceedings. And a series of federal appellate court cases added a judicial amendment to the APA's provision for informal actions by creating a new category called hybrid rulemaking, with various additional procedural requirements. See Verkuil, "Emerging Concept of Administrative Procedure," pp. 258, 318–19.

Elaborate court-imposed requirements have also expanded the access of interested parties to the administrative process by embellishing the concept of legal standing and extending the "notice and comment" requirements of the APA. The courts also multiplied and ritualized the steps that have to be taken, for which Martin Shapiro adopted the term *synopticism*, coined by David Braybrooke and Charles E. Lindblom. The synoptic test required agency decisionmakers to consider every possible means that might be employed to realize the legislative will; cursory or pro forma consideration of a few solutions would not do. In a way, synopticism marked a return to the gospel according to Frank Gilbreth, since it demanded that administrators take all steps to find the best way. Moreover, agency decisionmakers now had to keep elaborate records to prove that they had indeed made the search. Braybrooke and Lindblom, *A Strategy of Decision: Policy Evolution as a Social Process* (Free Press, 1963), p. 40; and Shapiro, *Who Guards the Guardians?* pp. 159–61.

43. See for example the opinion of Justice Stevens in *Chevron* v. *Natural Resources Defense Council*, 467 U.S. 837 (1974).

44. See Richard M. Cyert and James G. March, *A Behavioral Theory of the Firm* (Prentice-Hall, 1963), pp. 102–05.

45. James Q. Wilson, *Bureaucracy: What Government Agencies Do and Why They Do It* (Basic Books, 1989), p. 343; see also in this general connection, Donald P. Warwick, *A Theory of Public Bureaucracy: Politics, Personality and Organization in the State Department* (Harvard University Press, 1975), especially pp. 99–104.

46. By reducing the role of patronage in civil service staffing, merit appointments and tenure eliminated much of the incentive that members of Congress had to interest themselves in federal employees' pay and conditions of work. Gradually, the position of government workers began to slip relative to that of their counterparts in the private sector. Early in the 1920s, postal workers formed the first collective bargaining units of real importance within the federal government. Sterling D. Spero, *The Labor Movement in a Government Industry* (New York: Doran, 1924), pp. 26, 61, cited in Van Riper, *History of the United States Civil Service*, p. 156. But aside from the postal service and a few scattered teachers' groups, organized labor failed to make significant inroads into the public sector until much later. At the federal level, executive order 10988 is generally considered the decisive event in unionizing public employees.

47. This result is clearest at the federal level, but the dynamics of public sector collective bargaining at the state and municipal levels suggest the same thing. See Joel M. Douglas, "State Civil Service and Collective Bargaining: Systems in Conflict," *Public Administration Review*, vol. 52 (January–February 1992), pp. 162–69.

48. The judgment of the Subcommittee on Position Classification of the House Committee on Post Office and Civil Service remains as apt today as it was in 1967: "A major obstacle in the improvement of the classification in the postal field service is the attitude of employee organizations. Their attitudes are based on the craft approach to job ranking. This aims at all persons in the craft receiving the same pay and achieving higher pay through seniority alone. . . . The agreements with the employee organizations make transfers from one position to another, and one office to another, practically impossible because of loss of seniority." (H. Rpt. 91-28, February 27, 1969, p. 12, reprinted in Shafritz, *Position Classification*, p. 84.

49. For figures covering the 1970s see Robert W. Hartman, *Pay and Pensions for Federal Workers* (Brookings, 1983), pp. 22–23; and Carol A. Harvey, *The Status*

34     GERALD J. GARVEY AND JOHN J. DiIULIO, JR.

*of the Senior Executive Service, 1989*, SES 90-5 (Office of Personnel Management, 1990), p. 41.

50. Members of an influential group of contemporary scholars sometimes called the New Theorists contend that the employees are weak. They argue, essentially, as follows: personnel evaluators, especially when they operate from a central office removed from the position for which candidates are applying, cannot infer from qualifying exams and employment interviews how an employee will perform over a career. The Progressives' optimistic expectations for merit appointment notwithstanding, applicants have a much better sense than any personnel evaluator of their real reasons for preferring a job in the civil service to one in the private sector. The reason might be virtual immunity from firing unless underperformance becomes flagrant. Jobs that carry civil service protections—the Progressives' valued guarantee of job tenure—inherently tend to select adversely. Workers who seek career cushions rather than career challenges will feel more comfortable in organizations with assured promotion and predictable salary graduations.

Once applicants have been hired, the assurance of job security may induce them to do less than their best job. Less work for the same pay, some would suggest, is an all but inevitable consequence. See C. G. Veljanovski, *The New Law-and-Economics: A Research Review* (Oxford, England: Centre for Socio-Legal Studies, 1982), pp. 46–47, and sources cited there; Terry M. Moe, "The New Economics of Organization," *American Journal of Political Science*, vol. 28 (November 1984), pp. 762–65; and Garvey, *Facing the Bureaucracy*, chap. 2.

51. Herbert Kaufman, *Red Tape, Its Origins, Uses, and Abuses* (Brookings, 1977).

52. Alexis de Tocqueville, *Democracy in America*, Richard Hefner, ed. (New American Library, 1956), pp. 303–04.

53. See John E. Brandl, "How Organization Counts: Incentives and Inspiration," *Journal of Policy Analysis and Management* vol. 8 (Summer 1989), pp. 489–94; and Garvey, *Facing the Bureaucracy*, especially chap. 1. The New Theorists suggest that at any moment a balance exists between the ordering of work by the kind of classification system civil service systems traditionally use and its ordering by contract. If transaction costs on average fall throughout the economy, there will be greater reliance on free market exchanges, and bargaining and item-by-item contracting will increase. If, however, transaction costs seem on the whole to be rising, decisionmakers will increase their reliance on organizations and hierarchies "up to the point where the cost of an additional transaction within the firm [or bureau] begins to exceed the cost of the same transaction in the market. In equilibrium, some transactions will therefore be internalized within firms of various kinds and sizes, and some will be left to the market." Moe, "New Economics of Organization," p. 743.

Organizing work by contract rather than by civil service classification yields undeniable benefits—added flexibility in the personnel system, for example, and an increased ability to hire specialists who would never think of limiting themselves in a civil service structure. The tendency to organize the work of the federal government by contract represents a significant change in the way public business has traditionally been conducted. A vast literature has documented the gradual shifting of the equilibrium in favor of organization by contract, a process variously known as privatization, contracting out, or what Donald Kettl has termed "government by proxy." See *Government by Proxy: (Mis?) Managing Federal Programs* (Washington: CQ Press, 1988), especially pp. 7–14.

54. See for example John C. Goodman, "Privatizing the Welfare State," and Stephen Moore, "Contracting Out: A Painless Alternative to the Budget Cutter's Knife," in Steve H. Henke, ed., *Prospects for Privatization* (Academy of Political Science, 1987), pp. 36–48.

55. Charles H. Logan, *Private Prisons: Cons & Pros* (Oxford University Press 1990); and, in rebuttal to Logan's pro-privatization argument, John J. DiIulio, Jr., *No Escape: The Future of American Corrections* (Basic Books, 1991), chap. 5.

56. On union opposition, see Katherine C. Naff, "Labor-Management Relations and Privatization: A Federal Perspective," *Public Administration Review*, vol. 51 (January–February 1991), pp. 23–30. On legal limits, see Steven Kelman, *Procurement and Public Management* (Washington: AEI Press, 1990). Although Barry Bozeman has persuasively argued that most organizations in America's complex, highly regulated society display some elements of publicness, some functions seem inherently more public, more imperatively to be performed directly by government, than others. See *All Organizations Are Public: Bridging Public and Private Organizational Theories* (San Francisco: Jossey-Bass, 1987).

57. On December 1, 1992, the Office of Management and Budget released a devastating report on inefficiencies in federal contracting. Allan V. Burman, administrator of the Federal Procurement Policy Office at OMB, said that "agencies have spent a lot of time and resources in insuring that contracts are let and not on seeing to it that the contract is working effectively." The report bodes to be merely the latest round in a cyclical process of privatization and monitoring that ends by complicating governance rather than simplifying it. Keith Schneider, "U.S. Cites Waste in Its Contracts," *New York Times*, December 2, 1992, p. A1.

58. David Osborne and Ted Gaebler, *Reinventing Government: How the Entrepreneurial Spirit Is Transforming the Public Sector* (Addison-Wesley, 1992).

59. Graham T. Allison, "Public and Private Management: Are They Fundamentally Alike in All Unimportant Respects?" in Richard J. Stillman, III, ed., *Public Administration: Concepts and Cases*, 5th ed. (Houghton Mifflin 1992), p. 294. Allison adds, "There is little if any agreement on the standards and measurement of performance to appraise a government manager, while various tests of performance—financial return, market share, performance measures for executive compensation—are well established in private business. . . . Governmental managers rarely have a clear bottom line, while that of a private business manager is profit, market performance, and survival" (pp. 285–86).

60. Constance Horner, "Beyond Mr. Gradgrind," *Policy Review*, no. 44 (Spring 1988), pp. 34–35.

61. Significant efforts have been under way for some time to deliver on the promise of the 1978 Civil Service Reform Act for more decentralized, flexible

public personnel administration at the federal level. All references to deregulating the government should be read as incorporating existing ideas on rule loosening. Deregulating the civil service, then, refers to speeding a process that has not gone nearly far enough. Carolyn Ban, "The Realities of the Merit System," in Ban and Riccucci, eds., *Public Personnel Management*, pp. 17–28.

62. Bearing in mind that the required extent of privatization will depend on how much loosening occurs in the classification system.

# 3 ||| Can the Bureaucracy Be Deregulated? Lessons from Government Agencies

James Q. Wilson

NOTHING could be more striking than the emerging differences in managerial practice and theory between large corporations and government agencies. In response to foreign competition, market pressures, and the demands of dissatisfied shareholders, many corporations are becoming leaner, more decentralized, and more committed to identifying and serving customer interests. Though the details differ from one firm to the next, in general the strategies emphasize empowering lower-level employees and their immediate supervisors to make more decisions, flattening the firm's hierarchy so that messages and orders travel shorter distances, designing compensation schemes that reward good performance, and developing an organizational culture based on such concepts as total quality management. Some government agencies are also taking tentative steps along these lines, but for the most part public employees work in an environment of multiple constraints centrally imposed: decisions are made at the top, information filters through many levels, compensation is based on rank and seniority, and the organizational culture, implicitly if not explicitly, reflects an aversion to risk and makes compliance with rules more important than attaining goals.

For decades, private executives urged government agencies to adopt businesslike management techniques. Experienced public officials have always been somewhat skeptical of this advice because it ignored the profound differences between public and private organizations. Government bureaucracies must satisfy principles of accountability that are fundamentally different from those in industry. But despite their disparate perspectives, public and private executives often shared certain assumptions that made businesslike methods applicable in principle if not in practice: a belief that efficiency was the appropriate standard for evaluating procedures, a desire to control if not eliminate the discretionary authority of lower-level workers, and a commitment to clear chains of command that would minimize external pressures on managers. The executives shared, in short, a faith in Taylorism. When business managers entered government service, they were usually frustrated in their efforts to introduce Taylorite principles because they lacked the authority and resources, but these barriers to change did not diminish their commitment to the principles.

Today, private executives have a very different kind of advice to give to their government counterparts, advice that is distinctly non-Taylorite. The change is exemplified by the difference between the recommendations of the two Hoover commissions (1947–55) and those of a contemporary best-seller on public management, *Reinventing Government* by David Osborne and Ted Gaebler.[1] The Hoover commissions advocated achieving efficiency, establishing clear lines of authority, matching responsibility and authority, eliminating waste and duplication, and attracting expert, nonpartisan administrators. Osborne and Gaebler offer ten quite different criteria for guiding reform. To them, government should be catalytic, enterprising, anticipatory, decentralized, community owned, competitive, mission driven, results oriented, customer driven, and market oriented.

Osborne and Gaebler give many examples of government agencies at the local, state, and federal levels that have embraced one or more of their criteria. They end their account by applying the ten principles to three important policy areas—health care, education, and criminal justice. Their model for health care has many of the features of what has come to be called managed competition: independent providers supply the services, but within a government-structured market in which everyone is covered by insurance provided by employers or, as a last resort, the government. Education would be funded by the government but supplied by schools that compete for students. Criminal justice would be overseen by public safety coordinating councils that would fund specific programs based on how well they achieved measurable goals. All of this amounts, the authors believe, to a new paradigm for government.

One can argue with the examples of the new paradigm at work. For instance, I find it hard to imagine crime control being managed by a council (committees can rarely manage anything) that funds local agencies based on their measured outcomes (little of importance in criminal justice can be measured, that which can be measured is usually beyond the control of any police or correctional agency, and funding decisions in committees tend to be driven by interagency logrolling more than objectively assessed performance).

Nonetheless, many of Osborne and Gaebler's assumptions are correct, most of their examples fascinating, and all of their criteria stimulating. But three things are lacking. First, the authors take government for granted and ask only how it should operate, ignoring the fundamental question: "What should government do?" There are some things it must do whether or not it can do them well, but there other things that it need not do at all and, because it cannot do them well, should not try. The nation must have a government-supported navy and state department, but does it have to have a government Postal Service? A General Services Administration? A Health Care Financing Administration? By assuming that government can do nearly anything, provided only that it is "catalytic" and "enterprising," Osborne and Gaebler inadvertently revive Michael Dukakis's deeply flawed slogan that politics is not about ideology, it is about competence.

Second, the authors provide almost no guidance as to which reforms are suitable for which agencies. Surely we do not want the Internal Revenue Service to be competitive, community owned, and customer driven; we want it to be consistent, honest, and responsive. Consistency and honesty are best ensured by centralized control and immunity from citizen pressures; responsiveness requires some measure of decentralization coupled with a culture that takes citizens' questions seriously—not an easy mix to achieve. For many of the same reasons, Osborne and Gaebler's criteria do not seem very applicable to the responsibilities of the Social Security Administration, FBI, Secret Service, or Drug Enforcement Administration. But many of their emphases would improve the services citizens might want from public schools, veterans' hospitals, welfare agencies, and the Federal Emergency Management Agency. And there are many agencies for which it is hard to decide, without a lot more analysis than Osborne and Gaebler provide, which slogans fit, when, and under what circumstances. Americans want many regulatory agencies to be results oriented but not customer driven because the agencies' task is to regulate their customers. All parts of the military ought to be enterprising, catalytic, anticipatory, and mission driven, but anybody who thinks that every part also ought to be decentralized has never served on an aircraft carrier or in a strategic missile wing.

Finally, Osborne and Gaebler offer no strategy by which agencies can be freed from excessive constraints and motivated to be mission driven. Many agency heads, I suspect, might like to adopt some of their suggestions, but most do not. The executives' reluctance is not the result of personal rigidities or intellectual deficiencies; rather, they are responding to the incentives and constraints they encounter daily. These incentives include the need to manage situations over which they have little control and to manage them on the basis of poorly defined goals and in the face of a complex array of constraints that seems always to grow, never to shrink. Outside forces—elected officials, interest groups, employee organizations, professional associations, the courts, and the media—demand a voice in running the agencies and make that demand effective by imposing rules on them and insisting that all the rules be enforced all the time. Moreover, habitual patterns of action based on the lessons of the past, the memories of earlier struggles, and the expectations of co-workers narrow the area within which new courses of action are sought.

Bureaucrats often complain of congressional micromanagement, and indeed it exists.[2] In the past few decades, for instance, the Pentagon has had to cope with a dramatic proliferation of hearings, reports, investigations, statutory amendments, and budgetary adjustments.[3] But presidential micromanagement has also increased. Herbert Kaufman has noted that for half a century the White House has feared agency independence more than agency paralysis, and so it has multiplied the number of presidential staffers, central management offices, and requirements for higher-level reviews. Once started along the path of congressional or White House control, the process acquires a momentum of its own. "As more constraints are imposed, rigidities fixing agencies in their established ways intensify. As a result, complaints that they do not respond to controls also intensify. Further controls, checkpoints, and clearances are therefore introduced."[4] Much the same story can be told with respect to the growing involvement of the courts in agency affairs.

With some conspicuous exceptions, the result of this micromanagement has been to deflect the attention of agency executives

away from how the tasks of their agencies get defined and toward
the rules that must be observed no matter what the tasks may be.
Who, then, decides what tasks shall be performed? In agencies such
as the Social Security Administration with observable products and
routinized work processes, the answer is relatively simple—the
laws and regulations that created the agency also define its job.
But in agencies that lack such products or work processes or
both—police departments, public schools, the Forest Service, the
State Department—the answer seems to be nobody in particular
and everybody in general. The operating-level workers define the
tasks, occasionally by design, as when operator ideology makes a
difference, but more commonly by accident, as when experience,
professional norms, situational and technological imperatives, and
peer-group expectations shape the work. For example, much of the
behavior of the Environmental Protection Agency reflects the fact
that its mission is determined more by lawyers than by scientists or
economists.

The fundamental difficulty facing anyone attempting to implement the kinds of changes Osborne and Gaebler propose is that,
even if which criteria fit which agencies were known, the heads of
those agencies usually lack the incentives and the freedom to act in
accordance. Despite this, some will try and a few will succeed.
These brave attempts and (if the authors are to be believed) occasional successes make up the anecdotes in *Reinventing Government*. The book is useful as a challenge and a guide to these
motivated (or desperate) officials. And its teachings have become
the animating spirit of the 1993 report of Vice President Gore's
National Performance Review, a document popularly known as the
plan for reinventing government.[5] The report sets forth four goals
for federal administrative agencies—cutting red tape, putting customers first, empowering employees to get results, and getting back
to basics. Many of the recommendations designed to achieve these
ends involve reducing the constraints on federal executives so that
they will have the freedom to manage in ways that will better satisfy
their citizen-clients. For example, the report urges that authority to
hire workers be taken from the Office of Personnel Management
and given to the agency needing the workers. It also urges that the
time it takes to fire a federal employee be shortened, procedures for
purchasing goods and services be radically simplified, regulations
and accounting rules facing managers be reduced or consolidated,

and agency performance be measured against clearly articulated goals.

Were Congress to grant to agencies the freedom to run themselves in these ways, opportunities for more effective administration would be significantly improved. Government bureaus would be able to do some of the things that corporations have long been doing. But there are at least two reasons for being doubtful that this will occur on a large scale. First, Congress and the courts and the White House have been busily adding restrictions, not reducing them. With a few exceptions, government managers face far more limitations on their freedom of action today than they did thirty years ago. Second, government executives have no incentives as powerful as those private executives have to surrender power to subordinates, build work teams, and make customer satisfaction an overriding goal. Businesses must do these things to survive in an age of global competition, especially competition from low-wage producers, and if they do them successfully they are rewarded with higher earnings and the managers with fatter bonuses. Government can survive by fiat, and government officials get no significant financial rewards from putting customers first.

## Constraints: A Rising Tide Sinks All Boats

The constraints on government organizations have multiplied exponentially. There is no way to measure this change exactly, but a rough idea can be gained by comparing the texts of certain landmark laws passed thirty or forty years ago with their more recent counterparts. Here is one example.

The Federal Aid Highway Act (P.L. 84-627) was passed in 1956. In twenty-eight pages, it authorized the interstate highway system, levied the taxes to pay for it, and established the trust fund that would receive the tax receipts and disburse them for construction projects. It set certain constraints: the Davis-Bacon Act would apply so that highway contractors would have to pay prevailing wage rates, the Bureau of Public Roads would have to consult with state highway departments in drawing up plans, and public hearings would have to be held. There were also a few bits of advice: the authorities ought to study highway safety, and money could be spent on archeological salvage at construction sites.

Thirty-five years later, the program underwent a major reauthorization. The Intermodal Surface Transportation Efficiency Act of 1991 (P.L. 102-240) was passed, its very name suggesting the diverse goals that were now to be served. What the title implied the text amply confirmed. The law ran to 293 pages, more than ten times the length of its predecessor. In addition to building highways and aiding mass transit, the law mandated that the secretary of transportation relieve congestion, improve air quality, preserve historic sites, encourage the use of auto seat belts and motorcycle helmets, control erosion and storm water runoff, monitor traffic and collect data on speeding, reduce drunk driving, require environmental impact studies, control outdoor advertising, develop standards for high-occupancy vehicles, require metropolitan area and statewide planning, use recycled rubber in making asphalt, set aside 10 percent of construction monies for small businesses owned by disadvantaged individuals, define women as disadvantaged individuals, buy iron and steel from U.S. suppliers, establish new rules for renting equipment, give preferential employment to Native Americans if a highway is to be built near a reservation, and control the use of calcium magnesium acetate in performing seismic retrofits on bridges.

To this *partial* list of objectives Congress added extensive criteria to be used in planning. Transportation plans should be designed to relieve congestion and preserve existing facilities, be based on life-cycle costs, evaluate impacts on land use, encourage bicycle paths and pedestrian walkways, control water and air pollution, and take into account "all" social and economic effects. In addition, the law designates scores of specific projects—bridges, tunnels, roads, studies, experiments—that must be funded in specific states or cities or through specific organizations.

There was, of course, nothing in the act suggesting how the secretary ought to weigh these competing goals and constraints or manage the inevitable trade-offs among them, nor any indication how anyone other than God might foresee "all" the social and economic effects of a transportation plan. In essence the law is a list of every good deed anyone with access to Congress could think up. It does say something about federal transportation policy (Washington wants to encourage states and cities to develop a mix of highway, pedestrian, bicycle, and mass transit systems), but it implies much more about the interests that have political clout in the

nation's capital: states, localities, feminists, Native Americans, public interest lobbies, engineering and consulting firms, and the man-
ufacturers of certain kinds of equipment.

How will a secretary of transportation and his principal deputies, the
heads of the Federal Highway Administration, the Urban Mass Transportation Administration, and the National Highway Traffic Safety
Administration, cope with this law? If the past is any guide, they will
create special offices in charge of each major goal or requirement and
review procedures designed to ensure that pieces of paper are submitted discussing each before any money is spent. Time-consuming
attention to the law's mandates will take precedence in the minds of
many bureaucrats over building roads or funding commuter trains.
Then Congress will launch an investigation to discover why the money
it appropriated is being spent so slowly and the transit systems it
authorized are so long in taking shape.

The accumulation of goals and constraints for some agencies can
be mind-boggling. California elementary and secondary schools,
for example, are governed by the better part of five volumes of the
state's education code, 2,846 pages in all (including commentary).
And this is just the legislature's contribution to defining a good
education; to it must be added the rulings of the state superintendent of public instruction, the local school boards, and the district
superintendents of schools.

The lengthiest sections of the code are those pertaining to the
circumstances under which a teacher can be fired or a student
expelled. A teacher can be dismissed for, among other things,
incompetency, immoral conduct, or "evident unfitness," though the
courts have held that being arrested for a sex offense does not
constitute, in and of itself, either immoral conduct or evident unfitness. A dismissal first requires a written notice, filed the semester
before (and in no event less than ninety days before) the personnel
action, such notice to include detailed examples of incompetency
or unfitness. At the hearing, the teacher is entitled to be represented
by counsel and to select one of the three members of the hearing
panel. The evidence of the school is subject to discovery proceedings, and all testimony is to be under oath. An adverse decision can
be appealed to the courts. A pupil can be expelled (which is
defined as a suspension for more than five days) for a variety of
causes, but there is a right to written notice, a hearing, and representation by counsel.[6]

## Deregulation

To do better, we have to deregulate the government.[7] If deregulation of a market makes sense because it liberates the entrepreneurial energies of its members, then it is possible that deregulation may also help energize the public sector. The meaning of deregulation is relatively clear in reference to businesses. It means relying on market discipline shaped by government incentives (taxes, fees, and the rule of law) to balance the most efficient use of scarce resources with reasonable attention to collective goals. But what does deregulation mean when applied to government agencies? It means, I think, placing agency executives in a situation in which the rewards for attaining goals are increased and the penalties for ignoring constraints are reduced. To say the same thing in different words, deregulation means allowing agencies to operate in a regime where, to the greatest extent possible, they are judged by outcomes (what they achieve) and not inputs (who they hire, where they operate, and how they negotiate contracts).

Many government goals can be attained by relying on markets. Markets may serve public goals when both payers and producers are private (for example, when the government sets pollution charges), when payers are public but providers are private (for example, when government vouchers are spent on private schools), and when payers are private but providers are public (for example, when Australians or New Zealanders can choose to fly on either a government-owned or a privately owned airline).

The use of markets ought to be expanded in all circumstances where it is appropriate. Markets can work where there is no fraud, adequate consumer information, competition among purveyors, and real consequences (that is, a loss or gain of revenue) for successful and unsuccessful competitors. But many government services either cannot or will not be supplied through the market. In these instances the challenge for government is to find ways to make public agencies innovative, mission driven, and results oriented even when they retain their monopoly status. This is not easily done; indeed, examples of it will in all likelihood remain the exception and not the rule. But even if we cannot expect deregulation in the public sector to yield the same results as in the private sector, we can at a minimum agree that detailed regulation is rarely compatible with energy, pride in workmanship, and the exercise of initiative. The best evidence for this proposition, if any is needed, is that most people do not work well in an environment in which every action is second-guessed, every initiative viewed with suspicion, and every controversial decision denounced as malfeasance.

James Colvard, for many years a senior civilian manager in the navy, suggested that the government needs to emulate methods that work in the better parts of the private sector: "a bias toward action, small staffs, and a high level of delegation which is based on trust."[8] A panel of the National Academy of Public Administration, consisting of seventeen government agency assistant secretaries, made much the same point:

> over many years, government has become entwined in elaborate management control systems and the accretion of progressively more detailed administrative procedures, often heavily centralized. This development has not produced superior management. Instead, it has produced managerial overburden. . . . Procedures overwhelm substance. Organizations become discredited, along with their employees. . . . The attitude of those who design and administer the rules . . . must be reoriented from a "control mentality" to one of "how can I help get the mission of this agency accomplished."[9]

But how can government delegate and trust and still maintain accountability? If it is a mistake to foster an ethos that encourages every bureaucrat to go by the book, is it not an equally serious problem to allow zealots to engage in mission madness, charging off to implement their private version of some ambiguous public goal? Given the bureaucratic desire for autonomy and the political rewards of rule making, will anybody find it in his or her interest to abandon the control mentality and adopt the mission-accomplishment mentality?

Some parts of some agencies have managed to take important steps toward action, trust, and delegation. In 1987 the eastern region of the Forest Service, headquartered in Milwaukee, embarked on a serious effort to change its organizational culture. It shifted authority and resources from the regional office to the district forests, encouraged the building of interdisciplinary work teams in the districts, cut back on the number of regulations, and modified headquarters visits to local offices to emphasize collegial consultation and minimize rule enforcement.[10] This was a big change for the Forest Service, which had traditionally relied on detailed manuals, close inspections, and functional specialization to manage its far-flung employees and had insisted that all important policy issues be decided by the top brass.

In Minnesota, a program called Striving Toward Excellence in Performance (STEP) was begun to eliminate the all-too-familiar bottleneck created when headquarters staff insist that they and not the operating agencies know how best to purchase equipment. STEP was a systematic effort to induce staff to view line managers as their customers. It tried to redefine the process by which the constraints every government agency must work under—fiscal integrity, economical purchasing practices, fair employee supervision—were managed. Line agencies were given more authority and staff agencies less.[11]

Such innovations may survive the test of time and political counterattacks. But little bureaucratic improvement is likely if every step forward depends on the imagination and energy of a few motivated leaders. The key question is whether such changes can be made systematically and structurally. The Gore report was obviously written in the hopes of making it easier for all federal executives to do those things that parts of the Forest Service and a few other agencies have done (the report mentions the Air Combat Command and some other exemplars), but it provides no general incentives for government officials to act contrary to their current interests. And those interests, as the report itself acknowledges, are rarely to do a superb job or even to avoid doing a poor one; they are to stay out of trouble. "In Washington's highly politicized world, the greatest risk is not that a program will perform poorly, but that a scandal will erupt. Scandals are front-page news, while routine failure is ignored. Hence control system after control system is piled up to minimize the risk of scandal."[12] This problem is evident in the history of efforts to improve two government services, schooling and law enforcement.

## Attempts at Deregulation: Schools and Police

Some school districts and police departments have attempted to adopt important aspects of the deregulation philosophy by decentralizing operations and giving greater authority to line personnel and their immediate supervisors. In public education the approach is called school-based (or site-based) management; in law enforcement it is called community-based policing.

Site-based management is an effort to make the local schools more effective and responsive. This goal is to be achieved by giving principals wider authority to hire and reward teachers, redesign curricula, make purchases, and administer a budget. The hope is that such localized management will enable a public school to more nearly approximate the qualities of a good private school: to emphasize learning, motivate teachers, discipline students, and involve parents. This hope springs from the failure of earlier educational reforms that placed new and more detailed requirements on the schools—tougher graduation requirements, higher teacher certification standards, and centrally designed curricula. Such efforts have tended to multiply constraints without improving the quality of education. Though some may have had a marginal benefit, as a whole they have merely made public school systems more centralized and rule bound and thus more rule oriented.

In 1993 the Los Angeles Unified School District (LAUSD) adopted a version of school-based management developed by a coalition of education, business, labor, and community leaders called LEARN, the Los Angeles Educational Alliance for Restructuring Now. The plan calls for setting performance standards for students, teachers, and schools and assessing progress by means of standardized measures—all elements in the conventional armory of educational reform. But in addition, governance is to be decentralized to individual schools, making them semiautonomous units in as yet unspecified ways. The LEARN plan is being challenged by two rivals—a plan to break up the LAUSD into smaller districts and one to adopt voucher-based parental choice of schools. Advocates of the latter two strategies believe that site-based management in a system as large as the LAUSD is unlikely to succeed: pressures from teachers' unions, interest groups, and central administrators to maintain control over local schools will prove irresistible.

The critics may be right. A Rand Corporation survey of site-based management efforts in various parts of the country suggests that they succeed only where central authorities are genuinely willing to see their powers substantially diminished, and there are not many such authorities: "Site-based management will lead to real changes at the school level only if it is a school system's basic reform strategy, not just one among several reform projects."[13] The reason site-based management is a precarious reform is that for it to work, schools must be judged by outputs rather than inputs, and central school officials are overwhelmingly inclined to make inputs—rules, resources, hiring decisions, curriculum design, book purchasing— the standard by which school principals are held accountable. Because of this, the Rand study concludes, the best way to ensure that individual schools are accountable to output standards is to implement meaningful parental choice. It is too early to tell which pattern of accountability will prevail in Los Angeles or with what effect.

Police departments have also experimented with less centralized, less rule-oriented management systems, in most cases out of a desire to increase public confidence or respond to neighborhood complaints. Community-based policing is a law enforcement philosophy that tries to do two things—bring police officers and citizens into working partnerships in neighborhoods and give the police responsibility for identifying and solving neighborhood problems even if they are not conventional law enforcement issues. For community-based policing to work, patrol officers and sergeants must be given greater freedom from radio dispatchers and standardized duty schedules and evaluated on grounds other than arrests made or tickets issued. But enhancing the discretionary authority of patrol officers and loosening their ties to headquarters' priorities entail risks. The police chief and his principal deputies will have less control over how officers spend their time and fewer personnel with which to respond to calls. As a consequence the executives worry that they will be less able to prevent or cope with some of the pressures that usually spell trouble for law enforcement—allegations of corruption and complaints of slow response.

Few large cities have had any prolonged experience with community-based policing. New York is trying it in one precinct, Los Angeles has experimented with it in a few districts, and Philadelphia has launched it citywide. Houston made a major commitment to it under Chief Lee Brown but under a new chief reverted to a more traditional policing style. There are very few serious evaluations of the approach in practice and few indications of how such a strategy can survive in an environment—big-city law enforcement—in which political pressures tend to generate more, not less, central control and more, not fewer, operational constraints.

Attempts to implement bureaucratic deregulation have usually been responses to crises: pupils with sagging achievement scores, schools with high dropout rates, or neighborhoods upset by police indifference or brutality. Deregulation is embraced after everything else—appointing citizen advisory groups, launching public relations campaigns, writing new laws and regulations, or imposing additional bureaucratic constraints—has failed.

Not only is it uncertain whether crisis-induced change will last and make a difference, it is not yet known whether deregulation can occur without a crisis and by plan. The constraints that minimize an agency's commitment to achieve its goals and serve citizens are, after all, the product of politically powerful demands that government serve widely supported objectives. The constraints come less from the inherent conservatism of bureaucrats than from publics concerned about protecting civil rights, rooting out conflicts of interest, supporting due process, preserving fiscal accountability, protecting the environment, and ensuring citizen access. In short, they come from us.

## Deregulation, Autonomy, and School Choice

Because centrally imposed rules and goals are the chief threat to the kinds of energetic, decentralized, competitive, mission-driven agencies that Osborne and Gaebler want to encourage, it is worth taking up in some detail the use of markets to reduce constraints. Markets are already more widely used by government than many people realize. A significant part of the nation's security, maintenance, and supply needs are handled by private vendors. Because this practice reduces the number of federal jobs, it is often opposed by organizations representing federal employees. But contracting out has not provoked broad public debate because the public sees no vital interests threatened by allowing the government to purchase goods and services from the private sector.

It is a different matter when it comes to education. Although the country has had long experience with allowing people to choose between public and private colleges and giving college students tax-supported vouchers (such as the G.I. Bill) with which to pay their tuition, the idea of doing the same thing for elementary and

secondary school pupils has been highly controversial. It is important, therefore, to understand why many experts believe that market
competition among schools will improve the quality of education.

Osborne and Gaebler strongly endorse the conclusions of John
Chubb and Terry Moe about the advantages of competition in
schooling.[14] And they endorse them for exactly the right reason: if
schools are to compete for students, each school must have sufficient autonomy to design programs, run facilities, and hire teachers
in ways that appeal to parents. A centrally managed, big-city school
system that is in unchallenged possession of all the government
money spent in that area on elementary and secondary schooling
will have no incentive to confer on individual schools much freedom from central rules and every incentive to multiply those rules.
If the money comes from city hall or the state capital to the school
superintendent, it will come on the condition that he or she follow
the rules, mandates, and restrictions attached to that money. The
superintendent, in turn, will pass the funding to individual schools
only on condition that principals and teachers follow the rules,
mandates, and restrictions. Public schools, especially in big cities,
will lack the autonomy possessed by private schools.

By examining student achievement and organizational characteristics in 500 high schools across America, Chubb and Moe were able
to show that, controlling for the family background of the pupils
and the financial resources of the schools, students made greater
educational gains in private schools than in public ones. In this
respect they confirmed the findings of James Coleman and his
colleagues.[15] But they broke new ground. They showed that among
*public* schools, students did better, other things being equal, in
schools that were more autonomous. The more autonomous
schools were those that, in the opinion of the teachers and principals who worked in them, gave greater freedom to teachers and
principals to do their jobs than did other schools. The more autonomous schools were freer from personnel rules, curricular decisions,
instruction programs, and teacher discipline imposed by a central
school board or superintendent's office. The public schools that
were more autonomous tended to be located in the suburbs. Private
schools, by definition, are very autonomous, which helps explain
why, on the average, private schools do a better job of teaching
their students than public schools do and why suburban public
schools do a better job than big-city schools.[16]

This finding is of exceptional importance because the superiority of suburban public high schools to the the their big-city counterparts has usually been attributed to their wealth or their better staffing. But Chubb and Moe show that spending more money per pupil or reducing the student-teacher ratio has no discernible effect on learning. What does affect learning is freeing teachers to teach and principals to manage, and this effect operates in addition to, and independently of, the class status of the parents. (Once all the factors were taken into account, the race of the students had no effect on educational attainment.)

The reason many people, including Chubb and Moe, favor parental choice paid for by government vouchers is that it is almost the only way anyone can devise to produce autonomy for individual big-city schools. As long as a school system has monopoly control over public education funds, it will have no incentive to grant autonomy to any of its parts and every incentive to keep them on a short bureaucratic leash.

The Gore report is very cautious about turning government activities over to private firms. It proposes that the air traffic control system become a government corporation, private firms be hired to supply inspectors to enforce occupational safety and health rules, and the Defense Department rely more on private vendors for some of its functions (such as towing cars and providing automatic data processing). But it stops well short of any major privatization initiatives. The Postal Service is to remain a government enterprise, albeit one that has benefited, the report claims, from competition with private carriers such as Federal Express and UPS. And it is silent on Osborne and Gaebler's endorsement of voucher-supported parental choice in schools. Without the kind of incentives to improve that competition generates, the federal bureaucracy may not acquire a culture that is very different from what the report criticizes.

There may be, however, a middle course between voucher-funded schools and centrally decreed, site-based management. Being tested now in the public school system of a few states, this middle course may prove applicable to a variety of government agencies.

## Deregulation Charters

For lasting deregulation to occur in the absence of a market, it must be embedded in law and not merely generated by crisis. There must be a formal, written commitment from all sides as to the freedoms the agency is to enjoy and the standards by which it will be judged. One way to deregulate is now under way in California schools. Following a pioneering plan in Minnesota, the California plan, which took effect in 1993, allows parents, community groups, or teachers to petition the state for a charter to operate a public school (existing private schools cannot petition to become charter schools).[17] The petition must be approved by either 10 percent of the teachers in the school district or 50 percent of the teachers in a given school and by the local school board. (If the local school board rejects a charter, the petitioners can appeal to a special review panel.) When the state grants the charter, the school is exempted from all state laws governing local school districts. It must, of course, comply with the provisions of the state and federal constitutions, and so it cannot practice racial discrimination or offer sectarian instruction. The petition typically will spell out admission requirements (preference is given by the state to charters aimed at disadvantaged students), the qualifications that teachers must have, the desired educational outcomes for pupils, and the methods for measuring them. Once the school is in operation, it will get state funds on the same basis as regular public schools and can use this money to teach whatever it wishes, however it wishes, and to whomever it wishes. But its students will be tested to see if they achieve statewide educational goals. It is an experiment: in any given year, there may not be more than one hundred charters in effect in the state or more than ten in any school district, and no charter will last longer than five years (renewable for an additional five-year period).

There are parallels to this state experiment at the federal level. In the late 1970s the China Lake Naval Weapons Center was having great difficulty hiring competent engineers, in part because China Lake is in the California desert, miles from a beach or anything resembling a city, and in part because the government's inflexible pay system made it hard to offer attractive salaries or to reward employees who did good work. By the time junior engineers had learned enough on the job to do the job, they would leave for better-paying posts with industry and life in an attractive suburb. "We were becoming not the Naval Weapons Center but the Naval Aerospace Engineering Training Grounds," lamented one executive.[18] Reassigning a worker from one job to another required a snarl of paperwork; demoting a worker was considered nearly impossible. A similar problem was faced by the Naval Ocean Systems Center, mitigated only by the fact that the center is in San Diego where a lot of good engineers want to live even if it means working for an agency with a rigid personnel system based on generating reams of paper to show compliance with unrealistic job descriptions and uncompetitive pay schedules.

Then someone discovered a little-noticed provision of the Civil Service Reform Act of 1978 that authorized the Office of Personnel Management to conduct demonstration projects to see if changes in the personnel system would improve federal management. Not more than ten experiments could be conducted, none could last more than five years, and none could affect more than 5,000 employees. The result was the Navy Demonstration project, usually called the China Lake experiment.[19] Its goal was to give line managers greater authority over assigning, promoting, and rewarding subordinates. This was done by grouping all the jobs into five broad career paths (professional, technical, specialist, administrative, or clerical) and within each career path lumping the eighteen GS grades into (depending on the path) four, five, or six broad pay levels, or bands. About 5,000 employees at the two labs, mostly but not entirely scientific, professional, and technical personnel, participated in the project.

The managers benefited in several ways. At the San Diego center, simplified one-page descriptions of each career path replaced the detailed, multipage descriptions of each occupation. To classify a position they had to do little more than photocopy the simplified description and attach it to a form on which they checked a few boxes. When they recruited a new person, they had the flexibility to meet market-determined entry pay levels. The managers could increase the pay of outstanding workers within each pay band without having to justify promoting them to a higher grade or transferring them to a managerial position. Funds were given to all managers out of which they could distribute incentive pay increases and award one-time performance bonuses. The limited amount of money and the rules governing its use made it impossible to give pay increases or bonuses to everybody; thus the managers were forced to make choices based on performance. Had there been a reduction in force, higher-ranking employees would only have been allowed to bump persons within their own career path, and the right to bump would be determined first by performance ratings and then by seniority.

The experiment was immediately popular with the managers and grew in popularity with the workers.[20] The guerrilla warfare between personnel offices and line managers ended: the personnel staff no longer had to be cops telling managers what they could not do, and the managers no longer had to manipulate or evade rules to get their job done. Unlike the general merit pay program authorized by the Civil Service Reform Act, the two navy labs *really* based pay on merit in ways that rewarded good performers but not poor ones.

The enthusiasm in the field was supported by the evaluations conducted by the Office of Personnel Management. Over an eight-year period, OPM compared the California labs' experience with the experience of two similar navy labs located on the East Coast. It found that the center at China Lake was competing more effectively for engineers by offering them higher starting salaries and quicker opportunities for advancement. During the first five years of the project, the turnover rate at the West Coast labs declined; at the East Coast labs it remained the same.[21] More important, there was a change in who was likely to leave. In both experimental and control labs, the high-performing employees were less likely to quit than the low-performing ones, but the experimental labs did better than the control ones in this regard.[22] Managers at the San Diego center were unanimous that the demonstration project was helping them maintain or improve the quality of the skilled work force.

All this cost money. The payroll at the demonstration labs went up faster than it did at the East Coast control labs.[23] But that should not be surprising. If an organization's only objective were to minimize the size of its payroll, it would hire low-priced talent, get rid of senior people as soon as they started to earn a lot of money, and replace them with more recruits. Of course, quality would suffer. To maintain quality, one should hire the best people and keep them as long as possible, even after their paychecks become fat. That is what the California labs did.[24]

The California charter schools and the China Lake experiment suggest a strategy for negotiated deregulation. The number of units initially affected could be limited until experience was gained with them. Legislatures would have to pass enabling legislation that sets forth certain criteria of eligibility and standards for a charter, but the charter itself would have to be negotiated between a supervisory department genuinely committed to deregulation and the head of the field unit or bureau seeking greater autonomy.

Candidates for such charters are not hard to find. Schools, engineering groups, and research labs are obvious possibilities, but so are weapons procurement teams, veterans' hospitals, Forest Service districts, and regional offices of such agencies as the General Services Administration and the Federal Emergency Management Agency. Almost any agency would be eligible if its mission chiefly required it to be responsive to local conditions and needs rather than detailed national standards, especially if local responsiveness could be monitored by the clients (such as the parents of school children). The Internal Revenue Service probably is not suited for charter deregulation because it must assign the highest priority to the uniform application of a national tax code, but local public housing projects and certain regional offices of the Fish and Wildlife Service probably are.

No one should underestimate the enormous political resistance that will be generated by any deregulation proposal. The China Lake experiment was praised by managers, employees, and OPM alike, but for a long time the executive and legislative branches of government and some employee groups resisted extending it to other agencies. The Federal Managers Association polled its 20,000 mid-level civil servants and found that 70 percent were opposed to extending the merit pay principle of the China Lake project nationally.[25] Many federal employee unions were opposed. Unions are skeptical about, if not downright hostile to, the idea of merit pay; pay based on seniority is safer because it minimizes the authority of managers. Some members of Congress worried that a decentralized system would lead to pay inequity—engineers would be paid different salaries in different parts of the country. They were right, of course: wage rates vary across local markets. But what is understandable to a business executive is a threat to Congress because its members feel especially vulnerable to constituents' complaints of unequal treatment. Finally, resistance may stem from simple bureaucratic inertia. One person from the General Accounting Office who studied the demonstration projects said, "I'm not so sure there's anything really wrong with our current system."[26]

## Politics and Deregulation

What is required for agency executives to negotiate charters with their political superiors is an agreement on which regulations are essential and which marginal. This, frankly, may be impossible. The decentralization of authority in Congress (and in some state legislatures) and the unreliability of most expressions of presidential or gubernatorial backing mean that in most cases executives will discover that all constraints are essential all the time. But perhaps with effort some maneuvering room may be won. A few agencies have obtained the right to use less cumbersome personnel systems, and Congress has the power to broaden those opportunities. Perhaps some enlightened legislator will be able to get statutory authority for more flexible, decentralized procurement regulations.

If the number of regulations that require monitoring by a central office can be reduced, then an agency head can try to match the distribution of authority within his or her organization with the tasks it is performing. In general, authority should be placed at the lowest level at which most of the essential elements of information are available. Bureaucracies will differ greatly in what level that may be. At one extreme are the Internal Revenue Service or maximum-security prisons in which uniformity of treatment and precision of control are so important as to make exacting, centrally determined rules necessary for most tasks. At the other extreme are public schools, police departments, and armies, organizations in which operational uncertainties are so great that discretion must be given to (or, if not given, will be taken by) lower-level workers.

Between these extremes are many interesting possibilities, such as weapons procurement. Overcentralization of design control is one of the many criticisms of such procurement on which all commentators seem agreed. Buying a new aircraft is a bit like remodeling a home—the owner never knows how much it will cost until it is done, quickly finds out that changing opinions midway through the work costs a lot of money, and soon realizes that decisions have to be made by people on the spot who can look at the pipes, wires, and joints. The Pentagon procures aircraft as if none of its members had ever built or remodeled a house. It does so because it, and its legislative superiors, refuse to allow authority to flow down to the point where decisions can be made rationally.

In chapter 6 Steven Kelman explains what is wrong with government procurement regulations. In doing so he joins a long line of experts who have made similar criticisms, especially of defense procurement. Though the Pentagon has done much better in buying new weapons than the public seems to believe, it is not because of much congressional help. One author estimates that there are now 1,150 linear feet of laws, rules, and court orders governing defense procurement. In 1988 alone, Congress passed eight new laws that added fifty new rules to the process.[27] Many members of Congress believe in deregulating procurement, but in this regard they resemble the boy who said he liked oysters but was not well enough to eat them.

If an agency can acquire the freedom to focus on its principal goals and hold frontline personnel accountable for attaining them, then it is in a position to ask that it be judged by results. Of course, what constitutes a valued result in government is often a matter of dispute. But even when fairly clear performance standards exist, legislatures and executives often ignore them with unhappy results. When William E. Turcotte compared how two state governments oversaw their state liquor monopolies, he discovered that the state which did not have clear standards for its liquor bureaucrats produced significantly less profit and more administrative costs than the state with clear standards.[28]

Even when results are hard to assess, more can be done than is often the case. If someone set out to evaluate the output of a private school, hospital, or security service, he or she would have at least as much trouble as would someone trying to measure the output of a public school, hospital, or police department. Governments are not the only institutions with ambiguous products.

There are two ways to cope with the problem of evaluating government performance. One is to supply the service or product in a marketlike environment, shift the burden of evaluation from the shoulders of professional evaluators to the shoulders of clients, and let them vote with their feet. The client in these cases can be individual citizens or a government agency; what is important is that they be able to choose among rival suppliers on the basis of good information.

But some public services cannot be supplied, or are never going to be supplied, by a market. One can imagine allowing parents to choose among schools but cannot imagine letting them choose (at least for most purposes) among police departments or armies. In that case, the second way of evaluating a public service should be adopted: carry out a demonstration project in which the quality of service supplied by a deregulated agency is compared with that provided by a conventional one.

Cautious procedures like this probably seem thin fare to people who want Big Answers to such Big Questions as "how can we curb rampant bureaucracy?" or "how can we unleash the creative talents of our dedicated public servants?" But public management is not the arena in which to find Big Answers; it is a world of settled institutions designed to allow imperfect people to use flawed procedures to cope with insoluble problems. And the barrier to finding even small, partial solutions is not power-hungry bureaucrats, it is in us—speaking through elected representatives. Americans want a lean, efficient, responsive government, but they also want a carefully restricted government, one that will not only educate children or build highways, but will do so in ways that appear to broaden civil rights, improve the environment, subsidize minority-owned businesses, buy American-made products, hire employees on the basis of objective criteria, and empower legislators to address our grievances. Because constraints are usually easier to quantify than efficiency, we often get a fat government even when we say we want a lean one.

## Notes

1. David Osborne and Ted Gaebler, *Reinventing Government: How the Entrepreneurial Spirit Is Transforming the Public Sector* (Addison-Wesley, 1992).

2. Some of the paragraphs that follow are adapted from James Q. Wilson, *Bureaucracy: What Government Agencies Do and Why They Do It* (Basic Books, 1989).

3. Center for Strategic and International Studies, *U.S. Defense Acquisition: A Process in Trouble* (Washington, March 1987), pp. 13–16.

4. Herbert Kaufman, *The Administrative Behavior of Federal Bureau Chiefs* (Brookings, 1981), p. 192.

5. National Performance Review, *From Red Tape to Results: Creating a Government That Works Better and Costs Less* (1993).

6. *California Education Code*, sections 44932, 44938, 44944, 44945, 48900, 48914.

7. I first saw this phrase in Constance Horner, "Beyond Mr. Gradgrind: The Case for Deregulating the Public Sector," *Policy Review*, no. 44 (1988), pp. 34–38.

60    JAMES Q. WILSON

It also appears in Gary C. Bryner, *Bureaucratic Discretion: Law and Policy in Federal Regulatory Agencies* (Pergamon Press, 1987), p. 215.

8. James Colvard, "Procurement: What Price Mistrust?" *Government Executive*, vol. 16 (March 1985), p. 21.

9. National Academy of Public Administration, *Revitalizing Federal Management: Managers and Their Overburdened Systems* (Washington, 1983), pp. vii, viii.

10. U.S. Forest Service, Eastern Region, *Shaping a New Culture* (Milwaukee, n.d.); Karl H. Mettke, "Reinventing Government: A Case in Point," *Tapping the Network Journal* (Fall 1992), pp. 14–16; and "A Government Agency Transformed," *At Work*, vol. 1 (November–December 1992), pp. 1, 19–24.

11. Michael Barzelay, *Breaking through Bureaucracy* (University of California Press, 1992).

12. National Performance Review, *From Red Tape to Results*, p. 3.

13. Paul T. Hill and Josephine Bonan, *Decentralization and Accountability in Public Education*, R-4066-MCF/IET (Santa Monica, Calif.: Rand, 1991), p. v.

14. John E. Chubb and Terry M. Moe, *Politics, Markets, and America's Schools* (Brookings, 1990). Although President Clinton and Vice President Gore embraced most of Osborne and Gaebler's recommendations, they refused to endorse the voucher plan for public schools.

15. James S. Coleman, Thomas Hoffer, and Sally Kilgore, *High School Achievement: Public, Catholic, and Private Schools Compared* (Basic Books, 1982).

16. Chubb and Moe, *Politics, Markets, and America's Schools*, chap. 5 and app. D.

17. State of California, Senate Bill 1488, 1992; and "Senate Bill 1448, Charter Schools Act of 1992," memorandum from Joseph H. Stein, Jr., president of the California State Board of Education, January 13, 1993.

18. Quoted in Larry J. Wilson, "The Navy's Experiment with Pay, Performance, and Appraisal," *Defense Management Journal*, vol. 21 (3d quarter 1985), p. 30.

19. Office of Personnel Management, "Proposed Demonstration Project: An Integrated Approach to Pay, Performance Appraisal, and Position Classification for More Effective Operation of Government Organizations," *Federal Register*, vol. 45 (April 18, 1980), pp. 26504–26544.

20. Wilson, "Navy's Experiment."

21. Brigitte W. Schay, "Effects of Performance-Contingent Pay on Employee Attitudes," *Public Personnel Management*, vol. 17 (Summer 1988), pp. 244, 248; Office of Personnel Management, "A Summary Assessment of the Navy Demonstration Project," management report 9, February 1986, p. 41; Office of Personnel Management, "Turnover in the Navy Demonstration Laboratories, 1980–1985," management report 11, December 1988; and Office of Personnel Management, "Effects of Performance-Based Pay on Employees in the Navy Demonstration Project: An Analysis of Survey Responses 1979 to 1987," management report 12, December 1988.

22. Office of Personnel Management, "Summary Assessment of the Navy Demonstration Project," pp. 41–42.

23. Office of Personnel Management, "Salary Costs and Performance-Based Pay Under the Navy Personnel Management Demonstration Project: 1986 Update," management report 10, December 1987, chap. 1.

24. The Gore report specifically endorsed the lessons of the China Lake project and urged the adoption of more flexible personnel rules.

25. Susan Kellam, "Remaking the Grade," *Government Executive*, vol. 18 (November–December 1987), p. 14.

26. Quoted in ibid., p. 18.

27. Fred Thompson, "Deregulating Defense Acquisition," *Political Science Quarterly*, vol. 107 (Winter 1992), p. 729.

28. William E. Turcotte, "Control Systems, Performance, and Satisfaction in Two State Agencies," *Administrative Science Quarterly*, vol. 19 (March 1974), pp. 60–73.

# 4 ||| The Ethics of Deregulation— or the Deregulation of Ethics?

John P. Burke

THE EFFORT to ensure the ethical conduct of public officials provides a classic illustration of what is both good and bad about government regulations. As in private life, where ethical behavior is something more than avoiding bad conduct or wrongdoing, in government it can involve a positive commitment to public service. Ethical awareness can energize officials so that they are more actively committed to their jobs. Ethical values can foster a sense of direction, if not a more encompassing ethos, that points individual conduct toward a larger public purpose. Thus ethical conduct in government may be important in creating the kind of philosophy of public service that embodies the aims of a revitalized and effective federal bureaucracy.

The way ethics has been understood at the federal level, however, is a far cry from this more ambitious sense of a public philosophy or set of values widely held, regularly applied, and serving broad public ends. Much of the government's emphasis has been on ever more finely tuned regulations that seek to impose various criminal, civil, or administrative sanctions for inappropriate conduct. Ethics regulations, moreover, are concerned almost exclusively with petty criminality and the potential use of public office for private gain: detailed financial reporting requirements, intricate rules to control gift giving among employees, and a welter of guidelines to regulate job seeking in the private sector and a person's postemployment contacts with former colleagues. Few if any rules are directed toward improving the creativity and morale of government employees or encouraging the exercise of individual responsibility and discretion in ways that further the goals of the public sector.

62

The narrow and negative aspect of federal ethics legislation dates from the early days of the nation. In 1789 one of the first federal statutes created the Treasury Department and prohibited any person appointed to it from carrying on trade or commerce. In 1829 Postmaster General Amos Kendall issued eight ethics rules for his department, including one against "taking quills home from the office."[1] For the remainder of the nineteenth century and through the first half of the twentieth, Congress passed various statutes seeking to prevent unethical practices. Since the codification of the statutes in the Bribery, Graft and Conflicts of Interest Act of 1962, the federal government has followed essentially a two-pronged approach to regulating ethical behavior: criminal conflict-of-interest statutes passed by Congress and more stringent standards of conduct, enforced administratively and authorized by executive order, applied to a broader range of activities.[2]

The centerpiece of ethics legislation at the federal level, the Ethics in Government Act of 1978, which was largely a response to the Watergate scandal, is a comprehensive statute that seeks to bring order, uniformity, and guidance to ethics regulations. In particular, the law requires high-level executive branch officials to submit financial disclosure forms for government and, especially, public scrutiny and establishes the use of independent counsels for criminal investigations and prosecutions of senior executive branch officials. It created the Office of Government Ethics to oversee the disclosure process and enforce standards of conduct required by statute and executive order. (Originally part of the Office of Personnel Management, OGE became a separate agency in 1989.)

During the Bush presidency, ethics legislation again came under intense scrutiny. Immediately upon taking office in 1989, the president established the Commission on Federal Ethics Law Reform, chaired by former federal judge Malcolm Wilkey. Although the commission was heralded as a Republican and pro-business answer to existing legislation, its recommendations did not ease the burdens imposed by ethics regulations so much as even up the score between the executive and other branches of government. The commission focused on applying ethics regulations to Congress and the judiciary (along with some liberalization of policies on accepting gifts and travel reimbursement from outside sources).

In April 1989, following receipt of the commission's report, President Bush issued executive order 12674, which rescinded Lyndon

Johnson's executive order 11222 of 1965.[3] The new order made few substantive changes in administrative regulations, but it did call upon the Office of Government Ethics to promulgate a single, comprehensive, and clear set of standards of conduct for the executive branch (the standards were issued in August 1992 and went into effect on February 3, 1993). It also required OGE to coordinate annual training programs for certain executive branch employees and strengthened its role in reviewing agency and department ethics regulations and enforcement procedures.[4]

The same day he issued the executive order, the president sent his Ethics in Government Reform Act to Congress. Although the final version of this legislation, passed in November 1989, did not establish the common standards for all three branches that the commission had urged, it did include more stringent restrictions on postemployment lobbying and bans on some types of honoraria for employees of all three branches.[5]

The Clinton presidency will undoubtedly add yet more ethics regulation. Immediately following his election, the president barred members of his transition staff from involvement in public matters that might affect their personal finances or those of their clients and prohibited them for five years from lobbying the administration on matters in which they had been involved during the transition.[6] On December 9, 1992, Clinton required some 1,100 officials in the new administration to sign pledges that they would not engage in either formal or informal lobbying activities with their former agencies for five years after leaving government service, prohibited for five years White House officials from lobbying any agency or department with which they had dealings while in office, and set a lifetime ban on appointees becoming registered lobbyists for foreign nations. The president did not, however, prevent former lobbyists from joining his transition team or, later, his administration. Such a decision would have kept Vernon Jordan from heading the transition activities and other former lobbyists from joining the administration, especially Ron Brown as secretary of Commerce and Mickey Kantor as U.S. Trade Representative.[7]

Clinton's efforts to become the "ethics president," while perhaps laudable in intent, serve as a reminder that rules on ethics in government are not without consequences that often go unmentioned or fail to be anticipated. Although stricter rules may be regarded by some as "an index of civic virtue" (the tougher the regulations, the stronger the opposition to corruption), a demand for additional rules can reveal a certain moral righteousness that ignores the effects on the rights of those who are the objects of regulation or on other important government goals.[8]

President Clinton's quest for tighter rules has caused him some embarrassment. Transition chief Vernon Jordan was initially exempted from the new requirements but then, in the wake of public criticism, agreed to take a six-month leave of absence from his law firm and the various corporate boards on which he served.[9] Zoe Baird, Clinton's initial nominee for attorney general, was forced to withdraw from consideration following the revelation that she had hired illegal immigrants and had failed to comply with federal labor laws regarding their wages, information that was known to the president and his transition staff.

The administration's problems were compounded when it came to light that the replacement for Baird, Judge Kimba Wood, had hired an illegal immigrant to provide child care. Even though Wood's situation was different from Baird's—she had employed the alien before it was illegal for an employer to do so—the White House was apparently worried about the public's difficulty in distinguishing the two cases and withdrew her nomination. The prophecy proved self-fulfilling as Wood's nomination became—in the minds of many, unfairly—tarred by the brush of Baird's impropriety. In the aftermath of what now was termed Nannygate, Clinton also endured criticism from women's groups that he had unfairly scuttled the two nominations over standards that had not been applied to male nominees.

Other excesses of the more stringent ethics rules became apparent, and the White House narrowed the applicability of the rules preventing transition staff members from influencing areas of government that could affect their own financial interests or those of their clients. Disqualification would only be required when the actions would have a *direct* impact on personal finances or those of clients, and *clients* was more narrowly defined as personal clients, not those of a law firm or corporation to which a transition official might be connected.[10] By the end of November, when the transition was well under way, only one aide had been disqualified from making a staffing decision.[11] Nor did Clinton publicize the financial disclosure statements of transition officials, an action that had been announced with great publicity immediately after the election. The transition staff also found that drafting ethics rules for the new administration was a daunting task fraught with serious consequences: "There's not a big internal fight about pulling back," one official noted, "but it's very complicated stuff. Unlike the transition ethics rules, this is going to bind everyone. There are constitutional issues and legal issues."[12]

## Ethics Regulation: A Decentralized System

Oversight of federal ethics regulations and enforcement is largely the responsibility of the Office of Government Ethics, which was created to give central coordination and authority to federal efforts. Fearing the development of a large, intrusive, and overly powerful bureaucracy, however, Congress kept the agency small (in 1993 seventy full-time employees and a budget of $8 million), and charged it primarily with policymaking and oversight. OGE's responsibilities for the enforcement of ethics regulations are, however, significant. It develops, recommends, and reviews executive branch regulations, provides formal and informal advisory opinions on their interpretation, and establishes training and supporting materials for ethics officials at the agency level. It also reviews and approves the public financial disclosure forms of high-level executive branch officials, oversees the enforcement of ethics regulations at the agency level and refers possible violations to the Department of Justice, and evaluates and oversees the implementation of ethics programs at the agency level. OGE is organized into five administrative units: the Office of the Director, Office of General Counsel and Legal Policy, Office of Program Assistance and Review, Office of Education, and Office of Administration.[13]

Although OGE has significant oversight, coordination, and enforcement tasks, day-to-day administration of the government's ethics program is more decentralized. Each agency is required by law to establish a designated agency ethics official (DAEO), appointed by the agency but accountable to both it and OGE (which has the ultimate power—rarely exercised—to remove a DAEO). Some 100 DAEOs supervise 5,000 employees of their agencies who are charged with administration of ethics programs, which includes ethics training (now mandated annually for all government employees), review of financial disclosure forms, counseling and other responses to employee requests, and relevant agency enforcement efforts. According to Stuart Gilman, associate director of OGE, "the department and agency ethics programs emulate both the mission and the administrative structure of OGE."[14]

## An Enforcement Success?

If numbers alone are any indicator, OGE and agency ethics operations stand in marked contrast to those before 1978. Establishing OGE as an independent agency has undoubtedly given the concern for ethics in government more prominence, and the agency's regulatory authority has had a significant impact on the executive branch. Closer examination of OGE and agency activities, however, reveals a more complex picture.

One measure of the significance is the number of federal employees who are involved in matters relating to ethics in government. According to OGE's annual survey, 8,800 persons were involved in administering executive branch ethics programs in 1991, compared with 6,300 in 1989. The survey also estimates that $23 million was spent on ethics enforcement in 1991.[15] OGE's analysis of these statistics, however, reveals some potential difficulties underlying its enforcement efforts. Only 3 percent of the 8,800 employees were involved in ethics activities full-time. The remainder had other agency duties, which may indicate less attention to ethics than the numbers suggest. Only 4 of the 117 agencies surveyed had budget line items for ethics activities, even though separate budgets were encouraged by President Bush in executive order 12674. The absence of separate line items may indicate less concern for ethics regulation at the agency level than might be expected. Furthermore, the $23 million for enforcement is at best an estimate. It was based on numbers provided by 98 of the 113 agencies without separate line items; according to OGE, the remaining 15 could not even guess how much was spent.[16] Of the 4 agencies that had separate line items, the 3 that responded to the survey spent only $112,000 on ethics activities.

On the surface, compliance with regulations appears high. In 1991, the most recent year for which statistics are available, 99 percent of those required to file in three categories did so: 3,122 of 3,239 top-level federal employees filed public financial disclosure forms directly with OGE; 16,484 of 16,507 officials filed annual financial reports; and 868 of 960 filed financial reports at their termination from federal employment.[17] Data on the confidential financial disclosure reports, administered at the agency level and covering 250,000 lower-level and nonpresidential appointees, reveals a similar pattern of compliance.

Perhaps a more significant measure of OGE effectiveness is the number of administration nominees who, having filed financial reports, were required to make financial arrangements to comply with statutes and regulations. In 1990, as a result of OGE's examination of their financial disclosure reports, 107 of 306 top officials who required Senate confirmation were required to make 203 agreements regarding their financial interests. In 1991 the figures were similar. These arrangements included 139 recusal agreements on matters affecting the financial interests of nominees and their immediate families, 107 resignations from outside positions, 59 divestitures of assets, 37 waivers, 32 agreements concerning severance payments from former employers, and 4 blind trust agreements.[18]

## A Barrier to Entry?

Although compliance rates for filing financial reports and the number of actions that resulted indicate significant enforcement activity, they do not answer the crucial question of whether disclosure requirements deter people from entering public service. At best, the evidence is anecdotal. According to one account, "Of several hundred people approached for senior jobs in the Bush Administration, fully forty have refused service on financial grounds alone."[19] But even if this figure is correct, it is still not clear whether financial scrutiny deters so much talent that it compromises the quality of public sector performance. Those who complain about financial disclosure requirements, for example, may be using them as a less embarrassing explanation for having failed to secure an appointment. During the Clinton transition, more stringent ethics rules have caused delay if not embarrassment at times, but few reports have said that potential appointees have turned down positions because they feared the effects of ethics regulations. Even Edwin Meese, President Reagan's transition advisor and later object of an ethics investigation, was quoted as saying that "the problem was largely one of perception rather than reality." There were "good people in the pipeline," and the problems in getting them through it were never "as much as they were made out to be."[20]

Preemployment scrutiny is not without its benefits: it may screen out those whose previous financial dealings or attitudes about ethical matters make them unsuitable for public service. According to one OGE official, John Sununu's difficulties with the agency before his appointment as Bush's chief of staff should perhaps have warned of a certain insensitivity to the appearance of questionable conduct that emerged later. Sununu had been an adjunct professor at Tufts University and his children were entitled to free tuition as part of Tufts' benefits package. When OGE questioned the continuation of this benefit once he began service on the White House staff, he reportedly thought ethics rules that would have required him to give up the tuition benefit were a joke.[21]

Financial scrutiny may also let a president-elect off the hook or, as one OGE official told me, "save him from himself" by making it more difficult to offer positions to top contributors or powerful supporters when more competent but less well connected or financially advantaged candidates are available.

At first glance, the hurdles imposed by financial disclosure requirements during the appointment process, the various conflict-of-interest regulations that apply during the period of public employment, and the rules governing postemployment activity would seem useful barriers against those who might view public service as a means for private gain. Does the public really want someone working in the public sector for whom ethics regulations are viewed as burdensome or intrusive? The obvious answer is no. But such an easy response fails to consider the very real burdens, intrusions, and hardships that in fact can be imposed by the ways ethical behavior is monitored. Ethics legislation must do double duty: it should deter those who might seek public employment as a means to achieve undue personal gain or unfair advantage, but it should not discourage those in the private sector who are financially well-off and who may wish to return someday to private employment. The problem is compounded by partisan differences in recruitment patterns: Republican administrations are more likely to draw from the upper levels of the business community for whom financial disclosure problems and conflicts of interest more often crop up.

The goal of a revitalized, more effective public sector suggests a special need for removing unnecessary barriers that prevent experienced executives from entering public service. They may bring

fresh perspectives and new expertise to otherwise staid bureaucracies. They are likely to be less tolerant of delay, red tape, and waste.
And their services can be obtained at less than the market rate.
Principles underlying democratic government also implicitly encourage a certain ease of passage between the private and public
spheres: "One of the great traditions in American public life has
been the willingness of men and women to leave private jobs
temporarily and join government service. We do not want a government composed only of civil servants. The generous work of non-
career employees reflects our basic democratic view of government."[22]

Current regulations affecting entry into public service can clearly
stand improvement. The most obvious problem is the detailed
information required on the infamous SF 278 disclosure form. For
example, any type of income of more than $200 must be reported,
a threshold that seems too low. President Bush's 1989 Commission
on Federal Ethics Law Reform especially criticized the excessive
detail required by the disclosure forms: "The use of unduly narrow
categories for specifying asset value and income seems to the commission to result in a needless burden on filers without providing
particularly useful information to the public." The commission also
noted that excessive detail "increases the risk that filers will make
inadvertent mistakes."[23]

SF 278s must also be filed annually and upon transfer and termination. Because employees transferring from one agency to another
have already filed an annual report within the year, it is not clear
what purpose is served by an additional report; the most recent one
could simply be forwarded to the new agency for scrutiny. Termination reports (nearly 1,000 in 1991 and probably double or triple that
number in late 1992 as Bush appointees prepared to leave the
government following his election loss) also may not be needed.
Unscrupulous employees might, of course, engage in financial malfeasance in the period between their last annual report and termination, but is such a person likely to list questionable financial dealings on a termination report?

The Bush administration's introduction of tax rollover opportunities for nominees required to divest themselves of financial assets
helped reduce the burdens that result from disclosure. Similar efforts should be undertaken to ensure that appointees who must
make other kinds of financial arrangements do not suffer penalties.

Possibilities here include further exemptions from any tax liabilities incurred in complying with ethics regulations, which might not only prevent financial losses to appointees but force the government to calculate whether the benefits of such arrangements outweigh the cost of a loss in tax revenue. Blind trusts could be used more widely (OGE currently supervises only about thirty and seems reluctant to use them as a tool for compliance). OGE might also develop other, more creative ways of managing potential conflict-of-interest problems, such as negotiated purchase of stock options (if they are so valuable and such a temptation, why not have the government hold them?) or even a government buyout of ethically questionable assets.

Whether financial disclosure data on top officials should continue to be made public demands renewed consideration. The requirements resulted from the strong emphasis on regaining public confidence in the 1978 Ethics in Government Act and the Carter administration's goal of a more "open" government (government would be moral and free from the taint of corruption if potential sources of that corruption were made known to all). OGE reviewed 677 disclosure forms in 1990 and 1991; and in 1991 it received 751 requests for public inspection—293 from the news media, 61 from public interest groups, 26 from private citizens, and 371 from other sources—a considerable burden.[24]

Concerns about openness or public confidence may not, however, be so important today, especially if they compromise effective recruitment and retention. In fact, public disclosure, especially by the news media, may weaken public confidence in government by revealing only some of the facts or taking them out of context. Nor is it clear that public knowledge of potential sources of corruption or fears about the taint of corruption create ethical public service. Effective oversight and enforcement depend first on the efforts of OGE, not the news media. The media has a part to play if OGE fails in its duties, but the integrity of the agency would seem to be more strongly secured if attention focused on the conditions that enable it to operate in a nonpartisan manner, free of political pressure from the White House, Congress, or other sources. The success of these efforts, however, would not especially require public disclosure.

From the federal employee's perspective, disclosure requirements and any subsequent financial arrangements do shield officials from financial temptation and unwarranted allegations of impropriety. However, the shield from temptation would seem to work whether such matters were subject to public scrutiny or only that of OGE. Similarly, protection from unwarranted allegations would still exist if financial reports were confidential: the OGE would subject them to the same scrutiny and would still establish necessary financial arrangements. Indeed, protection would seem more readily compromised by public disclosure than by some more confidential system providing due process, informed scrutiny, and other procedural guarantees.

## A Problem of Principles and Purposes

Public financial disclosure is not the only requirement of ethics enforcement whose merits are difficult to evaluate, because ethics regulation has a peculiar quality that differentiates it from other types of public policy. The absence of ethical abuses could mean either that they have not occurred or that they have not been detected. The presence of ethics violations could mean that regulatory policy has failed or that it has successfully uncovered wrongdoing and has enforced compliance precisely as intended.

One way around the difficulty of evaluation is to consider whether the intentions of those who have framed ethics legislation or administrative regulation through executive order have been successfully implemented. But here too, confusion reigns: ethics regulation has an incremental and ad hoc quality rather than clearly defined goals, purposes, and underlying principles. As John Rohr noted, the 1978 act "has neither a preamble nor a statement of legislative intent."[25] New legislation or administrative regulations, furthermore, often arise as responses to a particular scandal—the 1978 act and Watergate—or the perception of a new area of questionable practices—the 1989 reforms and the acceptance of honoraria and, just recently, Clinton's lifetime ban on postemployment lobbying for foreign countries and its role as an issue in the 1992 presidential election. When broader ends are articulated, as in the report of President Bush's 1989 commission, they are, not surprisingly, subject to political compromise, replete with its welter of yet other goals. Thus the relationship between general principles of ethics and specific regulations is often obscure. No wonder we are unclear why we have the particular regulations we do, whether they are achieving what we think they should be achieving, and whether their costs are worth bearing, particularly by those who are directly affected by them.

Postemployment restrictions, so-called revolving door legislation, illustrates the effect of these disparate and sometimes conflicting goals. Steven Kelman contends that two general arguments might be made against the restrictions: the rights of jobholders to seek any employment they might wish and the possibility that discouraging movement in and out of government service "hurts the average quality of government decisions by putting decisions in the hands of people less likely to have appropriate knowledge, judgments, or attitudes."[26] Kelman also notes general arguments in favor of such restrictions: the unfair advantage of former employees in influencing former associates, the possibility of present officials going soft in carrying out their duties as they consider the prospect of future employment, and the possibility that officials might profit personally in the future by decisions made in the present.

The problem is that each argument or combination suggests very different and at times conflicting principles underlying restrictions in a particular piece of legislation, which makes it difficult to determine whether a regulation has been crafted well and is working effectively. For example, the Clinton administration's extension of some of the bans on postemployment activities from one or two years to five may be well or ill-advised depending on the reasons for the change (beyond the symbolic one that five years sounds tougher than one year). Given the high turnover among top officials in a particular agency, a five-year ban may have little import compared with some shorter period if the chief concern is one of unfair advantage in influencing former associates. However, if the main purpose is to prevent officials from slacking off in their responsibilities as they begin to think about their job prospects in industries they may currently regulate, a five-year ban may make better sense.

Increased attention to the purposes of ethics rules and procedures may also increase their legitimacy. When the principles are understood, it is less likely they will be seen as intrusive, burdensome, or the product of some malevolent "ethics bureaucracy." This would seem especially true for financial disclosure. Current procedures, especially those requiring public disclosure of assets and liabilities by top executive branch employees, stem in large part from the concerns expressed in the late 1970s for more open government. To the extent that openness and public knowledge continue to remain important reasons for financial disclosure, they should be emphasized; job candidates who are under scrutiny ought to understand why they are expected to endure such rigorous investigation. To the extent, however, that intrusive media scrutiny and misinformation pervade the process and open government is found to be of lesser weight when balanced against the privacy rights of individuals, then a redefinition of purpose and a revision of regulations may be necessary. Either way, those who are presently required to provide detailed information about their finances may be more satisfied. As Robert N. Roberts observes in what remains the most comprehensive study of federal ethics regulations, efforts to deal with the conflict-of-interest problem "have failed because of a general lack of understanding of how the system developed and as the result of disagreement over what constitutes a prohibited conflict of interest under current rules and regulations."[27]

Increased legislative, executive, and even public deliberation about precisely what ethical values are important, of course, runs against the grain of a political process that emphasizes practicality: political compromise at the level of the narrow and specific rather than reflection and agreement on broader ends and purposes. But such deliberation seems especially necessary in establishing whether particular areas of current scrutiny should in fact be subject to detailed regulation, especially when other values such as privacy or employee morale are compromised and when real persons are affected by regulation, bear its costs, and need to understand its rationale and legitimacy.

Whether present legislation violates the rights of employees may be particularly important in light of a recent court decision that struck down the ban on employees' accepting payments and other honoraria for writing articles and giving speeches. On March 30, 1993, the U.S. Court of Appeals for the District of Columbia ruled that the ban was unconstitutional because it violated First Amendment rights and was not narrowly tailored to serve an important government interest. Judge Stephen Williams wrote that although the law does not prohibit speech, "it places a financial burden on speech—denial of compensation." Quoting Samuel Johnson, Judge Raymond Randolph agreed: "No man but a blockhead ever wrote; except for money." However, Judge David Santelle, writing in dissent, argued that the ban imposed only a modest burden and that Congress had a reasonable basis for enacting it because such payments "undermine public confidence in government by creating an appearance of impropriety or corruption."[28]

Judge Santelle may be right: the ban on honoraria may indeed be only a modest burden. However, his rationale that it may create an appearance of impropriety creates yet another concern, namely that much ethics regulation, especially that dealing with conflict of interest, is not directed at actual violations but to possible acts that may only appear potential harms in the eyes of others. It is easy to forget, John Rohr has said, that "conflict of interest policies are *anticipatory* measures taken to head off *potential* harms to society."[29] Americans must be especially vigilant about the ritualistic and symbolic aspects of ethics regulations—that tough is good and tougher even better—because relying on coercive and intrusive measures to deter potential evils is dangerous. Society may even run the risk, as Bayless Manning (who advised President Kennedy on the 1962 legislation) warned, of indulging in "an orgy of virtue" where "we seem to lose our grip on decency."[30]

Deliberation on goals and principles raises issues about precisely which ethical values merit enforcement: why should gift giving among employees be subject to fairly stringent regulation but not friendships or other personal associations? It involves speculation about the ways in which the duties and obligations of persons working in the public sector differ from the duties in a private sector job or in one's personal life: to what extent and why should privacy rights be compromised by other more political and role-related values? More generally, are public officials bound to the same ethical principles as private citizens or are they bound by other perhaps more exacting standards? And it requires greater appreciation of precisely what political values underlie and otherwise define the kind of ethical behavior expected in public service: is open government, for example, the only democratic value that should inform thinking about how political considerations might be brought to bear on ethics in government?[31] At the same time, ethics regulations, particularly as they are communicated to employees through counseling and training, also need to be job centered rather than exercises in philosophical speculation.

Greater clarity in the principles underlying various ethics regulations not only involves determining relevant ethical values but also incorporating them within a framework that takes account of the organizational realities surrounding their implementation. Whatever the ethical purposes ultimately selected, they need to be tailored in light of their impact on the public sector's effectiveness in achieving its policy goals, their efficiency in the use of resources, and their contribution to the recruitment and retention of high-quality employees.

The kind of government service America may wish to create, therefore, may be compromised if it is subject to extensive scrutiny, mistrust, and denial of individual rights. Extensive regulation may yield public servants who are too acquiescent to government authority, especially intrusions upon individual privacy. As John Rohr comments, "Because they have had to sacrifice their privacy to the public good, they might not be terribly squeamish about asking the rest of us to do the same."[32]

Extensive regulation also may compromise the ability of officials to get their job done: it may destroy morale and promote excessive scrutiny, enforcement, and compliance. Regulating the conduct of public officials is different from regulating the conduct of potential burglars. One does not ask a burglar to run the government. Americans do ask public servants to do so, and we need to understand how ethics regulation fits into that larger definition of purpose.

Although undoubtedly a necessity of good government, ethics regulation, however defined, cannot be an end in itself; a public service sector populated by saints has no value in and of itself. It is only when the saints are busy at the Lord's work (in this case public sector work) and their values and insights are directed to working better that ethics takes on meaning and has real effect.

## A Penchant for Legalism?

Although a concern for ethics in government service has steadily grown in the past two decades, the emphasis has been on regulation and the approach legalistic. The dominance of legalism is best demonstrated by the fact that after any scandal the public demands tighter controls on the conduct of public officials.[33] The result, as one OGE official told me, is that "clarity in the definition of ethics policy has been sacrificed on the altar of legal precision."

Part of the legalistic cast undoubtedly stems from a problem noted earlier: the reasons behind ethics legislation are difficult to determine. Without agreement on ends and purposes, a more restrictive, legalistic frame of mind may develop among those who must implement ethics mandates. Thus OGE's enforcement and compliance strategy depends on legal drafting, interpretation, and other law-related skills, an approach reflected in the agency's internal organization.

The primary functions performed by OGE's Office of General Counsel seem especially to contribute to a legalistic emphasis in accomplishing the agency's mission. The office has five chief tasks:

—interpretation of administrative regulations, criminal statutes, and other ethics-related matters;

—consultation and assistance to agency ethics officials in applying regulations and statutes to specific situations;

—coordination with the Department of Justice in enforcing criminal conflict-of-interest statutes and managing OGE's enforcement efforts;

—administration of blind trusts and supervision of asset divestitures;

—provision of legal services for OGE in carrying out its own agency functions.

The tasks are carried out by ten attorneys—20 percent of OGE's policymaking staff—an arrangement that undoubtedly makes implementation of regulations subject to a more detail-attentive legal perspective. Indeed, the attorneys spend two-thirds of their time drafting and interpreting regulations. The remaining third is distributed among reviews of financial disclosure material; congressional and White House liaison; reviews of blind trusts, divestitures, and resolution of ethics agreements; and teaching and training.[34] The Office of General Counsel also tends to dominate the agency in other ways. Although the Office of Education has primary responsibility for training agency ethics personnel, General Counsel is represented in more than half the many presentations, speeches, and panels that provide information about government ethics programs.[35] And since the OGE's inception, only attorneys have served as director.

The more a legalistic perspective imbues OGE's mission, the less flexibility there may be in interpreting ethics regulations. For example, as one agency official told me, in 1992, following the institution of new rules on mandatory ethics training, the Department of Defense asked for a waiver in its proposed training schedule to enable it to train its 2.4 million employees over a period of one year rather than the six months required by OGE. It took more than three months of debate within OGE, extensive negotiation between the agency and Defense, and a letter from the OGE general counsel before agreement on a longer period was reached. In another case, OGE required a White House official to resign from the national board of the Girl Scouts for fear of potential conflict of interest. And in pursuit of financial disclosure forms required when an employee leaves, OGE attempted to gain compliance from one person who had been committed to a psychiatric institution and another who had committed suicide. In the latter case, the agency relented somewhat and allowed the person's widow to fill out the form.

Initial enforcement of ethics regulations, of course, occurs at the agency level under the direction of the designated agency ethics official. It is here that most financial disclosure forms are filed and examined, and advice on conflicts of interest and postemployment restrictions is provided. OGE is generally involved only for presidential nominees requiring Senate approval. But even at this level, efforts replicate many patterns in the parent OGE. The designated official, in particular, is located in the legal office in three-quarters of the agencies. The legal offices are also the most important providers of ethics counseling in half the agencies. The designated ethics officials or their deputies are responsible for ethics training in two-thirds of the agencies and for providing written advice on agency standards of conduct and on conflict-of-interest statutes in half.[36]

All in all, ethics enforcement at both OGE and the agencies occurs in an organizational context in which a legal frame of mind dominates. Clearly, legal interpretation of complex laws and legal means of enforcement are necessary parts of any ethics program, but other aspects may suffer if legal offices too heavily influence the programs.

One strength of the present system is that there appears to be a good balance between coordination and control by OGE and the use of agency-level officers to handle ethics problems for most federal employees. This balance allows the application of knowledge at the agency level that is necessary for informed and reasonable ethics regulation, while preserving some element of central oversight and governmentwide regularity in procedures and policies.

But as James Q. Wilson has pointed out, those aspects of an agency's mission that are not the focus of its attention—and, except for OGE, ethics regulation is not—require special protection. "This requires giving autonomy to the subordinate tasks subunit (for example, by providing for them a special organizational niche) and creating a career track so that talented people performing non-mission tasks can rise to high rank in the agency."[37] Ethics programs may be in need of such organizational protection. Not only do many of them appear to suffer from the effects of housing ethics officers in legal offices, but the programs may not have the kind of autonomy necessary to avoid other types of subordination.

Nor is it clear that OGE has been fully effective in its oversight functions. It has the power to fire ineffective ethics officers but has rarely exercised it. Although Congress tried to give increased status to agency ethics programs by designating the ethics officer as a high-level position, in most instances it is titular and a deputy runs the operation. In addition, although OGE does extensive auditing and collects information about agency ethics activities, it may need to do more program evaluation. As one OGE official pointed out: "What does it mean for an ethics unit to do its job? Is it just reviewing disclosure forms or meeting time deadlines? No one is really looking at how well staffed agency programs are or what is the depth of their review."

Recent revelations that bank examiners of the Federal Reserve system had taken loans at some of the financial institutions they were reviewing illustrates some typical organizational problems in ethics enforcement and the tendency to be overscrupulous about petty matters but ignore larger patterns of abuse. According to a 1993 report by its inspector general, the Federal Reserve's organization of its ethics program was largely at fault: regional reserve banks operate autonomously in administering the program, and ethical regulations were applied inconsistently in different regions of the country.[38] According to the *New York Times*, "ethical regulation was so confusing that some bank examiners never filed required personal financial disclosure forms. Others were uncertain what types of borrowing needed to be reported, and some reported improper borrowing but faced no consequences."[39] Of more than 200 examiners under review, 5 had improperly obtained various loans and another 13 had borrowed from banks affiliated with the ones they were examining. In one case, an examiner obtained a loan just a few weeks after completing an audit.

Some of the violations discovered by the inquiry, however, appeared trivial: examiners reviewing banks where they had obtained student loans years before or an examiner who had reviewed a bank where his wife held a credit card. In another case, a regional reserve bank ruled that it was permissible for examiners who held American Express cards to examine a bank affiliated with the American Express company because card balances must be paid each month and thus do not constitute a loan. However, the central Fed "decided otherwise, and the examination had to be staffed by examiners from around the country who did not happen to be American Express card holders."[40]

Tinkering with the organizational structure, simplifying rules, and emphasizing common sense will undoubtedly improve the operation and effectiveness of federal ethics programs. Greater attention must be given to ensuring the integrity of the agency programs so that they are not compromised by the mandated goals of their organizations. The enforcement of ethical behavior must also be freed from a tight embrace by lawyers and legalism. This is not to suggest, however, that rules and regulations and their drafting, interpretation, and dissemination should be abandoned; legal guidance is clearly needed at all stages of the federal ethics program. But the current regulatory emphasis may be overly concerned with legal precision and too heavily influenced by legal strategies of enforcement and compliance. There is certainly nothing wrong with regulation that tries to prevent financial impropriety or favoritism, but to the extent these become the exclusive focus of an ethics program, they may preclude attention to other facets of ethics in government. An exclusively regulatory definition of ethics may even become self-defeating, generating negativity, if not cynicism, antagonism, and an adversarial reaction, among those whose conduct the regulations seek to elevate.

## A Broader Understanding of Ethics in Government

Ethics in government must be concerned with wrongdoing and its prevention. The regulatory side of ethics protects citizens from "the abuse of power and authority" and provides "guidance for officials who find themselves faced with an ethical quandary that their own conscientious beliefs may not be sufficient to resolve."[41] But this function is only part of what should be the meaning or place of ethics in public life. First, attention to ethics cannot be limited to a concern for the somewhat narrow range of wrongdoing that is the object of current regulation. Rather, consideration of ethical behavior should be present in a wide range of situations that daily raise issues of personal honesty and integrity, fairness toward others, respect for others, and commitment to diligence and excellence in performing one's work.

Second, attention ideally requires a continuing appreciation for the requisites of on-going ethical decisionmaking and action. This calls for ethical commitment, a stimulation of a desire to do the right thing; ethical consciousness, awareness of ethical implications such as anticipating consequences and recognizing forces that tend to counter an ethical commitment (for example, self-protection and self-righteousness); and ethical competence, improving those skills essential to ethical conduct.[42]

Third, ethics programs must be attentive to those features of public office that may place special obligations and duties on people. Accountability to others and a proper sense of responsibility for one's actions are especially important because officials are entrusted with power and authority by others. So too is an understanding of broader values and purposes underlying public service: the fostering of a public philosophy, a democratic ethos, that will enable public officials to act responsibly as members of a democratic community that has entrusted them with carrying out, even defining at times, its political goals and public policies.

Finally, a concern for ethics cannot be an abstract theoretical or philosophical exercise. It must be understandable and have real import both to those in government service who must apply standards for ethical conduct and to the public that must support their ends and purposes. For both groups, understanding the particular features of ethics in government may be a difficult task: the ethical demands of public life differ from those in private life. Continual attention to how the ends and purposes of democratic government define public ethics thus seems especially necessary, both for democratic citizens and for public officials.

These four facets of a more inclusive understanding of ethics in government will likely make useful contributions toward reconstituting and revitalizing public service. The shift from a "don't do this" set of regulations to a sense of public purpose, for example, may increase the legitimacy of and commitment to ethics among public employees. As an ennobling effort that connects the actions

82    JOHN P. BURKE

of individual officials to a larger public purpose, ethical awareness will create a greater sense of commitment to that purpose. The seemingly burdensome parts of ethical behavior, such as filling out forms and following detailed regulations, may take on a different cast when placed within this larger, more positive context.

A greater sense of the public sector's legitimacy may also develop among the public. Although Americans believe that ours is a government of laws not men, as Bruce Jennings points out, "legitimacy rests on the fact that ours is a government of laws that are made, interpreted, and enforced" by men and women who must measure up to ethical standards that the public understands and supports. "Without such standards citizens would not know how to evaluate officials, and officials would not know how to evaluate their subordinates, their peers, or themselves."[43] Public trust in government, which has steadily deteriorated since the Watergate years, may be rejuvenated. And a public sector that is trusted by its citizenry is likely to be even more committed to the effective delivery of those goods and services that the citizenry rightfully expects of it.

## Notes

1. Stuart C. Gilman, "The U.S. Office of Government Ethics," *Bureaucrat*, vol. 20 (Spring 1991), p. 13.

2. For further discussion of the history of federal ethics legislation see Robert N. Roberts, *White House Ethics: The History of the Politics of Conflict of Interest Regulation* (Westport, Conn.: Greenwood Press, 1988).

3. President's Commission on Federal Ethics Law Reform, *To Serve with Honor: Report and Recommendations to the President* (Government Printing Office, 1989).

4. On October 19, 1990, President Bush issued executive order 12731, which superseded executive order 12674. The new order made few changes except for new regulations on outside earned income.

5. The 1989 act also empowered OGE to grant exceptions to gift-acceptance regulations and, in consultation with the General Services Administration, required the agency to develop new regulations on accepting travel reimbursements from outside sources. This ultimately resulted in greater agency discretion to grant dispensations from existing policies prohibiting reimbursements from "conflicting nonfederal sources." The 1989 act also revised the general conflict-of-interest statutes in 18 U.S.C. 208 by adding civil prosecution and injunctions to existing criminal prosecution provisions.

6. Michael Kelly, "Clinton Forming Tight Ethics Guides for Transition and Staff Aides," *New York Times*, November 12, 1992, p. A22.

7. Jordan, for example, was a senior partner in a prominent Washington law firm with an impressive list of lobbyist clients. He also earned $442,000 in director's fees for his service on the boards of eleven major corporations, held $911,000 in stock in these companies, and was eligible for $208,000 in pension funds and an unreported amount in stock options from them. See Jason DeParle and Stephen Labaton, "Lobbyists on Clinton's Team: Potential for Conflict Endures," *New York Times*, November 25, 1992, p. A18.

8. John A. Rohr, "Financial Disclosure: Power in Search of Policy," *Public Personnel Management Journal*, vol. 10 (January 1981), p. 29.

9. "Notebook," *New Republic*, December 7, 1992, p. 8.

10. DeParle and Labaton, "Lobbyists on Clinton's Team," p. A1.

11. The aide, Thomas McLarty, was eventually appointed White House Chief of Staff. McLarty agreed to disqualify himself from savings and loan matters because he had financial interests in an institution that was under regulatory investigation. Ibid., p. A18.

12. Quoted in Richard Berke, "Ethics Rules Bog Down the Transition," *New York Times*, December 2, 1992, p. B10.

13. Office of Government Ethics, *An Overview of the U.S. Office of Government Ethics* (1992), pp. 3–4.

14. Gilman, "U.S. Office of Government Ethics," p. 13.

15. Office of Government Ethics, *Second Biennial Report to Congress* (March 1992), pp. 44–45.

16. Ibid.

17. Ibid., p. 76.

18. Ibid., p. 79. At the agency level, 10 percent of the 20,000 disclosure forms filed by nonpresidential appointees resulted in some specific action. Ibid., p. 77.

19. Robert E. Norton, "Who Wants to Work in Washington?" *Fortune*, August 14, 1989, p. 77.

20. Quoted in Lou Cannon, "Appointments by White House Take Right Turn," *Washington Post*, June 18, 1981, p. A12.

21. Personal interview with OGE official. Subsequent comments from agency officials are also taken from interviews.

22. W. J. Michael Cody and Richardson R. Lynn, *Honest Government: An Ethics Guide for Public Service* (Praeger, 1992), p. 109.

23. President's Commission on Federal Ethics Law Reform, *To Serve With Honor*, p. 81.

24. Office of Government Ethics, *Second Biennial Report*, pp. 18–19, 78.

25. Rohr, "Financial Disclosure," p. 29.

26. Steven Kelman, "What's Wrong with the Revolving Door?" p. 4, draft manuscript of chapter in Barry Bozeman, ed., *Public Management: The State of the Art* (San Francisco: Jossey-Bass, forthcoming).

27. Roberts, *White House Ethics*, p. vii.

28. Robert Pear, "Judge Lifts Honoraria Ban on Federal Workers," *New York Times*, March 31, 1993, p. A19.

29. Rohr, "Financial Disclosure," p. 31.

84    JOHN P. BURKE

30. Bayless Manning, "The Purity Potlatch: An Essay on Conflicts of Interest, American Government, and Moral Escalation," *Federal Bar Journal*, vol. 24 (1964), p. 254.

31. For further discussion of these issues, see John P. Burke, *Bureaucratic Responsibility* (Johns Hopkins University Press, 1986); and Dennis F. Thompson, "Paradoxes of Government Ethics," *Public Administration Review*, vol. 52 (May–June 1992), pp. 254–59.

32. Rohr, "Financial Disclosure," p. 32.

33. Robert N. Roberts and Marion T. Doss, Jr., "Public Service and Private Hospitality: A Case Study in Federal Conflict-of-Interest Reform," *Public Administration Review*, vol. 52 (May–June 1992), p. 260.

34. Office of Government Ethics, *Second Biennial Report*, p. 9. Other factors also may have been at work in the general counsel's heavy emphasis on drafting and interpreting regulations. In 1990 and 1991 the general counsel staff "was virtually besieged with requests for guidance on the honoraria ban . . . which was part of the Ethics Reform Act of 1989." Ibid., p. 12.

35. Ibid., pp. 38–39.

36. Ibid., pp. 61–62, 70, 72.

37. James Q. Wilson, *Bureaucracy: What Government Agencies Do and Why They Do It* (Basic Books, 1989), p. 371.

38. Office of the Inspector General, Board of Governors of the Federal Reserve Board, "Report on the Audit of Potential Supervision and Regulation of Conflicts of Interest," Washington, January 1993.

39. John H. Cushman, Jr. "Some Fed Examiners Found to Have Abused Ethics Code," *New York Times*, February 25, 1993, p. D1.

40. Ibid., p. D21.

41. Bruce Jennings, "Ethics in Government: There Still Is Hope," *World and I* (May 1989), p. 24.

42. Michael Josephson, *Power, Politics and Ethics: Ethical Obligations and Opportunities of Government Service* (Marina del Rey, Calif.: Joseph and Edna Josephson Institute for the Advancement of Ethics, 1989), pp. 3–4.

43. Jennings, "Ethics in Government," p. 24.

# 5 ||| Deregulating the Federal Service: Is the Time Right?

## Constance Horner

CALLS TO UNBURDEN federal managers of gratuitous and obstructive regulations governing decisions on personnel, budgets, and procurement go back at least a decade. But although they are a staple of the expert's and insider's critique of government, they remain insufficiently answered by action. Recent changes in the political and economic environment, however, simultaneously raise the stakes for continued failure to loosen these constraints and present a rare opportunity for reform.

The stakes are raised because it has become important to the economy that America receive efficient and innovative performances from its federal managers. Not only has the Clinton presidency increased federal intervention in the domestic economy—the list of regulatory initiatives in its first three months runs to five single-spaced pages—but American business confronts intensified global competition. Now more than ever, economic growth is either assisted or impeded by the quality and character of government action.[1]

At the same time, if long-standing barriers can be overcome, opportunity for reform of federal management practices, an opportunity created by a confluence of political catalysts, is greater than at any time in the past decade and a half. As the 1992 Ross Perot presidential campaign showed, public demand for better government, however defined, is strong and the public newly attentive to the processes of government. Public attentiveness is a sine qua non of congressional willingness to act. President Clinton, with only 43 percent of the vote in 1992, not only must make a record of reform to respond to Perot supporters' demands, he also needs to defend his reputation as a New Democrat before the "reinventing government" element within the Democratic Leadership Council.

Meanwhile, public employee unions, which have historically opposed any reforms designed to cut employee pay or the size of the work force or to expand managerial discretion can continue their opposition only at the political expense of a Democratic president whom they supported for election and of a Democratic majority in Congress trying to work with him. At the least, the unions must be more open to negotiation than they have been through two Republican presidencies. By the same token, Congress cannot now "just say no" to either budget cuts or reform proposals, as it has in recent years. Finally, the pressure for reform has been increased by the president's assignment of Vice President Albert Gore, a potential future presidential candidate, to conduct a National Performance Review of the federal government that has produced recommendations for reform. It is a major, much-hoopla'd assignment for him.

But if the political stars are aligned for change, perhaps even for a grand bargain, it is not clear that prospects for accomplishing more than token improvement are yet other than meager. Reform means different things to different people, and some barriers that have deterred it in the past remain in place. Moreover, it is apparent that entirely different—and contradictory—strategies for reform are competing to satisfy disparate political needs. Bureaucrat-bashing rhetoric and budget-cutting proposals reminiscent of the best of Ronald Reagan have also marked the Clinton presidency, and Congress has begun, after a period of confused quiescence, to display its traditional support for government employee interests and opposition to presidential budget proposals.

Nevertheless, it is early days, and there are several budget and legislative cycles to go in this presidential term. There is time for learning and self-correction, time to find political compromises that will permit the deregulation of the systems curtailing the effectiveness of federal managers. It will be difficult, but it can be done.[2]

## What Ails Government?

Before devising the criteria for deregulation strategies, however, there must be consensus as to a clear diagnosis of the regulatory ailment and an ideal treatment for its amelioration. (There is no cure.)

Many Americans look at federal bureaucrats as lazy, indecisive, and incompetent. The practical consequence of this attitude is that the public has shown much less enthusiasm for reducing the paperwork and regulatory burdens on the civil service than for deregulating the private sector. Americans continue to support highly centralized controls on the bureaucracy, despite opposition to government intervention everywhere else. But deregulation of the public sector is as important as deregulation of the private sector, and for precisely the same reason: to liberate workers' entrepreneurial energies. Nearly a quarter of the nation's income is spent by or through the federal government. It matters a great deal how well or poorly that money is spent. A lean, resolute, productive civil service, able to decide and act rather than wait and see, would lead to smaller, more accountable government, allow more resources to remain in the private sector, and improve the quality of government services.

The federal government takes in $3 billion a day and spends $3.8 billion.[3] The federal payroll alone is $101 billion a year, with $35 billion more in retirement benefit outlays and $19 billion in health and life insurance.[4] No doubt, much of what the government does might be better done by the private sector, or in some cases not done at all. But some services are so important—National Institutes of Health cancer research, Department of Agriculture food inspection, Justice Department criminal investigation, Social Security Administration claims processing, Federal Aviation Administration air traffic control, and so on—that proponents of big government and small government alike can agree that they should be provided as effectively as possible, no matter who does the providing.

The senior bureaucrats charged with these responsibilities, though perhaps somewhat more risk-averse than private sector managers, are as competent, hardworking, creative, and motivated toward superior performance as any American executives. The problem is that they are trapped in systems that prohibit superior accomplishment. Some keep trying to serve the public, even without recognition. Others give up and become passive processors of paper. But all deserve a full-faith effort from political leadership to liberate their energies by removing the barriers to full performance. That means a serious effort to deregulate, simplify, and decentralize public management.

The efficiency and effectiveness of the government work force could be strengthened and its size reduced if managers in public service had more flexibility in making basic personnel, budget, and procurement decisions, and if reduced paperwork requirements freed them to focus more on the services they are supposed to provide. As it is now, federal managers are hemmed in by tens of thousands of pages of regulations restricting their every move. They have little discretion in decisions about their own personnel. Because of the complexity of reward processes and the inertia those processes induce, it is only with difficulty that they can use pay to reward and retain good employees. Nor can they more swiftly promote workers who show superior commitment and talent. Seniority remains the dominant ethos of civil service administration.[5]

With limited exceptions, federal managers are not allowed to use compensation to attract talent. Nor can they decide how many people to hire, for what jobs, or at what salary levels. Except for the Department of Defense, which has been exempted from personnel ceilings by Congress, the Office of Management and Budget decides how many people an agency needs (and sometimes where to put them). Sometimes OMB sets a maximum and Congress a minimum. It would be much better if senior managers could get their appropriated budgets and decide how many people to hire at what pay levels to get the job done.

The Federal Employees Pay Comparability Act of 1990 has created a little progress in reducing restrictions on managers. In certain circumstances it permits them to grant recruitment and retention bonuses to attract and keep good employees. It also permits hiring entry-level (GS-5 to GS-7) employees at any pay level in the entry-level range. However, it remains to be seen how far departments and agencies will go in actually permitting managers to use this discretionary authority. The impetus for the act was clearly to increase pay, not to expand management discretion in its award. (In the period leading up to negotiations over the act, the Bush administration was fearful that, without governmentwide legislation, agencies with pay-related recruiting problems and strong political support would persuade Congress to legislate selective and separate agency pay increases, thereby weakening the governmentwide system. Therefore, there was little incentive to demand that a reluctant Congress grant greater discretion in the award of pay).

Fixing the civil service classification system also had to take a back seat to dealing with problems in pay levels and methodology for arriving at them. Now forty-three years old, the system causes enormous frustration. Managers spend many hours negotiating with agency personnel specialists over the proper placement of jobs and employees in a system that has more than 700 occupations, 18 grades, and 10 steps a grade. There are seventy-three pages of rules on classifying—and therefore determining how much to pay—a secretary.[6]

Bracketing a decade of reformist thinking on classification are two studies by the National Academy of Public Administration that urge radical decentralization and simplification of job classification and dramatically increased empowerment of line managers to make classification decisions. The later study, reflecting broad consensus among federal managers, contends that in the current "moribund" system, "pay is distorted, managers are not accountable, too much paper is generated, and management and organization needs are not met."[7]

The system for disciplining employees also makes it hard for managers to take quick, effective, and fair action. Disciplinary action means coping with protracted and complex appeals procedures, including agency appeals, union-negotiated arbitration, Equal Employment Opportunity Commission (EEOC) determinations, and the federal courts. There are ceaseless disputes. In one typical case, for example, a postal employee was removed for inability to perform the job. With an accompanying panoply of staff and contending lawyers, the appeal went for hearings, review, and adjudication to the Merit Systems Protection Board, the EEOC, back to the MSPB, and then to a so-called special panel. The process took more than five years. The employee had worked for the government three years and nine months.[8] And this case did not include a union-negotiated grievance procedure or a trip to the Federal Appeals Court, which would have added months or years to the process.

There are union-supported proposals in Congress to move adjudication of discrimination claims from federal agencies to the EEOC.[9] If enacted, however, such proposals would not only prolong the process even further as federal claims joined the EEOC backlog, but also place additional restraints on the relations of federal managers with the employees they supervise.

Overregulation of the process for awarding contracts to procure work and equipment also hampers the effectiveness of management decisionmaking.[10] Awarding these contracts takes so long and requires so many levels of clearance that the equipment's technology is frequently out of date by the time it arrives or does not match equipment in other units.[11] Outstanding contractors are lost because they cannot wait or do not meet often unreasonable requirements. These are the day-in, day-out frustrations.

A very nonroutine example was the General Services Administration's effort to replace the government's quarter-century-old telephone system in the 1980s. The largest nondefense procurement in federal government history, Federal Telephone Service 2000 was intended to save the government tens of millions of dollars a year, improve the quality of service, and add much-needed capacity for data transmission. The three-year, hurry-up-and-wait procurement process was plagued not only by congressional intrusions but also by staggering technical and political complexities that GSA procurement officers were ill-prepared to deal with. According to Donald Kettl, "the complexity of the product and the structure of the market . . . required them to manage the arena in which they were buying. They were sucked into a role they did not want and were unprepared, with either staff or capacity, for the role they were forced to play."[12] It is self-evident that the purchase of information technology and other sophisticated equipment requires procurement officers who can compete in power, status, and pay with their private sector counterparts. The probability of congressional micromanagement and agency overregulation of decisionmaking will not attract men and women of such stature when they may work more autonomously and effectively on the other side of the negotiating table.[13]

## A Case For Deregulation

Federal managers frequently have no firm idea what their annual budgets are until the fiscal year is almost over. Agency leadership, uncertain over budget cutbacks, potential freezes, and so on, withholds spending until the last minute or moves it around in a kind of agencywide shell game. Even when agencies do know their budgets, managers cannot allocate funds according to their judgment. Instead, limitations on hiring imposed by OMB and agency central offices and congressional micromanagement through the appropriations process govern their decisions in ways that undermine sound administration. Permission to manage flexibly within assigned budget levels—and timely knowledge of what those levels are—would greatly strengthen the efforts of federal managers to produce the goods and services people say they want from government.

Each of the rules, regulations, and requirements under which the civil service does its work is well intentioned and designed to preclude unfairness or error. But together they have crippled the exercise of human judgment. (The personnel rules alone take up more than six feet of shelf space and have more pages than the Bible, the *Rand McNally World Atlas*, the Manhattan yellow pages, *Robert's Rules of Order*, and *A Tale of Two Cities* combined.) The systems that surround federal line managers are as convoluted and ugly as Medusa's snaky locks, and have much the same freezing effect—one good look and government managers lose heart, energy, and will.

Henry David Thoreau once said, "any fool can make a rule."[14] It is much harder to deregulate. To be effective, public sector managers need the power to make key decisions on personnel and budgets. They must be able to move employees from jobs they cannot do to ones they can, to award a contract for two weeks' work in less than three months' time, to hire another secretary or electronics engineer, whichever is more needed, without subjection to endless petty harassment by rules and clearances.

Some critics contend that allowing so much freedom would be a step in the dark, threatening at best disruption and at worst abuse. But there is a reassuring precedent in the success of the senior executive service. These 7,000 executives provide the prototype for autonomy accompanied by accountability. They administer many of the government's largest and most sensitive functions. They are accountable for the implementation of policy to the politically appointed heads of their agencies. If they succeed, they can be awarded large bonuses and advancement. If they fail, they can be removed. A modified regime of the same sort, proportionate to level of responsibility, should be implemented throughout the ranks. Increased autonomy is not a serious threat to supervised employees if the proper measures of accountability are in place in a culture that honors accountability and can react to success and failure with action.

A stronger reassurance that deregulation can work is a longstanding experiment conducted by the Department of Defense. Throughout the 1980s the department and the Office of Personnel Management worked together to institute a variety of personnel reforms. Their efforts took three forms: unilateral changes effected administratively by the agencies; legislation arising from that experiment, developed by OPM but ignored by Congress; and a major multiyear personnel experiment. These efforts delineated the outlines of possible governmentwide reform and indicated that it would succeed.

The experiment began in 1980 at the Naval Ocean Systems Center in San Diego and the Naval Weapons Center at China Lake in the Mojave Desert. The laboratories were engaged in research into undersea surveillance and weapons systems and Arctic submarine warfare and in development of the Sidewinder and Skipper missiles. But despite these interesting and challenging projects, they were unable to recruit and keep high-quality personnel. Working with OPM, the navy put in place a new and radically simplified system for defining jobs and hiring, promoting, and paying personnel.[15] The new system put managers more in charge of the work for which they were accountable. It grouped 120 occupational series into a few broad career paths. It abolished the 180-step general schedule and replaced it with four to six broad pay bands. Managers could move effective employees up within these bands or into different jobs without regard to rigid seniority or classification rules. The system replaced complicated, multipage job descriptions produced by the personnel office with a short, computerized list of job elements that managers, not just personnel specialists, could use. It also introduced some market-based pay at the entry level so managers could compete with the private sector for quality recruits. All pay increases were based on good performance.

These are common practices in the private sector but revolutionary in government. They are based on two principles historically anathema to government operations but necessary to sound management—relying on human judgment rather than overregulated systems to make decisions and rewarding employees for better work. The principles recognize that using discretion and judgment, exercising intelligence and character, enlarge human capacities. They recognize that material incentives spur effort and increase productivity.

How has the China Lake experiment worked? As James Q. Wilson comments in chapter 3, evaluations show resounding success. Management and employee morale is up, recruits have much higher college grade-point averages, managers spend less time on personnel matters (although they are making more of the decisions), and, most significantly, strong performers are more often staying and weak ones leaving.[16]

Burrell Hays, technical director at China Lake when the experiment began, told me, "under the system I grew up with, the first-line supervisor could pass the buck. Now he has to make hard choices. Productivity moves up, the weak worker moves back. We get more efficient and effective use of personnel." Eva Bien, China Lake's personnel director, also expressed enthusiasm:

> Both employees and managers have a lot more time to spend on the actual work, rather than taking up time trying to understand a complicated personnel system. They focus on what is important, the actual work. The navy is getting more productivity for its money. People feel better because they don't have to fight the system. Systems are dynamic. The federal personnel systems stayed stagnant while everything else moved forward. Our R&D work is dynamic, the whole world is dynamic, and the old personnel system is static. Under the new system, we in the personnel office don't have to do battle with the line managers anymore. We speak the same language and move in the same direction.

And Randy Riley, personnel director at the San Diego center, commented,

> One of the best parts of this system is that it is a bottom up program developed by line managers. After the project began, there was a fairly quick recognition by supervisors that the system worked. . . . The merit pay system . . . gets people interested in their jobs and performance and helps us define our goals and measure progress. . . . The system reduces the manager's paperwork.[17]

There have been other promising experiments in personnel reform: in "productivity gain sharing" at McClellan Air Force Base and the Defense Logistics Agency in California, in simplified classification and pay-for-performance at the National Institutes of Standards and Technology in Maryland and Colorado, and in the navy's "managing to payroll," that is, allowing line managers to decide the number and mix of staff needed to get the job done within the budget.[18] Such experiments could be echoed by similar reforms in budget, procurement, and other internal federal systems.

Although China Lake experiments cannot be put into effect governmentwide without legislation, the Office of Personnel Management has engaged in administrative simplifications and delegations that place more responsibility for decisions in the hands of managers, with central management agencies assuming more of an oversight role. For instance, OPM has devolved some of the hiring authority from itself to the agencies, allowed agencies to waive rigid qualification rules when they want to move employees from one job to another, and experimented with broad generic job standards that allow line managers rather than central personnel staffs to classify positions. Hundreds of restrictions and requirements were waived, simplified, or delegated in the mid-1980s.

How can the impact of these changes be characterized? At their best, they prevent the warping of common sense that occurs when observing rules takes precedence over using individual judgment or when decisions are made by distant regulatory overseers rather than by those who are affected by the results.

But there is opposition to these and proposed further changes coming from various institutions. The Office of Management and Budget fears loss of budget control and higher personnel costs. Unions fear further erosion of their power vis á vis management: if advancement and pay are based on performance, management—the judge of performance—is made more powerful and union representatives less powerful. Congress fears losses of union political support and the erosion of a regulatory basis for oversight to prevent abuse and protect constituent interests. Also, if decisions are decentralized, Congress will have more difficulty engaging in its customary and politically rewarding micromanagement. (One small example: I tried to consolidate three scattered and less-than-effective federal training installations into one well-managed site, but one of those installations was in Representative Pat Schroeder's district in Denver. She got an appropriations bill rider passed to prohibit the consolidation.)[19] Finally, if rules are simplified, there are fewer opportunities for the disputatious and litigious to challenge management action on procedural grounds.

The proposed changes, of course, would be undesirable if they increased costs, destroyed congressional oversight, allowed managers rampant opportunity to abuse employees, or removed necessary employee protections. They need do none of these. They will, instead, correct excesses that have developed over decades by applying successful private sector management practices to the public sector. Especially, they treat employees, from top to bottom, like the grown ups they are.

In 1987 the Reagan administration submitted to Congress the Civil Service Simplification Act, which would have instituted the China Lake reforms, voluntarily, gradually, and cost neutrally throughout government.[20] In the classic Washington parlance, and for all the reasons just cited, it was dead on arrival.

The objections to granting greater discretion to federal managers are sincere and substantive as well as illegitimate and purely political. Without an obvious or automatic limit, will managers grant performance-based pay increases too easily? Will costs spiral out of control? Will managers be unfair in their compensation decisions, favoring friends rather than good performance? Evaluation of deregulation and decentralization experiments suggests that although total costs can go up, they need not.[21] Controlling costs depends on proper system design, especially in introducing managing to payroll. The way to prevent managerial excesses is more, not less, discretion. Evaluation of personnel experiments also suggests that employee worries over fairness do not increase as a result of enhanced managerial power to set pay levels differentially among employees.[22]

## Political Barriers to Deregulation

Assuming substantive objections to deregulation can be overcome by experimental evidence and system design, political barriers remain. One is that there has historically been little political benefit in promoting internal government reform. Presidents and members of Congress have made stabs at reform via commissions and hearings (some, such as Reagan's Grace commission, considerable in scope), but rarely are they willing to expend serious political capital to achieve results because the value of reform is hard to explain to the public.

Another political barrier is the intense, long-standing opposition from unions. The Kennedy administration executive order that first recognized public employee unions did not allow them to bargain over pay. Therefore to generate support, they depend on grievances over workplace conditions, appeals of disciplinary action, and other means of defending employee interests.[23] Any increase in management discretion significantly erodes their already thin powers.

Congressional opposition to reform is tied to union opposition. There are federal employees in every congressional district in the nation. If they are mobilized by union leadership to oppose a reform considered unfair, they can have a strong impact on congressional decisions. Members of Congress with large constituencies of federal workers seek committees that oversee government operations and thereby become even more hostage to, as well as powerful over, employee issues.

Any further attempt to achieve reform will succeed only if it involves strategies that recognize and are designed to accommodate these political considerations.

## A Strategy for Deregulating

What might a reform strategy look like? Interest in reforming government is higher than at any time since the early days of the Reagan administration. President Clinton and his management advisors, especially those from the Democratic Leadership Council, have been energized by David Osborne and Ted Gaebler's ideas for "reinventing government."[24] Vice President Gore has been assigned reform duty. Yet the high expectations this interest has generated are already being disappointed by antibureaucracy, budget-cutting rhetoric and proposals. They are also being disappointed by an unfortunate tendency to repair to the language of mere enthusiasm and old nostrums: "waste, fraud, and abuse," "total quality management," "empowerment," "steering, not rowing."[25] These buzzwords appeal to various audiences with conflicting perspectives. They reflect a theoretical chaos that needs to be ordered by consistent ideas before political strategies, with all their compromises and concessions, can be attempted.

A successful strategy for reform would, however, contain provisions to meet the political needs of all parties to reform: for the president, cost cutting and efficiencies to save taxpayer money and redesign of government's internal workings to appeal to reinventors; for unions, strengthened bargaining power; for Congress, cost savings without loss of too much union support or opportunity for oversight. Can this be done? A case can be made for

DEREGULATING THE FEDERAL SERVICE 97

a series of trade-offs that would work in the next three years. The public wants a smaller, cheaper, better-run bureaucracy, but it is indifferent to the means by which this is achieved. By proposing to cut 252,000 employees and save $108 billion through the National Performance Review proposals, the president has established with the public his intention to save. If the cut is realized, he will have accomplished a major political goal. To pursue real reform, he retains considerable leverage with unions and Congress through future budget proposals. To accommodate union and congressional interests while seeking enactment of reforms that are difficult for them to agree to, he can offer concessions on pay and benefit levels. To date, he has adopted a different approach: to obtain union and congressional acceptance of his most politically visible but least substantively significant proposal—the 252,000 employee reduction—by agreeing to union demands that are most threatening to his significant proposals for change.

Specifically, the president appears to have garnered union support for personnel cuts by issuing an executive order instructing agencies for the first time to negotiate with unions over "numbers, types, and grades of employees."[26] Because pay is attached to grade level, the order has the effect of introducing some negotiation over pay, a long-sought union goal. Therefore, it reduces management flexibility to use pay to strengthen performance, a long-sought reformist goal.

The executive order also establishes a high-level labor-management council empowered to propose the statutory changes to the hiring and classification systems recommended by the National Performance Review.[27] This provides union leadership an effective veto within the executive branch over proposals for statutory change. For change to occur, the president will have to try to increase pay and benefits. This is not easy to do in an era of budget cutting, but it has been done to meet other goals and can be done to meet this one if the will to reform persists.

A successful strategy for change must also acknowledge Congress's need for a way to hold executive branch officials to account on behalf of constituents and taxpayers. Recent legislation, the Government Performance and Results Act of 1993, has created a vehicle by which Congress can meet its oversight needs even with a dramatic reduction of regulation.[28] By requiring agencies to establish performance goals, engage in strategic planning, and report annually on their progress, the new law provides a better basis than procedural regulations for congressional oversight.

The administration could offer to dramatize this vehicle as a way of affording Congress a politically viable alternative to oversight based on the statutory overregulation of federal managers. Such a strategy would only be effective, however, if the president wants reforms of the sort I have outlined strongly enough to negotiate to get them and to get them without yielding to union demands for participation that would tie management hands every bit as much as the regulations they would replace.

If this strategy or something like it does not work, a more modest but still valuable alternative would be to ask Congress for authority to put China Lake reforms and others in effect experimentally in selected agencies throughout government. This would allow recourse to revisiting issues of concern if needed. Yet success would breed imitation. It is important to explore the possibility that, given some degree of good faith, things can change for the better. Why does this matter? For good or ill, government competence has a broad impact on the American economy. For all that the critiques of government in American popular culture have been relatively good humored, the nation may be approaching a dangerous demarcation beyond which the criticism grows nasty and despairing. The potential for the public to lose confidence in government competence is serious. Unless the government changes its ways of doing business, it will eventually attract only the less able members of the American work force. Competent managers and professionals will not remain at jobs that give them only a passive role. They want to work where their strongest talents can be used, their efforts rewarded, and their intelligence and judgment allowed to influence decisions regarding production, service, and quality.

Experience in the private sector has shown that trimming headquarters staff and giving line managers more decisionmaking flexibility can improve performance and accountability. All the great management books say procedures should be simple, paperwork kept at a minimum, and line managers be given the tools they need to get their jobs done. The same is true of the public sector.

Although political and intellectual circles often emphasize the importance to democratic government of institutions such as the presidency, the political parties, and Congress, little attention is paid to the civil service. Yet, like political parties or the judiciary, the civil service is a basic component of democratic government. If it performs competently and is amenable to political leadership, democratic governance is strengthened. Even labor and socialist governments have looked to America's civil service as a model for overcoming paralysis of will and purpose in their public sectors. New or fragile democracies look to us for reassurance that they, too, can have a civil service that is responsive and uncorrupted and that serves the public interest with honor and pride. But without change in the way the nation's civil service is managed, time is not on the side of democracy, for them or for us.

## Notes

1. Sidney Jones of Carlton College, former assistant Treasury secretary, compiled the list of initiatives, to which he referred in a talk at the Brookings Institution conference, New Directions in National Policy Making, on April 26, 1993.

2. The ideas and observations in this chapter represent a revisiting, reiteration, and updating of my article, "Beyond Mr. Gradgrind: The Case for Deregulating the Public Sector," *Policy Review*, no. 44 (Spring 1988), pp. 34–38. Surprisingly little has changed in the past five years in the organization of government work, especially its personnel practices. What has changed is the political environment, which is potentially more receptive to reform.

3. Based on 1992 receipts of $1.091 trillion and outlays of $1.381 trillion. *Budget of the United States Government, Fiscal Year 1994.*

4. For the payroll, see Office of Workforce Information, *Federal Civilian Workforce Statistics: Employment and Trends as of November 1992* (Office of Personnel Management, 1993), p. 23. For retirement benefit outlays, and health and life insurance benefits, see *Budget of the United States Government, Fiscal Year 1993*, appendix 1, pp. 906, 908.

5. Stephen Barr and Bill McAllister, "Del. Norton Claims 'Locality Pay' Victory for Federal Workers," *Washington Post*, May 13, 1993, p. A11. As part of House negotiations over pay in the budget reconciliation bill, a deal was cut that included the suspension of all cash awards for superior performance through fiscal year 1998.

6. Office of Personnel Management, *Position Classification Standard for Secretary Series GS-318* (January 1979).

7. Alfred M. Zuck and others, *Modernizing Federal Classification: An Opportunity for Excellence* (Washington: National Academy of Public Administration, July 1991), p. xiii. The earlier study is National Academy of Public Administration, *Revitalizing Federal Management: Managers and Their Overburdened Systems* (Washington, November 1983).

8. Horner, "Beyond Mr. Gradgrind," p. 35.

9. American Federation of Government Employees, AFL-CIO, *Revitalizing the Federal Government, A Report to Vice-President Gore* (March 1993), pp. 5–6.

10. Executive Office of the President, *Budget Baselines: Historical Data and Alternatives for the Future* (Office of Management and Budget, January 1993), p. 135. The federal procurement process costs more than $200 billion a year, with about 70,000 contract actions each day involving some 250,000 firms and 150,000 federal employees.

11. The latest example of undue delay is the Federal Aviation Administration's attempt to procure a $4 billion modernization of its air traffic control computers. In early 1993 the new equipment was scheduled for delivery three years late. John Burgess, "Out-of-Control Contract," *Washington Post*, March 8, 1993, p. F1.

12. Donald F. Kettl, *Sharing Power: Public Governance and Private Markets* (Brookings, 1993), chap. 4.

13. According to Fred Thompson, "Deregulating Defense Acquisition," *Political Science Quarterly*, vol. 107 (Winter, 1992–93), p. 729, Congress continues to add to the "existing 1,150 feet of legislation and case law governing procurement."

14. Henry David Thoreau, *The Journal* (February 3, 1860).

15. For a succinct summary of this system, as well as other federal personnel experiments, see Brigitte W. Schay, *Broad-Banding in the Federal Government: Management Report* (Office of Personnel Management, February 1993).

16. On job satisfaction see Office of Personnel Management, "Effects of Performance-Based Pay on Employees in the Navy Demonstration Project: An Analysis of Survey Responses 1979 to 1987," management report 12, December 1988. Grade point averages at China Lake increased significantly, and offer-acceptance ratios increased at both demonstration labs: Office of Personnel Management, "Recruitment of Scientists and Engineers in Four Navy Laboratories," management report 14, August 1991. Managers spend less time on classification: Office of Personnel Management, "A Summary Assessment of the Navy Demonstration Project," management report 9, February 1986. Turnover of high performers is significantly lower at the demonstration labs: Office of Personnel Management, "Turnover in the Navy Demonstration Laboratories 1980–1985," management report 11, December 1988. Turnover of marginal performers averaged over ten years was 20 percent at China Lake and 30 percent at San Diego, compared to 4 percent for outstanding performers. Turnover of unacceptable performers (who did not improve) was 34 percent at China Lake and 46 percent in San Diego between 1982 and 1992; data from Nancy Crawford, China Lake.

17. These remarks are excerpted from interviews I conducted in 1988, eight years into the experiment.

18. Schay, *Broad-Banding in the Federal Government*, p. 18.

19. *Treasury Postal Appropriations Act*, H. Rept. 2622, 102 Cong. 1 sess. (GPO, July 1991).

20. Constance Horner, *Civil Service Simplification Act: The Unfinished Business of Civil Service Reform, Purpose of CSSA* (Office of Personnel Management, July 1986).

21. Although salaries rose disproportionately at experimental sites, the increases resulted from controllable factors such as higher starting salaries and the overall configuration of positions that formed part of the conversion design. Following conversion, the rate of increase was the same under both comparison and experimental systems. In any event, salaries rose dramatically for outstanding performers. Schay, *Broad-Banding in the Federal Government*, pp. 14–16.

22. Recognizing the potential for abuse or unfairness if regulatory requirements are waived, the Civil Service Reform Act of 1978, which established experimental authority, prohibited waivers of rules relating to benefits, equal employment opportunity, political activity, and merit principles. The law also required congressional notification and consultation with employee organizations before a demonstration project was begun. According to one study, "None of the evaluation reports of the demonstration projects reported any management or OPM abuses. Even a local labor union representative . . . stated that he has not seen the management abuses that the union was concerned about at the start of the project." Merit Systems Protection Board, *Federal Personnel Research Programs and Demonstration Projects: Catalysts for Change* (December 1992), pp. ix, 20.

23. In a letter to Vice President Gore on March 25, 1993, John Sturdivant, head of the American Federation of Government Employees, AFL-CIO, the largest federal employee union, asked that the unions be "participants and partners" in the vice president's National Performance Review and highlighted better management-labor relations as the first of his goals in working with the Clinton administration. In a May 6, 1993, interview he reiterated an interest in trading increased management flexibility for increased bargaining opportunities.

24. David Osborne and Ted Gaebler, *Reinventing Government: How the Entrepreneurial Spirit Is Transforming the Public Sector* (Addison-Wesley, 1992).

25. Stephen Barr, "Bureaucracy Review Opens with a Rally: Officials Told to Adopt 'Entrepreneurial' Spirit," *Washington Post*, April 16, 1993, p. A23. In a kickoff gathering of federal employees serving on the "reinventing" teams of the National Performance Review a professional "motivator" "led all in a chorus of 'hi ho, hi ho, it's off to work we go.'"

26. Executive order 12871, "Labor-Management Partnerships," section 2(d) (October 1, 1993), referring to material quoted from 5 U.S.C. 7106(b)(1).

27. Executive order 12871, section 1(b)(2).

28. The Government Performance and Results Act starts with pilot projects but will eventually involve the entire bureaucracy in developing long-term strategic plans and annual performance plans and achievement reports, all designed to ensure solid measurement of outcomes. The act also lets the OMB grant waivers to agencies that want more flexibility in setting nonstatutory budget, salary, and personnel levels. This combination of planning, accountability, and flexibility is the paradigm for successful reform, providing that the OMB permits its real exercise.

# 6 ||| Deregulating Federal Procurement: Nothing to Fear But Discretion Itself?

Steven Kelman

MANAGING THE PURCHASE of goods and services from private firms is an increasingly important part of managing the public sector.[1] The federal government undertakes 20 million contracting actions a year, and they account for one-fifth of the federal budget. Everyone agrees this procurement system is in trouble. The conventional explanation is that government officials have excessively cozy relationships with contractors or that people who oversee the spending of someone else's money get lazy. The government ends up paying contractors too much and gives "wired" awards to favored contractors who do not deserve to get them. The conventional solution to these problems is more competition.

I, too, believe that the government often fails to get the most it can out of its relationships with suppliers. But the system of competition as it is often envisioned and the typical controls against favoritism or corruption are more the source of poor performance from vendors than the solution to it. The basic problem with the current system is public officials' inability to use their common sense and good judgment to encourage higher quality, less costly services. The system must be significantly deregulated to allow officials greater discretion. The slogan for procurement management should be "competition for performance."

## The Current Procurement System

Probably the most dramatic evidence of problems with the current procurement system comes from cost overruns and perfor-

---

I thank John J. DiIulio, Jr., Constance Horner, and the other authors in this volume for helpful comments on an earlier draft.

mance inadequacies of major weapons systems. To be sure, the purchase of large systems being developed from scratch presents a strong challenge for even the best procurement system, partly because development itself is so difficult and partly because it is inherently risky to buy a new system using a fixed-price contract of the kind used to buy proven products for which there is an existing market. But if the government abandons fixed-price contracts, where can it find incentives for suppliers to keep costs down?

Significant problems, however, exist even in the purchase of goods and services at fixed prices. In a survey of top information systems managers in government agencies and large private firms, I asked each, "Thinking about your information technology contracts in general, about what percentage of the time would you say you end up being dissatisfied overall with the performance of your vendors?" Government managers were dissatisfied nearly 25 percent of the time; private sector managers 16 percent.[2] Those accustomed to horror stories about government performance might find this difference trivial. But it does show that government managers are far more likely than private managers to be dissatisfied with the services of their computer vendors. This is not a screaming scandal, but it is hardly a record of distinction.

These results are confirmed by the managers' judgments of vendor performance on the most recent major contract they let.[3] On average, government officials gave their overall level of satisfaction as 6.9 out of a possible 10. For private managers the average was 7.8. Forty-eight percent of government managers rated overall vendor performance at 8.0 or higher, compared with 74 percent of private-sector managers. The managers were also asked about their satisfaction with various specific elements of the job suppliers have done. The differences between the government and private sector closely reflected those for overall satisfaction, with two exceptions. Government managers were even less often satisfied that vendors kept their promises and that they stuck to the contracted delivery schedule.

## The Current Regulatory Structure

Government agencies may not simply buy what they want from whom they want. The rules governing both contract award and contract administration are embodied in statutes, in the 744-page

Federal Acquisition Regulation, and in thousands of pages of sup-
plementary rules for specific agencies (the Defense supplement is
most important) and specific kinds of acquisitions (the Federal
Information Resources Management Regulation governing computer-
related procurements is the most important).[4] The rules cover
everything from how to determine and specify needs to how to
select vendors to how to administer a contract. The regulatory
system has three goals: to provide fair access to bidders in competing for government business, to reduce the chances for corruption
in the procurement process, and to pay the lowest possible price
for goods or services of the quality desired.[5] Nowhere among these
goals, however, and not emphasized in the theories of public
administration out of which they grow, is *excellence* in performing
the organization's tasks. Perhaps this was because agency tasks in
the nineteenth century when the doctrine was developed were
rudimentary and straightforward, so that if they were accomplished equitably, honestly, and economically, excellent results
would follow more or less automatically. When the federal government distributed land to homesteaders or pensions to war veterans
or bought pencils or coal, equity, honesty, and economy was all
that was necessary.

Although the three goals underlie all public administration doctrine, perhaps only the arrangement of awarding contracts through
competition simultaneously promotes all three. Competition lowers
prices, extends access to everyone, and if decisions are based on
full and open competition, makes bribing officials more difficult
because a corrupt decision in favor of a bidder who would have lost
is easy to detect.

Defining the three goals did not by itself produce the highly
regulated system that has developed. The goals might simply have
been proclaimed and officials trusted to achieve them. The statutes,
regulations, and cultural norms that now govern the system reflect
the public's fear that, left to their own devices, officials will award
contracts tainted by cronyism, partisan backscratching, or outright
bribery. In addition, the public suspects officials of being slothful
and heedless, of failing to get good products at good prices because
they are not spending their own money and there is no bottom line
to worry about. Finally, agencies are suspected of being pressured
to award contracts to politicians' constituents or contributors.[6] To
achieve the goals of the procurement system, it was believed neces-

sary to limit the discretion officials enjoyed in awarding contracts. Requiring competition was a means to do this as well.

Traditionally, the ideal institutional expression of equity, integrity, and economy was the practice of advertising procurements to all comers, accepting sealed bids, and awarding contracts to the lowest bidder who met the specifications. This process went the furthest of any possible in removing discretion from those involved in it. But much of American procurement regulation reflects the tension between the practice of sealed bidding and the grudging realization that it was often hopelessly inappropriate for much of government procurement. Specifications could be too complicated or imprecise to admit of a simple declaration by bidders that they could meet them. The government also wanted to buy products, mainly weapons, that had never been produced before, so a fixed price could not be quoted at the time of contract award. Allowing trade-offs between quality and price often made more sense than specifying a single level of quality and having vendors bid their lowest price to obtain it.

During much of the twentieth century there has thus been an alternative procurement method involving the selection of a contractor after bidders present proposals (in response to a government request for proposals) explaining what they plan to do and for what price. Government officials then evaluate these proposals for price and quality and choose a winner. This is called procurement by competitive proposals.[7]

Procurement by competitive proposals allows officials more discretion than does procurement by sealed bid. But because it could allow officials unbridled freedom, three kinds of limits have been imposed. These rules and practices establish the government's requirements, the criteria by which proposals are to be evaluated, and the information that may be used in the evaluation. The hope has been to discipline managerial discretion by making the awarding of contracts as much as possible a structured reaction by officials to the initiatives of others.

The system domesticates what might otherwise be undisciplined discretion by first specifying what the government wishes to purchase. The basic idea is that government may ask for no more than what it requires to meet its needs (indeed, its "minimum needs," to use the language of the Federal Acquisition Regulation).[8] The theory is that those needs are established by program missions that in turn are ultimately based in statute. In theory, too, the people involved in purchasing specify needs in detail and shape them into the language of specifications. This sequence, if correctly carried out, should allow little discretion because officials do not themselves determine needs but only translate existing needs established by Congress into specifications that suppliers can bid on. In pursuit of these goals, however chimerical, agencies initially perform expensive and time-consuming requirements analyses to prevent officials from seeking the unnecessary and to preclude favored vendors from getting a procurement wired by having specifications written to match their capabilities rather than agency needs. It is one of the main reasons procurement takes so much more time for government agencies than it does for private businesses.

Procurement regulations allow agencies considerable discretion in selecting criteria to evaluate bids. The regulations insist that "price or cost to the Government shall be included as an evaluation factor in every source selection." There is no requirement, however, that price be the dominant criterion or that the contract award be made to the lowest bidder. Agencies may also consider a bidder's technical excellence and managerial capabilities. Still, discretion in determining evaluation criteria is not unlimited. Just as specifications must be related to the agency's requirements, so too the criteria. Technical or management evaluation factors "should be justified on legitimate agency requirements, like any mandatory requirement. [They] need not and should not be included unless clearly relevant to the agency's mission."[9] This proviso tends to exclude criteria whose benefits to an agency are hard to quantify. Thus, for example, most users of complex computer software packages would regard as a positive sign the existence of customers who compare notes and meet with company representatives to discuss ways to apply the product and to make suggestions for product improvement. But the government may not consider presence of a user software group as an evaluation factor unless "there is a clear showing that the direct, identifiable, and quantifiable benefits of membership in such an organization outweigh the attendant costs."[10]

The system for developing evaluation criteria also limits discretion by requiring that all criteria be established in advance and stated in the request for proposals: "An agency," the Federal Acquisition Regulation states, "shall evaluate competitive proposals solely on the factors specified in the solicitation."[11] Officials cannot decide what criteria to use in judging suppliers' proposals, or how to weigh them, after they have seen the proposals. If that were allowed, officials could throw the contract to a favored vendor simply by inventing new evaluation criteria after they had read the proposals or by decreeing that the areas where the favored bidder's proposal turned out to be strong were precisely those that the agency regarded as crucial.

The third way the system seeks to tame discretion is through the practice that suppliers may be judged only on what they have presented the government in their written proposals. This feature, like others in the evaluation process, results from the culture of procurement and not the regulations, although evaluating vendors based only on their proposals may be seen as an application to procurement of the general doctrine that administrative decisions be based solely on the written record. What the doctrine means is that government officials may not evaluate suppliers based on information the officials have sought out on their own initiative or on information and impressions they have accumulated simply as living, breathing human beings. Officials may not base a contract award on an article in a magazine or a phone call to a friend who has had experience with a supplier. Otherwise, officials might select just the facts that would justify a corrupt or biased decision. If, by contrast, evaluation is based on information that vendors themselves provide, then the possibility of biased selection of facts by government officials is eliminated. The problem, of course, is that the possibility of biased selection of facts by the suppliers is heightened.

The system also seeks to ensure preservation of equity, integrity, and economy by establishing extensive mechanisms for bidders to protest procurement decisions to outside bodies. These include opportunities to protest both before an award is made (over the nature of specifications or evaluation criteria, for example) and after an award has been announced.

The current system thus creates two primary kinds of problems: it makes it difficult to use important information that would help the government choose the best vendor, and it reduces incentives for vendors who are awarded contracts to do a good job. Current procurement practices and regulations are thus a major source of the mediocre performance of the government's suppliers.

## The Inability to Consider Past Performance

The most bizarre problem the current system creates is that it has been interpreted to prevent officials from taking into account the past performance of vendors. Agencies have frequently had earlier contracts with one or more of the suppliers bidding for work on a new contract. Yet evidence about how they performed has generally been considered inadmissible when an agency is considering the same supplier for a new contract.[12]

There is no provision in the Federal Acquisition Regulation that prohibits using information from the past performance of vendors on contracts with one's own organization. The refusal to use the information in practice has grown out of the doctrine that suppliers may be evaluated only on what is in their written proposals. Judgments about how a contractor did in past dealings do not fit into the model of limiting the exercise of officials' discretion to a structured reaction to the actions of others. Such judgments are a composite of countless individual incidents and experiences—the time the project manager came (or did not come) after a power outage, the indifference or solicitude shown when unexpected problems arose, the attitude during price negotiations on a technology upgrade not priced in the original contract.

Because past performance is such a composite, specific evaluation criteria are difficult to design in advance, so that any information used has been seen to risk being unsystematic. To allow officials to choose among endless facts and impressions may allow arbitrariness or outright prejudice. Furthermore, to reduce the likelihood of their becoming subject to unfair influence during the evaluation process, members of a technical evaluation team have generally not been permitted to talk with colleagues at their agency about experiences they may have had with the bidders, or even to tell others who the bidders are.

In addition to all this, taking account of past performance in contracts with one's own organization has been interpreted to conflict with full and open competition. A supplier with no past experience at the agency could not get the credit for good performance given to another. And the greater the incentive provided for performing well—that is, the more past performance counts in making new awards—the less open the competition for new contracts.[13]

In the survey of senior government information systems managers that I conducted, 85 percent answered no when asked, "Are you allowed to factor in your own prior experience with a vendor here in this agency in making award decisions?" "There is," one respondent lamented, "no history in government procurement." And another said, "our procurement process is such that taking our past experience with a vendor into account is extremely hard to do. It seems to start from scratch each time around." A person of enormous good will and devotion to his job who was in charge of one of the procurements at the Internal Revenue Service said that one other person involved in the procurement knew about one bidder with which the agency had had terrible experience in the past but "was careful not to tell anyone on the panel so as not to bias the evaluation process."

A recompetition for an IRS computer-support-services consulting contract provides an appalling example of what happens when past performance may not be taken into account.[14] Of all my case studies the customer was the most enthusiastic about the vendor in this contract. The customer's phone calls had been returned quickly at any hour of the day or night and the vendor had redone at no extra charge reports with which the customer was dissatisfied. In recompetition for renewal of the contract (which occurred after my research was completed and the reactions of IRS people to the vendor's performance already recorded), however, the incumbent lost to a supplier the IRS had not worked with. It lost because the request for proposals had included a hypothetical situation to which the bidders were to respond, and the incumbent's response was judged poorer than that of the winning bidder. The fact that the incumbent had prodigious experience responding to such situations was not taken into account. "Evaluating performance is something that's frowned upon," according to one official involved in the recompetition. "Just because the contractor does work for the government and does a good job, it doesn't mean he can get the business again." The same official went on to say that he took "pride in the fact that we're so objective."

The procurement system thus has prevented public officials from providing what is probably the most useful information to help predict the performance of contractors. There are simply too many important aspects of a vendor's future performance that cannot be gauged based on what is included in a written proposal. Will the vendor deliver what has been promised? Will it try to exploit the inevitable ambiguities or incomplete features in contract language, or change orders that need to be negotiated during the contract, after the contract has been signed? Will the vendor switch senior personnel out of a project the moment the contract allows and replace them with people who are much less impressive, or staff a contract with inexperienced trainees who are sent off to other jobs as soon as they have gained some experience? Will it do the minimum work necessary, or go beyond that? Information about how a vendor has performed in these respects is the best way to predict how it will perform in the future.

The refusal to take past performance into account affronts common sense. Even children know that if they have tried a candy bar once and liked it, they will probably want to eat one again, and if they have disliked it, they probably will not. And past performance typically plays a crucial role in contract awards in the private sector. When informed that government procurement processes do not look at past performance, private sector managers I have interviewed were generally incredulous. All stated some version of "how can they say you can't take into account the single most important factor in making those decisions?"

The current system's emphasis on written proposals encourages suppliers to promise far more than they can deliver. Such promises are of course a problem in any sales context, but my survey showed that government managers were far more likely than their private sector counterparts to agree that "vendors frequently overpromise in a major way about what their products can deliver, how fast they will be ready, and so forth."

The current system also reduces incentives for suppliers to do a good job on contracts once they have won them. One textbook on purchasing management makes the point succinctly: "The greatest reward a customer can give is assurance of future business in response to satisfactory performance."[15] Good performance may require vendors to make transaction-specific or idiosyncratic investments tied to dealings with specific customers.[16] There are many transaction-specific, idiosyncratic investments that generate value. A supplier might invest in special tools or production technologies to produce a version of his product that is adapted to a customer's unique needs. Likewise, a customer might invest in employee training in techniques or procedures specific to the operation of a supplier's equipment. Perhaps the most pervasive investments are those in learning—suppliers learning about special features of customers' operations and customers learning about special features of suppliers' products and how best to use the equipment in their specific environment. The supplier who has invested in learning is in a position to bring more value to the relationship with the customer than one who has not.

Customers, of course, know the features of their sites as well or better than vendors. Nonetheless, vendors who learn about a customer's operation are still in a good position to make helpful suggestions. Vendors can provide greater knowledge of their own products and how they might be applied to the specific problems of a customer's operation. Vendors can bring a fund of experience from dealing with other customers and knowledge derived from their own research. They might also notice things that customers do not because customers may be too accustomed to their way of doing things to see alternative possibilities. Finally, vendors can be helpful as sounding boards for their customers' ideas.

As a result of all this, a vendor who has invested in learning about a customer's operation is not only in a better position to solve problems the customer knows it has, but also to uncover better ways of doing things. For example, a computer supplier who has learned that some researchers take copious notes on books or journal articles for later use in their work could show researchers how to adapt a software product to serve as a filing and keyword search system for the notes—a capability of which the researcher, who has perhaps used computers only for word processing, might not have considered.

Reaping the benefits of these transaction-specific investments requires rewarding the firms that have made the investments. It is sometimes suggested that the fact that government frequently signs multiyear contracts with vendors in itself promotes investments in site-specific knowledge. Unfortunately, this is not so. Suppliers with long-term contracts will invest in site-specific knowledge to the extent they can recoup the investments out of savings to themselves but will not invest for the sake of creating value for the customer. They will invest only if they get rewarded for good past performance the next time a contract is awarded. Lacking the ability to recoup transaction-specific investments because agencies have not been able to take past performance into account, vendors simply fail to make them.

My research involving computer procurement showed significant differences in the extent to which vendors make investments in transaction-specific knowledge for their government and private customers. I asked managers of information systems the dollar value of their investment with their most important supplier and how many people the supplier had on site full time working on contracts with the organization. For private firms, vendors had one full-time employee on site for every $3.9 million of customer investment; for government agencies, one for every $6.4 million. Even these results were skewed in favor of the government by two agencies (out of thirty-one) with a much larger number of vendor employees than any of the others. Thirty-two percent of the government sites had no full-time vendor personnel present, but only 20 percent of the private sector sites had none.

Those missing employees deprive the government of something. When I asked managers whether any of their organizations' current vendors took the initiative in identifying the needs or the applications that were eventually addressed in their most recent major computer contract (thus asking about the prevalence of vendor advice on problems the customer had not known about), 67 percent of government managers said there was no vendor involvement in needs identification, but only 20 percent of the private sector managers agreed. Twenty-nine percent of private sector managers, compared with 12 percent of government ones, placed vendor involvement at the midpoint of a 7-point scale or higher.

It should be remembered that the managers were asked about contracts that had actually been signed, so that unnecessary or simply self-serving supplier suggestions would likely be excluded, since they probably would not have passed internal review to proceed to contract award. And it should also be remembered that the managers were asked about a major contract, so that the suggestions should not be seen as of marginal importance. These results suggest that the site-specific investments of current vendors in learning about the customers' business do add value for customers.

The results also suggest that the worst part of the government procurement system may be that public managers do not know what they are missing in terms of potential value that suppliers can bring to their organizations. Customers will never know they missed the opportunity to get an idea from a vendor if the idea involves a problem they did not know could be solved. In assessing the costs of the current procurement system in government, therefore, one must consider not only the costs that agencies attach to dissatisfaction with vendor performance, but also the costs agencies do not detect—of missed solutions to unaddressed problems.

### Developing and Responding to Government Specifications

Basic to the model of domesticating discretion in government contract awards is that public managers must tell suppliers in advance not only what the government wants but also how much it wants it. What the government wants is set forth in its specifications; how much it wants it is set forth in its evaluation criteria. Specifications and evaluation criteria are established at the beginning of the process. Embodied in a request for proposals, they are then shown to vendors for response. Because evaluation criteria must be set forth in writing, the government is prevented from changing the grounds for contract award after it receives proposals, something that would open the way for favoritism.

To be fair, establishing criteria in advance and then judging proposals against those criteria does correspond to a common idea of how one ought to make rational decisions. This system, however, creates two problems. First, it artificially and detrimentally cuts short the period during which government may learn about what it wants and how much it wants. Second, it creates incentives for vendors to respond to inappropriate specifications rather than to help the government improve them. Most organizations acting outside the constraints of a procurement regulatory system do not make decisions this way. A 1960s study of how corporations made their first purchase of a computer concluded that in only 4 of 233 situations did decisionmaking correspond to the classical model.[17] Nor was information gathering of the kind necessary to elucidate goals concentrated toward the beginning of the process. Instead, learning continued at high levels throughout, reaching its peak, in fact, around the time the final decision was made.

It is a mistake to require that learning about what one wants and how much one wants it be limited to the early stages of the procurement process because people are unlikely to focus on such matters until much closer to the actual time of decision. Translated to procurement, thinking abstractly and out of context on questions such as whether the capability of a supplier's management should count for 5 percent or 50 percent of the award decision, differs significantly from confronting a real decision with real information about various suppliers. If, for example, a vendor is barely able to provide service sufficient to be judged responsive to a proposal's specifications, should the worst that happens be that the vendor gets a low score on something that counts a mere 2 percent toward the contract award? If the resum of a key manager in the vendor's proposal looks suspect but not in a way that fits the preestablished criteria for evaluating resums, does an agency really wish to bear with the criteria?

Buyers public and private frequently make mistakes in specifications, and suppliers are often in a position to detect the mistakes. Yet the government system produces among many vendors an attitude of "bid what they ask for, not what they want." As one government manager I interviewed stated, "the problem is that they give you the answer to the question you ask, not to the question you should have asked but didn't know how to ask." In a Department of Agriculture local office computerization effort, the office ended up with an expensive Rube Goldberg solution because none of the suppliers informed it of the defects in the specifications that made such a solution the only way to meet them.

Competition requirements also make it difficult for government to gain the benefit of supplier insights about defective specifications. The basic philosophy is that if a vendor points out problems, the government should change the specifications and reopen the contract to bidding. "Why bother to be altruistic?" a marketing manager for a large computer company said. "You just go back to a level playing field." In an Immigration and Naturalization Service local office computerization procurement, the supplier pointed out that specifications in the request for proposals were inferior to another approach. When the INS gave the supplier credit for the suggestions, the losing competitor protested the contract award, stating that if the government liked the suggestion, it should reopen the contract with new specifications. A General Accounting Office report portrayed the INS gesture as a scandal.

Frequently, it is profitable to vendors to bid on defective specifications, either because they allow a vendor to sell the government more expensive products or because they allow a vendor to negotiate lucrative change orders when the solution asked for in the specifications does not work.

The problem of vendor reactions to defective specifications is difficult to solve within the current regulatory structure. One would wish to be able to reward suppliers for pointing out defects. However, this requires granting managers a great deal of freedom to use their good judgment. When an agency allows vendors to comment on draft specifications, they typically raise large numbers of questions. But almost always vendors raise questions only where a proposed specification creates a competitive disadvantage for them. Although the Department of Agriculture put specifications for its local office computerization out for comment before making them final—and received voluminous comments on them—not a single vendor pointed out the defects that were later to prove so expensive. All the suppliers were happy to bid on specifications that would allow them to sell the government unnecessarily expensive equipment. To change this, the government must be able to reward vendors for pointing out defects even when such defects do not competitively disadvantage any vendor. Creating that freedom requires letting government officials use their judgment to distinguish between issues raised by a potential bidder simply to remedy a competitive disadvantage for that bidder and comments that genuinely help the government.

## A Strategy for Reform

Rule boundedness in the management of the public sector fits well with goals limited to equity, integrity, and economy. But in a complex and changing world it is more difficult to achieve excellence simply by following the rules. In such a world, goals that give important place to the quality of government's performance are likely to require that public officials be given more discretion. This applies especially to procurement.

To the observer who worries about the performance of the system but whose cynical view of government officials leads him to believe that suppliers perform poorly because lazy or corrupt bureaucrats let them rip off the government, I ask, what is the alternative for improving supplier performance? Such an observer would presumably want the government to "be tough," to withhold payments or initiate lawsuits against those who perform poorly. But although it is relatively easy to translate the injunctions to be honest, fair, and economical into rules, it is much harder to do so with the injunction to be tough against vendors. Decisions about when and how to be tough will require considerable judgment. And if the cynical observer does not trust government officials' discretion, he has no program for improving vendor performance.

The grant of more freedom to public managers should not be unconditional. Much greater freedom should be given them to make decisions that affect their ability to accomplish their work. But managers should then be held responsible for the results. There should, in other words, be greater freedom to select the means with the best chance of realizing agreed-upon ends. Evaluation of performance is often not easy. But the energy now going into developing rules to restrict public officials in using their judgment should be redirected toward thinking about how to develop performance evaluation measures.

Unfortunately, in a government context *accountability* is often used as a synonym for achieving equity, integrity, and economy, rather than as a description of behavior that gives important place to excellence. Indeed, some who use the term suggest by the way they use it that it means following the rules. Grants of greater discretion are thus often presented as decreasing the accountability of government agencies. What is being proposed here is not an end to the accountability we rightly expect of government managers. It is a change in focus toward accountability for results.

I support increasing the freedom of judgment public managers are permitted to exercise. This might, for example, involve statutory authorization for experiments that would eliminate most procurement rules and institute a regime with only two broad procedural requirements: written justification for each procurement decision and multimember evaluation panels to reach decisions. The written justification would, within the constraints that nonrevelation of proprietary information impose, lay out why one bidder and not another was selected. The document would be publicly available, like the statements that government agencies currently provide in connection with administrative decisions on rules.[18] Use of multimember evaluation committees (ad hoc groups of agency employees, usually users of what is being bought) should remain the primary way to judge supplier proposals. The panels do dilute somewhat the sense of responsibility that individual participants feel for decisions they are making, but they also tend to encourage excellence. When a manager must justify a decision in front of others, the situation favors those behaviors that can most easily be justified. Standards for excellence normally constitute our publicly stated ideals, sloth a guilty private vice, and poor judgment a source of embarrassment. Institutions that bring behavior before others whose opinion we value encourage behavior to move in the direction of our ideals.[19] Multimember committees also make corruption considerably less likely.

If one chose to proceed more cautiously toward deregulation, by far the most useful change would be to add past performance in contracts within the agency as a factor in evaluation, and one given significant weight. Firms that had done well in the past would get a good score; firms that had done badly would get a poor score. If a certain supplier has had no previous experience at the agency, it would indeed have a harder time getting a contract than one that has performed well.

The more the scoring on the new evaluation factor depends only on objective measures of performance (such as meeting contracted delivery schedules), the less radical the departure from the current system would be. But because so many dimensions of good performance are difficult to quantify, officials should be allowed to use their judgment in determining how good past performance has been. The factors with which performance might be judged should not be arbitrarily limited. Judgments about past performance should be able to be influenced by such a story as that the vendor's project manager came to the customer's site at 3:00 a.m. to figure out why a computer was not working right. Judgment about criteria for evaluating performance should be constrained only by the requirement that the agency explain the basis of the judgment.

The effort to take past performance into consideration should not be doomed from the start by demands that a vendor's performance be measured only by mountains of data that nobody is likely to have the time to develop or review. Information about past supplier performance must be both inclusive and simple. The way to meet that double test is for agencies to gather two kinds of information. First, managers should be asked to fill out a simple form once every six months rating vendors with whom they have contacts. The form should have three or four fixed-response questions, where each manager must simply check in a box listing overall satisfaction with the supplier's performance (using perhaps a scale of 1 to 10) and satisfaction for a few specific factors. The form could ask managers who wished to do so to provide additional written commentary, but it should be made clear that this is not required. Second, when contracts are being let, members of an evaluation committee should each be assigned to conduct a half-hour interview with managers who have experience with any vendors bidding on the contract. The interview would use a standard set of questions. The resulting information should be part of the bid record. If such interviews are done at the time of contract award, there should be no problem getting agency managers to focus on the questions.

One agency in the government where some contract award processes have begun to use performance information is the Department of Defense.[20] Most of these efforts have involved small purchases of spare parts through a sealed-bid system that has traditionally awarded a contract to the lowest bidder. Programs that take account of performance are now under way in all three services and the Defense Logistics Agency, which buys spares for the three services. The program at DLA, which is further along than those at some of the other agencies, began in 1988 as the Quality Vendor Program. The inspiration, as for similar efforts within the department, was the 1986 report of the Packard Commission on Defense Procurement, whose recommendations included making defense procurement more closely resemble private sector procurement practices.[21] The idea was to allow vendors to apply for blue-ribbon contractor status at the Defense Logistics Agency. The vendor could be awarded such status after having achieved a sufficiently good record for on-time delivery, absence of product defects, and various other criteria in a certain number of past contracts with the agency. When a blue-ribbon contractor bid, the officer making the decision about the award was authorized to allow the vendor to charge up to 20 percent more than competitors.

But various factors have inhibited use of the system. These small awards are made not by users but by contracting officers who may feel no direct interest in the quality of products the government gets.[22] Contracting officers have to present a written justification for making the award to a blue-ribbon contractor, but an award to a low bidder needs no justification. Of DLA's small-purchase base of

25,000 suppliers, 575 have received the blue-ribbon designation. Since inception of the program, a blue-ribbon contractor provision has been written into a fifth of the 600,000 small-purchase solicitations DLA has issued and a price preference paid 600 times.

DLA is now changing the blue-ribbon contractor system to a vendor rating system. The system will use DLA data regarding vendor delivery and product quality under existing contracts (quality will be measured by the number of complaints about defects and the results of lab tests on incoming products) to give every supplier a rating between 0 and 100. A vendor's quality rating will be part of the file on a contract. The evaluation of bids will be changed so that, unless the contract solicitation says otherwise, price and past performance will count equally. A contracting officer will thus need to justify not only an award to other than the lowest-price bidder but also one to a low-quality bidder.

The new system is still being developed, and one concern DLA officials have is the quality of their data, particularly regarding product defects. Users frequently have failed to report defects, procurement people believe, because they assumed it did no good. DLA expects that defect reports will increase as the rating system is developed.

A more ambitious program involving major weapons systems has begun in the air force. The program includes performance risk as a criterion in the technical evaluation of proposals. Evaluation committees get information on performance risk through one traditional source, vendor-provided references, and two nontraditional ones, interviews with users who have had experience with one or more of the bidders and a contractor performance assessment reporting system file compiled each year on every vendor. The file is based on reports of performance written by program managers. Vendors may contest features of these reports, and a final report must be approved by the program manager's superior. (Early experience with the rating system suggests that three-quarters of vendors are rated satisfactory and the other quarter either higher or lower.) The idea behind using these three sources is that references provided by suppliers will be slanted in their favor, interviews with users will provide information slanted against, and the annual written report will provide information somewhere in between. It is still too early to evaluate the impact of the system.

## Possible Objections to Reform

What would be the effects of these changes on the equity and integrity of the procurement system? Will vendors be arbitrarily excluded from government business? Will the greater discretion granted managers return government to the days of Boss Tweed and the shame of the cities, of sweetheart deals and payoffs?

I do not suggest that suppliers be arbitrarily excluded from doing business with government. Arbitrary exclusion is exclusion for no good reason, so if there are good reasons not to choose a bidder, the exclusion is not arbitrary. I suggest only that public officials be given greater freedom to determine that there were indeed good reasons not to give a vendor a contract. And no defender of the current system would openly suggest (although some appear to believe) that vendors have a right to receive government business, only that they not arbitrarily be excluded.

Left to their own devices, why might public officials choose one vendor over another for other than good reasons, that is reasons related to how well they believe the vendor will do the work? Perhaps the officials might do so because they are lazy. This is a problem that should be dealt with by results-oriented performance measures, not through procurement regulation. Perhaps the officials might choose because they have been bribed (a topic I deal with later). Often the suggestion is made that public managers stay with vendors they know because they feel more comfortable with them. Insofar as this is more than a variant of saying that the official is lazy, such comfort frequently constitutes genuine value to the government that has been achieved through ongoing relationships and hence may not be arbitrary.

To suppliers who complain that they too are taxpayers and have the right to bid for government business, one must be willing to state that taxpayers in general have a right to expect that dollars spent on procurement be spent so as to maximize the value the public receives. One must, in short, be willing to state that much of what some vendors perceive as arbitrary behavior is not arbitrary at all. And one must therefore be prepared to conclude that a change in the system need not imply any compromise of the goal that government treat citizens equitably as long as the concept of equity is properly understood.

DEREGULATING FEDERAL PROCUREMENT 121

I take very seriously the goal of keeping corruption out of government. The current procurement system, however, exacts such an enormous toll on the quality of government performance that the nation must seek other ways of keeping corruption out. The basic approach should be to fight procurement corruption through the criminal system, not the procurement regulatory system.

Combating corruption through regulation is of dubious effectiveness. Once I had a different view, namely that a genuine trade-off existed between procurement effectiveness and the reduction of corruption. But the 1988 defense procurement scandal, involving the sale by officials of information about what specifications the government was likely to list in an RFP convinced me that the procurement regulatory system functions as a sort of Maginot Line, an imposing defense reduced to impotence because it simply redirects dishonesty into other forms. Almost unnoticed in discussions of that scandal was that the system worked, at least on its own terms. Nobody was able to throw a contract directly. Instead, some contractors bought early access to information that later became publicly available, giving them more time to prepare their proposals. They could then present proposals that "legitimately" made it through the hoops of the formal procurement process and won because they were indeed the best proposals.

The scandal showed that the elaborate procurement oversight did not even generate the paper trail to catch the crooks. According to press accounts, the trail began instead with a tip to government fraud investigators from an employee at a defense contractor who had been approached by a defense consultant about purchasing inside information.[23] Government investigators then proceeded to use wiretaps and the people first implicated to provide information about further illegal actions. It has become easier to uncover procurement fraud because of investigative techniques such as these, previously used almost exclusively in narcotics and similar cases. But there is no mention in the press accounts that any records the procurement system produces were helpful in investigating the scandal. One former inspector general at the General Services Administration attempted to uncover procurement fraud by examining procurement records. His conclusion was that no matter how gross the corruption, one would "not find anything in the documents."[24]

To say that the current system may do less to reduce corruption than one would think is not the same as suggesting that some hypothetical procurement system where nobody looked and nobody cared would have levels of corruption no higher than the current one. The current system may, at least to some extent, increase the effort and ingenuity required to cheat and hence serve as a disincentive: even the Maginot Line made France more of a challenge to conquer than if it had not been there.

Combatting corruption through regulation also unjustly punishes the many for the crimes of a few. The current system puts too much of the burden on honest government officials trying to do their jobs and on citizens who are the victims of poorer government performance. It would be better if the cost of efforts to combat corruption could be targeted on the corrupt themselves rather than spread out over everyone.

Deregulation of the procurement system should therefore be accompanied by an increase in penalties for corruption. The corrupt do not bear the full social costs of their corruption, since corruption is costly not only because of the particular procurement that is "thrown" but because of the pressure it creates for new regulatory controls. Any loosening of the regulatory straitjacket should be accompanied by, and linked to, increased resources for public investigations of corruption. These resources should be given not only to investigative units outside line agencies responsible for procurement but also to units within the agencies, so that no agency administrator need stand naked against the criticism that the operation under his watch was buried in scandal and that it took a team of outsiders to expose it.

Another phenomenon the current procurement system seeks to minimize is intervention in contract award decisions by members of Congress who wish awards to go to constituents. The current system's main (and not inconsiderable) virtue in this regard is that it provides government officials with an easy, unthreatening way to say no to elected officials: "I'd like to help, but I've got to follow the rules." The system also allows members to make a show of intervening on behalf of constituents or campaign contributors, secure in the knowledge that the agency will not change its behavior.

I would therefore urge in conjunction with changes in procurement regulation a requirement that the dates and topics of any contacts between elected officials or their staffs and an agency regarding a procurement decision be made part of the published record of the procurement. This would allow the news media, in effect, to enforce limits on political intervention. Members of Congress might resist such a proposal, for fear its very ability to make intervention less likely will eliminate a benefit constituents or financial contributors believe they get from a member of Congress. But it is hard to imagine a convincing public policy argument on behalf of this deception, and Congress might be shamed into adopting the publicity requirement if it were vigorously advocated.

If no such requirement could get passed, a general duty clause might be developed in a pared-down version of a future Federal Acquisition Regulation, stating, "contract award decisions must be made solely on the basis of a judgment about which contractor will provide the best overall value, considering quality and cost, in performing the objectives stated in the procurement. No other factors may be taken into consideration." The official who needs a rule to cite for a member of Congress can then have a rule without needing the other hundreds of pages of regulations.

Two narrow objections to using performance information in making contract awards should also be noted. One is that using it would put small new businesses, or businesses trying to break into the government market for the first time, at a disadvantage. The second is that the information may punish a vendor for bad past performance when the vendor may no longer employ the people responsible.

Suppliers with no past performance record with an agency should be treated neutrally, compared with those who have a past record. The Department of Defense has done this by giving them a performance rating average for vendors bidding on a contract who do have records. The lack of performance history will not help the vendor who has never worked at the organization before, but it will not hurt either. Suppliers with a performance history may be helped by the record but may be hurt as well. This solution is fair. An established firm that has successfully satisfied its customers should be given credit for that. But small new firms may also have lower costs, greater innovativeness, and ability to react more quickly than established companies. There is no reason to believe that making past performance count will preclude small businesses from getting contracts.

As for the objection that a vendor might have fired bad people and improved (or that a previously good vendor might have lost good people), this is why government officials need more discretion in judging past performance. If a change has occurred, the agency ought to be allowed to note that in the procurement record and use it as an explanation for why a score for past performance departed from what it otherwise would have been.

Another problem for devising systems to evaluate past performance is the extent to which vendors may be allowed to challenge low ratings. Due process concerns that are so important to American administrative law in general and to procurement regulations in particular allow extensive opportunities for vendors to question ratings. But if suppliers are allowed formally to protest ratings, agencies may be unwilling to give bad ratings for fear of occasioning long expensive lawsuits.

It is fair to ask how federal managers who buy and use computers might react to new freedoms I have advocated. Classic accounts of problems created by adherence to bureaucratic rules suggest that if bureaucracies become excessively rule bound, it is because devotion to rules has become part of the bureaucrats themselves. Descriptions of such bureaucrats certainly seem to fit the behavior of contracting officials I have encountered. Contracting offices gain their standing by being experts on the rules. And because people in these offices lack responsibility for accomplishing the missions furthered by the products or services acquired, they also lack any countervailing pressures against pressures to stick to the rules. Contracting offices thus become the source of the negative features of the procurement culture that they present to unsuspecting program people as if these customs were law.

But evidence regarding program people who are responsible for accomplishing something is not nearly as dreary. An examination of how the few federal agencies that are not subject to the Federal Acquisition Regulation procure computer systems suggests that government officials will take advantage, in appropriate ways, of greater discretion.[25] The study I conducted showed that government computer managers chafe under the current system. Furthermore, surveys of senior government managers suggest considerable dissatisfaction with the rules and clearances required in procurement, personnel, and similar systems.[26] And it should be kept in mind that just as powerful in discussions of organization theory as the image of the rule-obsessed bureaucrat is the image of the autonomy-seeking professional. The close supervision that rule boundedness embodies is normally thought to engender resentment from those subject to it, not the willing submission of escapees from freedom.[27]

## Recent Moves Toward Procurement Reform

Some potentially important moves toward procurement reform have recently been initiated by the Office of Federal Procurement Policy, the unit of the Office of Management and Budget responsible for procurement policy in the executive branch. The office worked hard to obtain a provision in procurement legislation initiated in Congress that would authorize experiments to waive some or all procurement regulation. The provision was included in a bill passed by the House in 1992 but was not included in legislation passed by the Senate.

There have also been important developments involving performance information. On January 11, 1993, the Office of Federal Procurement Policy issued a policy letter that stated, "Executive agencies shall . . . specify past performance as an evaluation factor in solicitations for offers for all competitively negotiated contracts expected to exceed $100,000 except where the contracting office determines that such action is not appropriate. Such determinations shall be in writing and included in the contract file."[28] The letter also allowed contractors the right to comment on past performance reports that agencies developed (and the right to have the comments become part of the procurement file the agency keeps on its vendors) but not formally to protest them. Office of Federal Procurement Policy letters are supposed to be reflected in the Federal Acquisition Regulations, and the January 1993 letter directed that this occur with 210 days.

The experiments at the Defense Logistics Agency have been greeted skeptically by the House Government Operations Committee, which feared they would make it more difficult for small firms to compete for government business. The Small Business Administration has agreed. Some agency comments on the draft letter from the Office of Federal Procurement Policy worried that considering past performance would introduce too much subjectivity into evaluations.

## Conclusion

The federal procurement system has worked better in practice than in theory. The most conscientious and devoted public officials have sought and at least sometimes found ways to apply their common sense and good judgment to the process. But rather than encouraging excellence, the system has kept it the province of the heroic few. According to a manager I encountered who withheld a contract award from a firm that had done a poor job, "It was uphill. The system doesn't make it natural or easy. But you can either be victimized by the system or say, 'I'm a thinking human being.' " Simply to display common sense, such as favoring vendors because they have done good work, is to court questioning, disgrace, or even prison. Unfortunately, those responses are the pattern in far too much of the public sector. The nation owes public officials and all those affected by the quality of government performance more than that.

## Notes

1. Much of the material in this chapter is adapted from Steven Kelman, *Procurement and Public Management: The Fear of Discretion and the Quality of Government Performance* (Washington: AEI Press, 1990). That book gives fuller evidence supporting the propositions presented here.

2. For details on the survey design and administration, see Kelman, *Procurement and Public Management*, pp. 3–4, 106–08.

3. Respondents were told they could define *major* however they wished.

4. The Federal Acquisition Regulation is CFR 48, chap. 1 (the page length is as of the October 1985 edition). The Federal Information Resources Management Regulation is CFR 41, chap. 201. For a discussion of procurement law, see Ralph C. Nash and John Cibinic, Jr., *Federal Procurement Law* (George Washington University Press).

5. For a discussion, see Michael Barzelay, *Breaking through Bureaucracy: A New Vision for Managing in Government* (University of California Press, 1992), chaps. 1 and 2. I am indebted to Barzelay for helping me put my thinking about the goals of the procurement system into the context of the development of the doctrine of American public administration. Mark Moore has written extensively on alternative conceptions of the task of public sector management. See, for example, "Small-Scale Statesmen: A Normative Conception of the Role and Function of Public Management in Contemporary American Government," Cambridge, Mass., 1988.

6. Much of the impetus for procurement regulation has come from the very Congress that many regard as one source of the problems. In passing procurement

laws designed to stamp out favoritism, Congress appears to be acting in the manner of the dieter who padlocks the refrigerator so that he will not, in a weak moment, lunge for the whipped-cream cake.

7. An earlier phrase was *negotiated procurement*. In recent years the phrase has been banished for political incorrectness because it suggests to some a lack of competition.

8. Federal Acquisition Regulation 10.004 (a)(1).

9. General Services Administration, Information Resources Management Service, "Guidance the Standard Solicitation Document for ADP Equipment Systems," June 1987, p. 32.

10. Ibid., p. 19.

11. Federal Acquisition Regulation 15.608(a).

12. The exception is for the bare-bones determination by a contracting officer that the vendor meets procurement regulatory requirements for responsibility. Responsibility refers to the ability of the supplier to perform the work if awarded the contract. Bidders may be declared nonresponsible because the contracting officer has doubts about their integrity, perseverance in completing the work, or their financial or operational soundness; see Nash and Cibinic, *Procurement Law*, vol. 1, pp. 186–87. In all cases, the officer must look for relatively objective evidence of problems—for example, indictment or convictions of a company or its officers for tax evasion or violation of federal labor laws. Records of contract terminations for poor performance may show lack of perseverance or lack of ability to perform work. Contracting officers may also seek evidence from other agencies, or (in particular when the question is over the ability of the company to perform the work in question) make a preaward survey of the firm's facilities before making determinations of responsibility. (See Federal Acquisition Regulation 9.105.6. The quotation about "verifiable knowledge of personnel" appears in Federal Acquisition Regulation 9.105-1(c)(2).)

Protest arbiters almost always delay determinations of nonresponsibility by contracting officers, which implies that such judgments lie almost entirely within a contracting officer's discretion; Nash and Cibinic, *Procurement Law*, vol. 1, pp. 180, 201. Nonetheless, it would be fair to say that determinations of responsibility generally certify a bare-bones minimum standard of company ability and that most contracting officers do not make declarations of nonresponsiveness casually, since such determinations exclude a potential competitor. (A more extreme determination than that of nonresponsibility is a decision to bar a contractor. Debarment decisions result from fraud or antitrust violations in connection with bidding on or performing government contracts or from a repeated history of bad performance. Such decisions, which require overwhelming evidence and provide vendors with many procedural safeguards, are normally governmentwide and last for three years. See Federal Acquisition Regulation 9.4.

13. The inability of an agency to use information from past performance should be distinguished from what is often called incumbent advantage in contract rewards. This advantage generally exists independently of the quality of past performance and simply because of the vendor's past presence at the customer's

128    STEVEN KELMAN

site, which allows a vendor to develop a good written proposal more easily because it understands the agency's requirements better.

14. For the research in *Procurement and Public Management*, I examined each of the procurements for computer hardware, software, or services with an expected value over $25 million awarded by civilian federal agencies during fiscal year 1985 (a total of nine).

15. Michael R. Leender and others, *Purchasing and Materials Management*, 8th ed. (Homewood, Ill.: Richard D. Irwin, 1985), p. 210.

16. Oliver E. Williamson presents these ideas in *Markets and Hierarchies Analysis and Antitrust Implications* (Free Press, 1975). See also Arthur M. Okun, *Prices and Quantities: A Macroeconomic Analysis* (Brookings, 1981), particularly chap. 4.

17. Eberhard Witte, "Field Research on Complex Decision making Processes: The Phase Theorem," *International Studies of Management Organization*, vol. 2 (1968), pp. 516–82.

18. The elimination of such rules would not, of course, prohibit officials from choosing to use sealed bids and other traditional techniques where appropriate, as in buying pencils or toilet paper. But it would give people much more freedom in deciding how to go about acquisitions.

19. There are, of course, instances in which the group's ideal may be laziness, as cases in which blue-collar workers have restricted production. These are products, however, of a group ideology that sees bosses as exploiters and uses restricted output as a way to restore justice. Such results are unlikely to obtain in the kinds of settings I have discussed.

20. This discussion is based on Tom Neufer and Dan Smith, "DLA Vendor Rating System: A Second Generation, Best Value Buying System," Defense Logistics Agency, 1992, and on interviews with Ed Martin at the Air Force Materiel Command and a number of officials at the Defense Logistics Agency.

21. President's Blue Ribbon Commission on Defense Management, *A Formula for Action: A Report to the President on Defense Acquisition* (Washington, 1986).

22. These officers are also separate from those who administer contracts and must deal with complaints by users about poor vendor performance.

23. Stephen Engelberg, "Inquiry into Pentagon Bribery Began with a Telephone Call," *New York Times*, June 19, 1988, p. A1.

24. Interview with William Block, U.S. Attorney's Office, District of Columbia.

25. Kelman, *Procurement*, pp. 101–02.

26. I am indebted to Robert Reich for making this point.

27. See, for example, Alvin W. Gouldner, *Patterns of Industrial Bureaucracy* (Free Press, 1954).

28. *Federal Register*, vol. 58 (January 11, 1993), pp. 3573–76.

# 7 ||| Is Deregulation Enough? Lessons from Florida and Philadelphia

Neal R. Peirce

*I*f we were doctors in an emergency room, and had a patient come in
telling us "Doc, I have cancer, but I've also just been shot in the chest,"
*our first goal would be to get the bullet out, stop the bleeding, so the patient
can survive for the long run. Then we worry about treating the cancer.
What we have done, with help of the city council and the business
community, is to take care of the bullet wound problem. The patient is
living for the short run. Now we have to cure the cancer—the erosion of
the tax base of the city of Philadelphia, crime and violence and the whole
panoply of crippling social problems that have literally been dumped on
our cities.*[1]

> Mayor Edward Rendell of Philadelphia, fifteen months after
> taking command of his nearly bankrupt city

*O*ur premise was the state was spending money at the wrong place in
almost every endeavor—at the crisis end. We only deal with things
*when something becomes a crisis. Politically, that's the only way you get
the vote. I call it the Herman Talmadge philosophy—"Don't never try to
solve a problem that people don't know they got." The idea of getting in
front of problems is very mindboggling to people that have always waited
until called upon to find the solution.*

> Governor Lawton Chiles of Florida, former U.S. senator,
> twenty-seven months after taking office

---

Robert Guskind conducted the Florida field research for this chapter.

130     NEAL R. PEIRCE

AFTER VISITING the leaders of Florida and Philadelphia, two of America's most hard-pressed government jurisdictions of the early 1990s, one comes away with the conviction that neither deregulation nor any other tinkering at the edges of official structures is sufficient to the challenges of the decade. Deregulating the public service is certainly worthwhile. But as these cases suggest, other reform strategies are needed.

Florida, on the heels of decades of tumultuous growth (from less than 2 million people in 1940 to 12.9 million in 1990), began the 1990s facing large budget shortfalls and major crises in health care, social services, and corrections. The pressures of rapid growth, the state's traditionally low levels of spending for social services and education, and a revenue system constrained by historic resistance to an income tax all left Florida with the dubious distinction of having some of the nation's worst public health indexes, most intractable poverty, lowest educational achievement, and highest levels of violence and crime.

Without major structural, budgetary, and tax reforms, equally sobering crises threatened to unfold throughout the 1990s. Spending by the state's massive Department of Health and Rehabilitative Services (HRS), for instance, threatened to balloon to as much as two times the entire projected state budget for 2000, thanks to both the demand for service brought on by rapid growth and the traditionally low front-end expenditures for human services and preventive health care. Again, should current crime trends continue and the state's controversial early release program for inmates be abandoned, documents prepared for Governor Chiles's Commission for Government by the People warned of a spiraling prison population—from 43,000 in 1990 to 132,000 by 2000, accompanied by spending that would increase from $907 million to $3.047 billion.[2]

Philadelphia experienced major industrial closures and lost 450,000 people, mostly middle-class residents, to its suburbs between 1960 and 1990. Its social fabric and solvency alike are imperiled by homelessness, AIDS, crime, and shattered families. One-fifth of its residents are living in poverty. The city experienced nineteen tax increases in the 1980s and has the nation's highest wage tax. By one estimate, the taxes cost the city 130,000 jobs in the 1980s.[3]

Spiraling human service costs, meager state and federal aid, lucrative union contracts, and the city's obsolete tax system led to a fiscal crisis in 1990–91 in which the Philadelphia City Council refused Mayor Wilson Goode's request for yet another tax increase. Since 1972 the city had been issuing short-term tax anticipation notes (in recent years 5.5 percent to 6.0 percent) to cover cash flow problems. But in August 1990, when City Controller Jonathan Saidel went public with concerns about long-term structural problems in the city's budget, buyers' appetites for the notes disappeared. Moody's Investor Service gave the city a CCC (junk bond) rating. After months of effort in the private markets, the city finally secured $150 million from a consortium of local banks and two government pension funds but was obliged to pay an effective interest rate of 27 percent. This galvanized the city's politicians, especially black leaders, who had previously resisted any kind of state fiscal review board. In June 1991 the state of Pennsylvania created PICA, the Pennsylvania Intergovernmental Cooperation Authority, a fiscal oversight board designed to make emergency loans to the city on the condition of continuing adherence to state-set rules of fiscal prudence.

In December 1991 a Philadelphia civic organization, the 21st Century League, issued a report in which the basic challenge to the city was laid out. Based on interviews with seventeen former and sitting cabinet and subcabinet officials of the city and written chiefly by Theodore Hershberg of the University of Pennsylvania, the paper called for two kinds of reform:

First, there must be a complete transformation of the *organizational culture* of government: the dominant mind set, attitudes and customs of politicians, labor leaders, city managers and employees that now impede effective service delivery and mar the city's reputation and credibility. Second, there must be fundamental change in the *structure* of government: the City Charter, the Civil Service system, and union contracts, work rules and collective bargaining procedures that affect the basic rules through which Philadelphia is governed.[4]

Elections at the start of the 1990s brought fresh executive leadership to both Florida and Philadelphia. Democrat Lawton Chiles, former U.S. senator, was elected governor of Florida in 1990 with a running mate, former U.S. Representative Buddy MacKay, who shared his interest in government reform. Edward Rendell, a former

Democratic district attorney, was elected mayor of Philadelphia in 1991 on a platform of spartan, efficient government to rescue a city teetering on the edge of bankruptcy.

While officials in many other states and cities were attempting major reforms, deregulation, and "reinvention" to match the challenges of the 1990s, Chiles and Rendell embarked on ambitious reform agendas to respond to challenges of extraordinary severity. The Florida and Philadelphia experiments speak directly to the complexities, challenges, and promise of public service reform in large and complex state and local governments. Their experiences were selected for this chapter precisely because they seem so far removed from the Sunnyvale, Californias, and other comfortable middle-class communities often cited in the literature.

## Florida: The Chiles-MacKay Experiment

Chiles and MacKay chose to team up in the 1990 campaign with the precise intent of making Florida a laboratory of state government redesign and achieving the type of fundamental change they had found so elusive as federal lawmakers. The agenda they developed encompassed three broad kinds of reform.

—Internal management. Assisted by dozens of outside consultants and aides versed in private sector restructuring, Chiles and MacKay developed internal reforms aimed at transforming state management practices. These efforts ranged from adoption of total quality management methods to investment in communications and computer technology to budget reform.

—Agency restructuring and decentralization. Chiles and MacKay intended a complete restructuring of some of Florida's largest bureaucracies through agency mergers, elimination of layers of management, and movement from a vertical organizational structure of narrowly defined roles to a broad horizontal orientation of management teams sharing responsibility and authority. Agencies were also to be decentralized to shift authority, and the responsibility for producing results, from remote managers to employees who delivered the services.

—Programmatic overhauls. As progressive Democrats, Chiles and MacKay were also anxious to alter the scope, structure, and goals of major state programs. Programs were to be reoriented to emphasize preventive investment. (They claimed, for example, that for every dollar spent on primary and preventive health care, the state could save $8.00 in subsequent health care charges. Early intervention and treatment of emotionally disturbed children would save $1,500 a child. For every dollar spent on substance abuse treatment, $11.50 in future costs would be saved.)

Grim reality faced them, however, as soon as they reached Tallahassee: a $1 billion state budget shortfall. Spending increases that were being planned for education, health care, social service, and other programs critical to the reform effort were postponed. And Chiles was forced to make deep cuts across a range of state programs. Significantly, the governor did manage to gain approval of a $100 million Healthy Start program to provide prenatal and early infancy health care, a reform typical of the kind of "front-end investment" strategy he hoped to institute.

Chiles and MacKay wanted eventually to get the state to accept either an income tax or a broad services tax (which it had had briefly in the 1980s but had repealed). Without such a major overhaul of finances, they argued, Florida would be forced to continue its dangerous underinvestment in critical programs and would continue to face fiscal crises. But they were also convinced the public would not stomach higher taxes until state government was better run and could command some respect.

Their reform efforts would be crucial to rebuilding public confidence in government. To begin to lay the foundation for reform, they appointed the Governor's Commission for Government by the People, popularly called the Right-Sizing Commission, charged with developing a framework for the most important changes to the institutions and programs of Florida government. Representation on the commission included government, business, and citizen leaders and was chaired by the mayor of Orlando, Bill Frederick. Several out-of-state "reinvention" consultants, including David Osborne, were brought in to work with the commission.

The commission proposed six principles that should drive Florida government: the goal was to be "catalytic, community-oriented, customer-driven, value-oriented, results-focused and market-oriented."[5] It also made very specific recommendations for reform in five key areas: human investment, education, governance, public safety, and growth policy.

The human investment strategy, said the commission, should focus on radically decentralizing the Department of Health and

Rehabilitative Services to transfer control to fifteen community-based councils around the state. For education, the agenda should be "choice, competition, decentralization, measurement of results, public-private partnerships, and a community role in the schools." And for governance, the commission laid out an ambitious plan for the early 1990s:

> A strategy to gain the trust of the people by 1) equipping state managers and staff with the skills and motivation to be innovative and to continuously improve service to the taxpayers, 2) revamping key management systems, including budget, procurement, and personnel—to provide flexibility to management, and 3) developing accountability systems to evaluate the performance of state agencies based on how well they serve their customers and on the outcomes of their work.[6]

The legislature had already agreed to Chiles's proposal to place Florida's entire career service system under sunset laws in 1992, a move to force serious redesign of the system. The Right-Sizing Commission's call for reducing the number of state agency management layers would be reflected within a year in new career service rules eliminating 1,000 job classifications and allowing managers to award outstanding employees with better pay instead of creating supervisory job titles for them. Chiles created a Florida Total Quality Management Committee to spur management reforms in state departments, with pilot projects inaugurated in four agencies.

Most of Florida's state workers, who under total quality management theory ought to be consulted early and treated well in any reorganization, felt neglected by the new administration. Not a great many were asked early in the process about their ideas for organizational improvement. And because of the state's financial problems, the legislature and governor reneged on a wage increase for state employees that had been voted in 1991. Not until two years later, as a result of a court suit, were the workers able to get their raise, and then only effective in mid-1993. The effects on morale were predictably poor.

Pilot budget and personnel projects were, however, launched in the Departments of Revenue and Labor. The idea was to give government managers a mission to accomplish and then almost total freedom to run their operations, pretty much like a private business, as long as they could bring in the needed results. The director of the Worker's Compensation Division of the Labor Department, for example, was given that freedom and used it to merge seventy job classifications into fourteen and eliminate ten middle-manager positions. With the savings, incentive bonuses ($50 to $200 a month) were set up for data entry and other clerks in the department.

Such paring down does involve pain. As Jerry Koehler, deputy secretary of the Florida Labor Department, commented,

> People in senior management positions are asking me "But what would I do if I lose this job?" These people are so dependent on government protection that it's frightening. In industry, people are dependent on the company they work for, but they also know the company can go broke or get bought out. So I ask myself: Do I have an obligation to the employee, or to the taxpayer, when I don't need the employee? I think my obligation is to the taxpayer.

The Right-Sizing Commission had also recommended a permanent follow-up body to adopt state government performance measures and report publicly on accomplishments and shortcomings. In November 1992 Chiles created the fifteen-member Commission on Government Accountability to the People, with nine private and six public members. The hope was that GAP's work, in conjunction with administration efforts, would produce accountability standards to monitor and assess reforms. Equally important, the administration hoped that substantive standards leading to significant change should help sell the reforms to skeptical Floridians.

It soon became clear that Chiles and MacKay intended nothing less than the total overhaul of critical components of Florida state government. A bevy of true believers in reinvention, many of them private management consultants with limited experience in government, were brought on board. A climate open to any and all new and bright ideas, to the most wide-ranging experimentation, was generated.

But in the interest of creativity and breakthroughs, political expediency was relegated to a back seat. The administration ran into heavy difficulties getting its programs approved by the legislature. A number of the reform proposals were rejected, altered to soften their impact, or approved with only a small portion of the funding the governor had sought. The lawmakers, accustomed to micromanaging state operations, were predictably protective of existing power relationships. They proved very skeptical of the idea that it is often better to invest in the present to avoid far greater expenses and crises later.

A "productivity enhancement initiative" proposed in 1991, for example, set up a pool of funds from agency budget cuts to be returned to the agencies to help them streamline and increase productivity through technology improvements, employee bonuses, training, and research projects. Chiles and MacKay intended the $101 million in budget reductions that came from cutting 3,000 state jobs to have been returned to agencies that made the cuts. But the legislature approved returning only $30.8 million to improve productivity.

The legislative opposition may have been heavier and more effective than Chiles and MacKay anticipated, but as practiced politicians they were aware of what they were doing, and its risks. MacKay explained:

What we're doing doesn't compute with people looking at this through a political framework. The new frame of reference is like a corporate restructuring. The American people have lived through all the restructuring of institutions in the private sector. They have seen a payoff—a better product, whether it's Ford, GM, or any other kind of firm, now more oriented to the customer, plus costs coming down. The American people are saying to government, "Until you do the restructuring we aren't going to put up any money. I won't put any more money in there because these guys will keep wasting it." Ross Perot captured that feeling. The guy's right. Instinctively people have figured it out. Here I am a progressive Democrat and the only way I can get my agenda done is to recognize the legitimacy of that argument.

MacKay also acknowledged, however, that while the administration had "won some people over" to the idea of full restructuring of state government, it had not "made the case to the voter in Florida, and that is very frustrating."

Critics might say that Chiles and MacKay lacked political finesse. But their task was complicated immensely by such unanticipated events as the recession-driven fiscal crisis that hit Florida state government in the early 1990s and the devastation to south Florida of Hurricane Andrew in 1992. The administration was obliged to cut $2 billion in projected spending in its first two years in office, reductions substantially larger than Florida had ever before faced. In 1992 Chiles presided over the largest tax increase in state history, even though the legislature had refused to approve half of the $2.5 billion in net new revenue he had requested. In tune with his agenda of proactive public investment, the governor had sought $600 million in expanded education spending ($414 million alone for an anticipated 97,500 new school children by 1995), $142 million for expanded public safety (including 6,100 more prison beds), and 214 million to make government work better through upgraded technology in government agencies, total quality management training for workers, and investment in productivity enhancement. The legislature cut especially deeply into the funds for improving agency productivity.

Chiles's popularity plummeted as a result of the budget crisis and his quarrels with the legislature. (The proportion of Floridians calling his performance excellent or good dropped to 23 percent in early 1992.) Even after a less contentious 1993 legislative session, during which the state passed a sweeping statewide health care plan that guaranteed medical coverage to all the state's residents, the administration's political standing remained weak. The governor was philosophic about the difficulties: "In all of this people have to understand that change does not come about without a bow wave or tidal wave [of opposition]. You can't even chart the direction from which it will come, the speed or velocity. We just didn't realize how strong the bow wave would be."

Chiles mused that "the hardest thing is to have the press understand what you're doing." MacKay echoed him, noting that economists and business people understand more quickly than reporters and political scientists the concept of present value—the future returns for timely investment. Despite the administration's success in conceiving and pushing through the legislature prevention-oriented social programs and management reforms that would eventually "save billions of dollars," MacKay said, "I can't get the political press corps or the academics to acknowledge there's any virtue in that. It's almost a gap in how the political scientists think. It's ignorance. But you can't tell someone they're ignorant and convert them."

It is worth noting that Chiles and MacKay had to operate in a less than ideal administrative-political setting. Florida's governor is obliged to share his authority with a cabinet of independently elected executives; indeed he exercises direct executive control over only twelve of the state's twenty-five agencies. An increasingly popular Republican party in the state has also brought the dynamic of two-party partisanship (although a number of the administration's defeats have been at the hands of fellow Democrats).

Relations with the legislature while an administration attempts reinvention are particularly important, according to Bill Lindner, secretary of the Department of Management Services. So that legislators will not feel threatened, he suggested, they need to understand that the administration's goal is "an implementation, operation and management strategy, not policymaking. Legislators should like the idea of holding managers accountable."

The chief laboratory for government deregulation in Florida became the effort to decentralize the Department of Health and Rehabilitative Services. From the start the idea was to pare back by at least 25 percent a Tallahassee-based bureaucracy that typically busied itself sending orders to the field and trying to ensure compliance with federal rules and mandates. At the same time the plan proposed to transfer employees and responsibility to field offices. Chiles and MacKay aimed to place significant control in regional citizen-based boards, giving more freedom to them and local administrators and then holding them accountable for results.

The legislature approved the decentralization plan in 1992. But in 1993 the administration found itself acutely embarrassed when it turned out the HRS caseload, and so the department's need for a large budget increase, had been grossly overestimated because a computer system had run amok. Legislative Democrats took the political heat for voting $250 million in additional taxes that were not in fact needed. In the resulting furor, the HRS secretary resigned and MacKay agreed to run the agency personally. When he arrived on the scene, he discovered that the legislative mandate for decentralization had scarcely proceeded and that the agency's notorious bureaucracy was as staunchly unwieldy as ever.

The HRS incident suggested a potentially serious lack of focus and coordination of effort within the administration. Jane Hayes of the State Budget and Planning Office said, "If there isn't truly strong coordination [in the near future], you could see all of this going away. The issues of social services, education, criminal justice will always take precedence over the good government issues. [Government reform] only gets pushed when you have a crisis. It's very difficult to capture peoples' attention and keep their interest in management."

Florida's experience has also pinpointed how easy it is for an uninterested bureaucracy to stonewall reform efforts, even in the face of legislative or gubernatorial direction. The chief internal resistance to government right-sizing and reinvention in Florida does not, Chiles administration officials reported, come from the quarter many people often anticipate, the government employee unions. Rather, it has emanated from management. Florida's public employee unions have been leery of the career service reforms and testy in some negotiations, but they have on the whole been accommodating. Rank-and-file workers are reported to like the idea of increased freedom and responsibility in return for accountability. But in many departments the administration's reform agents said they had hit solid resistance from managers fearful of losing control and authority or, in departments such as HRS, losing entire levels of management through decentralization.

On taking command at HRS, MacKay appeared to be pushing decentralization with alacrity. The 25 percent reduction in personnel—specialists in food stamps or mental health, for example—was moving forward as responsibility was shifted to the field. MacKay confirmed management resistance to the overhaul: "There's a huge feeling that if they lose their assistant deputies, they're going to lose their clout, or that they won't have enough people to maintain internal controls and satisfy the feds and avoid critical audits." His reply was that "the new district system administrators and local boards have to have the authority to run the programs themselves, and if they screw up, they'll be held responsible."

The local boards and staffs, MacKay reported, were elated that they were being taken seriously and given real autonomy. And he foresaw a political dividend.

This agency will never be funded properly until its true constituency—the United Way, Children's Home Society, Salvation Army—concludes we've finally gotten our act together. The most powerful people in the state are on the local boards. They'll eventually become our advocates. We'll suddenly have some credibility back and have some very powerful local constituencies up there lobbying for us, and HRS will be healed.

Being perceived as delivering services effectively would be a major accomplishment because neither HRS's clients nor its constituency groups nor the public held the agency in very high regard.

But it would also be necessary, said Glenn Robertson, a consultant on the HRS overhaul and former budget director under Governor Bob Graham, to reform the executive approach to the legislature.

If we ever want to get the legislature out of micromanaging executive agencies, we have to assure them that when they appropriate money they will get appropriate outcomes they can hold us accountable for. To get them to appropriate money to achieve better results on the number of low-birthweight babies in each county, for example. The localities should figure out the right strategies—education, health, training for the workers, and how they want to achieve better outcomes. And then hold us accountable for figuring out how to get the money to the localities.

There are, Robertson acknowledged, perils in decentralization.

As soon as funds are misused—and someone somewhere in one of the fifteen districts will misuse the HRS funds, we know that will happen—then it will headline time and there'll be editorials about "How can the legislature allow this?" And of course there will be a political tendency to go to a control-oriented, micromanagement system. We have to set up the ability to do decentralization and outcome expectations without micromanaging them. We don't know the answer to that question yet.

Decentralization is imperative, Robertson added, to enable officials at the local level to take the multitude of agencies and programs, federal and state, and to get them to coordinate service to families and communities. Eventually, he added, it would be necessary to bridge the efforts of HRS and Education, "two of the biggest entrenched bureaucracies."

In the meantime, the productivity enhancement initiative of the administration's first year had turned into the Innovation Fund, with monies garnered from budget savings. The fund was administered by a new Department of Management Service, a merger of the old Department of General Services and Department of Administration Services. The new department, one of several mergers pushed by Chiles, was designed to be a consultant to the other agencies, to motivate them on reinvention steps and provide them with guidelines for improving their processes. (It also staffed the Innovation Fund).

Total quality management, meanwhile, was spreading to more departments. All state agencies were encouraged to undertake strategic planning to clarify their future directions and agree on performance measures. Indeed, the reform effort as a whole was taking root across Florida state government. The results could be seen, for example, in internal changes that reduced from thirty days to five the time employees wait for expense reimbursements, or in the Labor Department's reorganization of unemployment offices, which cut applicants' waiting time from a full day to one hour. And the effort appeared in fundamental changes in policy such as reorienting social service spending to proactive investment and prevention strategies. Some agencies dragged their feet, of course, while others moved more aggressively. But the administration's intent was to bring all on board, even though there were clearly problems in coordination among the departments and between them and the governor's office that required attention to ensure the success and continued progress of reform.

Civil service reform proved far more complex than the administration anticipated, notwithstanding the legislature's initial agreement to subject the career service system to sunset rules at the end of 1992. The old rules were left in place while the administration immersed itself in an arduous process of evaluating the status of management within each agency and then tried to negotiate new rules with government employee unions. The goal was to give agency managers the flexibility to develop incentive systems for their employees and to avoid the practice called bump and roll, workers jumping from agency to agency and to new jobs to qualify for salary increases rather than increasing their skills and developing expertise in their current positions.

The outcome of the career service reforms remained unclear in mid-1993, and opinions about them were still divided. Some officials believed a new system was critical to ensuring the success of internal management reforms; others argued that substantive change was possible without a final resolution. Some within the Chiles administration believed a new system could be worked out with the unions. Others characterized the process as "trench war-fare—hand-to-hand combat with progress measured in inches." (In the absence of agreement with the unions, the issue of personnel rules would be thrown back to the legislature). As one official commented, "we can solve the problem if we can stay alive politi-cally long enough. Some people are trying to use the political actuarial table against us—if [we] can hang in there long enough, these guys will be gone."

Yet a review of Florida's circumstances suggests it was almost chimerical to believe another election, another gubernatorial ap-proach, would disperse the challenges the Chiles-MacKay adminis-tration was attempting to confront. Florida's population continues to grow at 250,000 persons a year, with an accompanying annual growth of 5 percent in the state government work force. Each employee is entitled to a substantial benefits package. Unless the growth in the number of employees can be limited by using tech-nology and getting more productive, better trained workers, state costs will grow far faster than tax revenues.

Another factor slowing reform is the unrelenting pressure to provide more services to an ever expanding populace. Bob Brad-ley, the state's deputy director of planning and budget, cited one telling example: during the 1990s the number of eighteen- to twenty-four-year-olds was expected to grow by 280,000 a year compared to an annual average of 50,000 in the 1980s. That meant no relief for the criminal justice system; to the contrary, it repre-sented a potentially huge increase in cases and incarcerations. The expanding population also meant new demands (90,000 new stu-dents yearly) on a higher education system what had been getting by with heavy reliance on community colleges and only nine uni-versities. The increased enrollment, said Bradley, would be the equivalent of three new colleges a year. And, he continued, "95 percent of our general revenue fund now goes to five agencies—HRS, Corrections, Education, the legislature, and judiciary. All the other agencies are less than $1 billion. If we are going to start cutting, we have to get a handle on those systems—including med-icaid, now growing at 30 percent a year."

Such projections suggest, in fact, that Chiles and MacKay's broad, multilayered reforms might represent just the first steps to prevent the bleak, costly dilemmas confronting Florida government in the early 1990s from turning into fiscal and human catastrophes by the turn of the century.

## Philadelphia: Rendell's Revolution

Gregarious, hard-charging, articulate, alliance-building— Philadelphia's Edward Rendell developed all the attributes normally associated with successful politicians. And in 1991 he was elected mayor of a city steeped in some of America's most partisan, patronage-based politics. Rendell differs from the stereotypical politician in two critical respects, however. First, he ran for office telling Philadelphians to expect hard times, that only doses of fiscal castor oil could rescue their town from bankruptcy. And he indicated he would be as a tough with one of the city's most entrenched political forces—its government employee unions—as might be necessary to save the city's fiscal skin. Second, Rendell ran as an advocate of broad experimentation in government.

In his unsuccessful run for mayor in 1987, he had talked about the need to downsize the city's government, to obtain the same or better services for less cost. Specifically, he had said the city needed an office of management and productivity and a private sector task force to advise on management reforms. In the following four years, as he prepared for another run, Rendell became a much more serious student of government reform. He read the Grace commission report on reforming the federal government; he read comparable reports on state and local government reform prepared by commissions in New York State, Ohio, and elsewhere. In 1990 he visited Phoenix to learn firsthand about specific efforts there: a program inviting employees to submit suggestions for improved departmental performance and then share in some of the savings; departments earning credit for their next-year budgets through good performance; and privatization of trash collection and how the municipal work force had won back the contract. Rendell also conferred with officials in Los Angeles and with former Newark Mayor Kenneth Gibson about a program Gibson had initiated to privatize 50 percent of trash collection but keep the other 50 percent public. "I tried to be a sponge for all the good ideas," Rendell said. In the words of David L. Cohen, Rendell's chief of staff and close confidante, "by 1991, Rendell had ten file drawers of documents on these types of [management and productivity] issues. For four years, he literally studied how to be mayor."

Rendell said that the most successful of the business-led management and productivity efforts he discovered was conducted under Governor Richard Celeste in Ohio.

I tried to find the executive director, a woman named Karen Nowak. We called out to her at the Ohio Office of Management and Productivity only to discover she'd moved to Chester County, outside Philadelphia. So I called her, told her my plans to run for mayor again. She became my first campaign worker, early in 1990, and stayed with me throughout the campaign, and then became co-staff director of our Mayor's Private Sector Task Force on Management and Productivity. She's the driving force behind a lot of this stuff we're doing.

Government reform moved on two related but different tracks—fiscal reform and reform of how the government works—during Rendell's first fifteen months in office. The fiscal track meant righting a severely listing ship. Philadelphia was "poised on the brink of total disaster," Rendell said on the day he took office. He moved immediately to formulate a five-year plan to restore fiscal balance and satisfy the requirements of the Pennsylvania Intergovernmental Cooperation Authority (PICA). The plan rejected any new tax increases. But interestingly it contained no massive across-the-board service cuts, proposals to sell city assets, or other classic emergency measures. Instead it called for reducing personnel costs by $492 million over four years, coupled with $658 million in savings from management improvements and a series of smaller cuts in services—"a fine mist of pain across the city," Fred Voight, executive director of the Committee of 70, a local civic watchdog organization, told *Governing* magazine.[7] Within a year the administration was able to cover almost all the projected $208 million structural deficit in the city's $2.3 billion 1992–93 budget (using PICA borrowings to fill the gap of $53 million to $60 million) and to produce a fully balanced budget for 1993–94. A five-year cumulative deficit of $1.4 billion had been slashed to less than $150 million.[8]

The success of the entire effort depended, however, on the conclusion of an agreement with the city's leading unions. Rendell offered a stiff set of conditions. The work force would have to go three years without a pay increase. Paid holidays would be chopped from fourteen to nine (saving the city $9 million yearly). Sick leave would drop from twenty days a year to ten. Employees would lose their right to free legal aid. The city would take from the unions the management of health plans, saving $60 million to $70 million each year.

In the final analysis, the city gave a little—but very little—on those conditions. One of its tactics to soften up the unions was to issue a long paper describing inefficient outmoded work rules the city had agreed to in past negotiations. It was alleged, for example, that city building custodians resisted cleaning walls above shoulder height, claiming that wallwashers (a separate category of worker) perform that task and that if custodians were obliged to do it, they should receive extra pay. Sludge truck drivers were reported to do a "great circle route" at the dump, a distance far greater than they needed to cover, to work up overtime, and union representatives alleged harassment when the city questioned the practice. The report also claimed it was taking the city years to terminate oft-reported goldbrickers and that the unions tried to prevent layoffs even of workers with criminal records.

The historic pattern in Philadelphia labor negotiations, Deputy Mayor Joseph Torsella explained later, had been for mayors to give away all manner of management rights in exchange for modest wage increases.

> Initially there was a belief, even among our own managers, that we weren't serious about this stuff, that we just wanted to cut health benefits, that all the rest was talk. But we had in fact spent a lot of time talking with our managers, seeing what was critical for them, before the negotiations started. In the end we didn't make the historic trade-off; we put equal priority on finance and management issues. The contract was a token of our determination to make this government work.

The chief unions representing Philadelphia's 32,000 city workers, AFSCME District Councils 33 and 47, representing (except for fire and police) most of the nonuniformed white collar and blue collar workers, respectively, were put on the defensive by Rendell's tactics. But after a sixteen-hour strike on October 15, ten months into the mayor's term, they crumbled, agreeing to virtually all his demands, which were projected to save the city $374 million over four years. Some bitterness followed the settlement; a staff member for District Council 33, for example, was quoted as saying, "We were the scapegoats. We were demeaned, belittled and denigrated. He's pushed back thirty years of history."[9]

One reason Rendell was able to triumph so easily was the close alliance he had made with an erstwhile political rival, City Council President John Street. A colorful political leader from heavily black North Philadelphia, Street had been an uncompromising, table-pounding renegade in his early political career. But by 1992 he seemed a new man, working closely and adeptly with Rendell and producing nearly unanimous council votes on critical issues. (The council, which former Mayor Bill Green had once called "the worst in the free world," had changed sharply in the 1991 elections with the defeat or retirement of many of its most contentious and self-dealing members, replaced by newcomers running on the same austerity and reform platform as Rendell.)

The alliance with Street also defused potentially divisive racial tensions as Rendell, a white who had succeeded a black mayor, began to make painful cuts in city personnel roles and services. "With Rendell and Street working hand in hand, the race card has been almost totally removed from the public debate," Theodore Hershberg of the University of Pennsylvania commented.[10]

Rendell's five-year plan enabled PICA to sell $474 million in bonds to close the immediate deficit facing the city. By later in 1992 the city's credit rating was raised to a B or BB level by various rating agencies—not high, but at least above the junk level.

Righting Philadelphia's finances through labor agreements and smart political alliances represented only half of Rendell's approach, however. The other half involved instituting some of the government reinvention models he had been studying for years and championed in his campaign. Rendell's interest in privatizing some government functions tended to grab and keep peoples' attention. By spring 1993 some half-dozen city services—custodial services at City Hall, security at the Philadelphia Museum of Art, operation of trash transfer stations, maintenance of a major expressway—had been privatized. Operation of the city warehouse was also contracted out on a just-in-time ordering system in which no inventories were kept, contractors agreed to deliver items rapidly, and typically long delays for supplies were effectively terminated.

Rendell insisted, however, that "privatizing is not my goal—delivering the same or better service for the same price is my goal." David Cohen explained:

When Rendell campaigned for mayor, he tried to draw a distinction that the media consistently rejected. And the point was that he was not for privatization, he was for competition. And that the end goal of privatization was to introduce competition into city services. He always said that if the net result were not a single service privatized, but the quality of city services up and the cost driven down, he would have hit a home run.

Cohen said the city had picked its contracts carefully, that thirty-eight services were on a list for consideration, and that while every one except public safety was theoretically a candidate for privatization, certain functions—intake of homeless persons and prison social services, for example—had been offered for bids but failed to produce satisfactory ones. The most startling part of the privatization experiments, said Cohen, was the impact on the municipal work force. Productivity was up sharply at the city's sludge treatment plant. The *Philadelphia Inquirer* quoted a worker at the facility: "You don't have any job security. They have the right to privatize whole units. It's a terrible state of being for a lot of people right now."[11]

The unions had not softened in their resistance to privatization. But Deputy Mayor Torsella reported,

There *is* a change in the tone of debate. Initially there was some belief on their part that we were not serious, would not want to follow through and actually privatize anything. There was also a belief that if we did, we'd do it in a draconian way, out of spite, out of misguided philosophy of not recognizing the importance of people. But in fact we've handled it quite differently. We've worked hard to hammer down the economics of each case, not do it gratuitously, to see the costs and benefits. Second, we've worked very hard to place the employees elsewhere in city government or with the contractors replacing us as primary service providers. The net result is there is now more reality, less posturing in our discussions with the unions.

A major issue, in fact, was how Rendell and his associates, having engaged in a hard-nosed standoff with the unions and having reasserted management rights, could make the long-term switch everyone seemed to agree was necessary—to supporting individual workers in their jobs, adopting total quality management, and creating a better-trained, more competent, motivated work force that in turn would increase the quality of, and citizen confidence in, the city's performance.

Rendell said he had tried to be conciliatory from the day the strike was settled. Cohen defended the labor agreements as "inherently fair to the municipal work force," adding that city workers "still had the best benefits package that any worker in Philadelphia has." But, he added, "it is incumbent on us for the long-run functioning of the city to get on a cooperative level with the municipal work force. The choices we have made are to move slower, build bridges, meet and consult with unions, and try to get unions' acquiescence and participation in changes we could, by contract, make without them. We have made a lot of headway to make the work force feel included."

Along the same lines, Torsella emphasized that the city managers were sharing personally in the sacrifices necessary to make the city solvent, having accepted not only the same benefits cuts as the unions but an actual 5 percent wage cut in 1992. He hoped the unions would eventually agree to support Rendell's program "if they see us pursing management excellence with the same tenacity as we pursued management rights." It would be too much, Theodore Hershberg said, to expect rapid transformation in Philadelphia's labor-management relations. "You can't go real fast. It's cultural. It takes time—maybe two full terms."

Criticism was voiced, in part by business leaders, that Rendell and Cohen were micromanaging changes in departmental operations, failing to decentralize authority or involve the line managers who decide day to day how money is spent and work is done. The two were also criticized for bypassing the city's managing director and chief civil servant, Raymond Shipman. PICA Executive Director Ronald G. Henry told one reporter, "you can negotiate a labor contract without a managing director, but as you get further into an administration, the idea of having a parallel structure is very inefficient." Henry was also quoted as saying, "there is no system, no one responsible on an ongoing basis, to make sure initiatives happen." One consequence, he said, had been a slowdown of progress on human services, privatization, and revenue collection.[12]

The criticism was vehemently rebutted, however, by Rendell, Cohen, and other administration leaders. The mayor noted that 700 middle managers had been going through a two-to-three-week training course and that he had spoken with each group. The administration encouraged the business-led group, Greater Philadelphia First, to set up a public service award for outstanding management performance. The first award (with a $10,000 stipend for continuing education) went to a career service employee who managed development of the Philadelphia Water Department's first privatization project, promising the city multimillion dollar savings during the coming years. A detailed manager's guide for implementing the 1992 collective bargaining agreements was published, and administration officials produced weekly reports on contract compliance and a monthly city managers' report on budget compliance and goal achievements department by department. "We're doing all we can," said one, "to involve as many levels of management as we can and establish a real esprit de corps."

Inheriting a patronage-encrusted and sometimes grossly inefficient municipal bureaucracy does, however, involve many headaches. The Philadelphia Housing Authority, responsible for the city's public housing stock, was plagued by so many vacant residences and allegations of mismanagement and political influence that the federal Department of Housing and Urban Development seized control of the agency early in 1992. A year later, with federal management scheduled to end, charges of incompetence and patronage favoritism were still flying. Housing advocates despaired of any opportunity to renovate the thousands of vacant units or relocate families to satisfactory shelter in the city's large supply of moderately priced, privately held row houses. Rendell administration officials reacted with unusual defensiveness, noting the legislature had not given them full authority over the PHA.

At the Philadelphia Parking Authority, however, a major purge of patronage-based jobs had been effected. Both Rendell's strengths and weaknesses, knowledgeable observers suggested, sprang from his being a skillful politician. If he were to abandon the city's tradition of patronage-based politics entirely, they said, he would expend his political capital and effectiveness. The city lacked a strong citizen-based constituency for inventive, high-quality government, making it necessary for the mayor to move more slowly on some fronts than he might like.

Rendell did, however, tap the business community, as he had seen done in Ohio and elsewhere, for advice on management reform across agencies. The Mayor's Private Sector Task Force on Management and Productivity was formed soon after his election. The appropriate selection for its chair was Joseph E. Paquette, Jr., chairman and CEO of the Philadelphia Electric Company. Several dozen CEOs (no substitutes allowed) joined the task force. All the work was done by corporate, law firm, or university people, with none of the large accounting firms or other paid hands allowed into the process. Several hundred volunteers from the business community actually went to work for the city so that they could review operating departments. Karen Nowak served as project consultant and David Pingree as project director (he had served in earlier years as a member of Florida Governor Bob Graham's inner circle, including a period as HRS secretary.)

The task force did seventeen reviews, some focused on one department, others spanning several. The subjects ranged from real estate management to communications to human resource administration. In one case a single corporation wrote an entire review: Bell of Pennsylvania, which has a large motor fleet, analyzed the city's fleet operations, proposing a coordinated system to keep all the city's vehicle and repair shops busy, cut the share of the fleet that was in for repair from 20 percent to 10 percent, and saved $5 million a year. In other areas many companies were involved—management information systems, for example, in which a wide array of mainframe and software vendors contributed to a massive review of how the city could improve information gathering. (This task force proposed an integrated tax administration system within the city's Department of Revenue, providing for the first time a way to cross-check tax payers and payments—wage taxes against business profits against property taxes, for example. The new system was projected to increase revenue $50 million a year.)

The Private Sector Task Force met intermittently with Rendell and once a month with Cohen, Tom Knox (Rendell's deputy mayor for management and administration), Director John Claypool of

Greater Philadelphia First, and Chair Ronald Rubin and President Charles Pizzi of the Greater Philadelphia Chamber of Commerce. Friendly tension arose over the size of the savings the task force's recommendations could effect—the task force figure was $150 million a year; Rendell and Cohen fought for low estimates for fear the city council or police and fire arbitrators would spend the extra money. But the administration considered the task force activity highly important, not only for the cost-saving recommendations, but also in helping win the confidence and involvement of the business leaders (who had routinely seen their suggestions ignored during the Goode years) and reminding the public of Rendell's intention to run the city in a more businesslike manner. Although the task force operations formally ended in April 1993, Rendell said he was looking for ways to keep alive the new, strong ties between business leaders and city administrators.

Revision of Philadelphia's city charter was also on Rendell's agenda. A reform document when it was adopted in the 1950s, its protections against the corruption and political favoritism that had historically bedevilled Philadelphia city government had become an albatross around management's neck by the 1980s. Months were required to approve small contracts, for example, and heads of major departments were free to appoint only two aides exempt from civil service rules and union discipline.

A charter commission was formed and Rendell had Street appointed chairman. The result was a clear trade-off: avoidance of political issues (far-reaching civil service reform or a change between at-large and district city council districts, for example) in return for increased management flexibility. Among the revisions that seemed most likely to be recommended: broad authority for the mayor and council to create new departments and abolish obsolete ones, modification of the rather absurd civil service "rule of two" (restricting appointment to a post to the top two candidates by numerical grade on a test, even in situations with hundreds of applicants), and some substitution of experience for numerically ranked tests for job placement. Some business people thought Rendell was sacrificing a golden opportunity, at a moment of reform fever in the city, to do a stem-to-stern reorganization of the city government. But at least after years of stalemate some action of significance seemed likely. Despite repeated attempts in the preceding forty-one years, not until November 1991 did voters approve a first charter change—to raise the contract bidding threshold from $2,000 to $10,000.

However vigorously Rendell used the start of his administration to trigger a turnaround in the reputation of Philadelphia governance, he had to contend with continued oversight and second-guessing from the Pennsylvania Intergovernmental Cooperation Authority, the state's watchdog on the city's progress toward the goals of its five-year plan. Sometimes PICA was so pointedly critical that Rendell exploded with streetwise directness. In December 1992 he had this to say about a draft PICA report that faulted the city's management, productivity, and revenue initiatives: "if they want to pick a fight, I'll kill 'em. I'll absolutely kill 'em." (Cognizant of a mercurial touch to the new mayor's personality, neither the PICA board nor Philadelphians took the threat very seriously.)

In its April 1993 evaluation of the five-year plan and the administration's performance, PICA offered accolades to Rendell, Street, and the council for "drawing Philadelphia back from the brink of insolvency and debt" and making a start at addressing underlying budgetary problems. But the report added,

> the "fiscal equilibrium" which has been attained is but delicately balanced, and rests upon the thinnest of edges. . . . Philadelphia [is] within striking distance of fundamental reform. . . . [Yet] only a small shortfall in either projected revenue or the results of efforts to address the operational problems of government, even after what has been achieved to date, would quickly cause the momentum of expenditure growth to once again outstrip the increases in City revenues. In short, Philadelphia still stands only steps away from insolvency.[13]

The basic challenge facing the city administration, PICA reported, was to upgrade its management systems and practices. The authority especially noted such challenges as restraining runaway growth of expenditures (20.9 percent a year in the Department of Human Services, for example), paying vendors more promptly, instituting a much improved capital project management and reporting system, and releasing clearly unqualified employees rather than counting almost exclusively on attrition to reduce city employment rolls.

Finally, PICA noted the cancer eating away at Philadelphia that had so concerned Rendell and his inner circle: the steady attrition of jobs occasioned by restructuring of the economy away from manu-facturing, which had been relieved temporarily by the economic boom of the early to mid-1980s but had worsened in the recession of the early 1990s, costing Philadelphia 10 percent of its job base. The closing of major defense installations (the Philadelphia Naval Yard and others, with a potential total loss of 17,500 jobs), and a constant succession of closures by traditional Philadelphia firms, made the outlook all the more glum. Federal health care reform threatened to harm the health care industry, the only sector of the local economy to continue adding net new jobs. And each loss hurt the city's wage tax receipts (4.96 percent of the wages of city residents, 4.31 percent of the wages of nonresidents.)

There was hope for some respite as the economy recovered from the recession of the early 1990s, yet fear that most of the economic reversals the city had suffered were structural. Rendell and his colleagues placed great hope on increases in tourism and conven-tion attendance. The new $522 million convention center on Market Street in the heart of downtown opened with an eleven-day cele-bration in late June 1993. With posh decor and artwork, the massive center catapulted Philadelphia to the front rank of U.S. convention cities. Also in downtown an Avenue of the Arts revitalization plan for South Broad Street received a heavy state government subsidy (another evidence of Rendell's political finesse).

But in David Cohen's words, "we need a sign—'It's Economic Development, Stupid.' Because everything else we're doing is treading water. None [of our reforms] gets us out of deep crisis if the tax base continues to erode with the 1 percent-a-year job loss we've been experiencing. If that happens, if ten years from now, in real terms, our revenues are 10 percent less, where will we be? All our [fiscal and political changes] will be for naught." Torsella, the dep-uty mayor, talked of the totality of labor, budget, and management changes as a critical first *perestroika* for Philadelphia. But a larger vision, including fundamental social reform and careful economic planning, would be necessary, he said.

A critical first step in that direction, a comprehensive city strategic plan to be launched as a joint administration–city council–business community–labor effort, was announced by Rendell in May 1993. The mayor said he was grateful to the PICA board and his own Private Sector Task Force for the original idea. The basic economic prospects and potential for Philadelphia would be part of the strate-

154    NEAL R. PEIRCE

gic plan, as well as such pressing social problems as "care for abused, neglected and dependent children, primary health care for uninsured Philadelphians, and the homeless."

*The Philadelphia Inquirer*, the city's leading newspaper, jumped to endorse Rendell's initiative: "Mr. Rendell summoned the right sense of urgency. The cost of prisons, child welfare services, public health facilities and courts could send city finances spinning out of control at any time—why one local budget expert calls them 'the Four Horsemen of the Apocalypse of Municipal Finance.' Beyond that, the social problems creating those costs are the main force driving businesses and middle class residents out of the city."[14]

## Conclusion

One is left with a question: are the reform challenges faced by a historic, declining Northeastern industrial city such as Philadelphia the same or fundamentally different from those confronting the fast-growth Sunbelt state of Florida? Major dissimilarities of course spring to mind: not simply population growth versus decline, but fundamentally different economies (one expanding, one in apparent decline), contrasting racial and ethnic mixes, a state's ability to tax as opposed to a city's limited authority.

Yet the challenges of making government and civil service systems more responsive to consumers, of centralized control versus decentralization, of employee training and motivation, and the basic question of long-term fiscal feasibility are strikingly similar. Of Philadelphia's Four Horsemen of municipal finance—the needs of children, public health, corrections, and the port—all but the port bear strong resemblance to any leading Four Horsemen of Florida state finance one might care to name. And in state and city alike, a critical question for the future of every citizen and business will be the capacity of government to remake itself in an era of deep and rapid economic and social change.

## Notes

1. Unless otherwise indicated, all quotations in this chapter are from interviews with sources conducted by the author or his research assistant, Robert Guskind, in April and May 1993.

2. Neal R. Peirce, "Recasting State Government for the Harsh '90s," remarks prepared for the Year 2000 Conference, Florida International University, May 17, 1991.

3. Neal R. Peirce, "Philadelphia Redefines Its Role as the Employer of Last Resort," *Philadelphia Inquirer*, August 31, 1992, p. A9.

4. 21st Century League, *Reforming Philadelphia City Government* (Philadelphia, December 1991), Executive Summary.

5. Governor's Commission for Government by the People, *Government by the People: A Prescription for Florida's Future*, vol. 1 (Tallahasee, 1991), pp. 10–11.

6. Governor's Commission, *Government by the People*, vol. 2.

7. Charles Mahtesian, "Maybe Philadelphia Is Governable after All," *Governing* (April 1993), p. 38.

8. *City of Philadelphia Five-Year Financial Plan, Fiscal Year 1994–Fiscal Year 1998* (January 21, 1993), pp. 3–6.

9. Neil Barsky, "Bootstrapping Mayor Raises Hope of Revival In, Yes, Philadelphia," *Wall Street Journal*, February 22, 1993, p. A1.

10. Ibid.

11. Marc Duvoisin, "Changing Business as Usual," *Philadelphia Inquirer*, April 18, 1993, p. 1.

12. Mahtesian, "Maybe Philadelphia Is Governable after All," p. 38; and Randolph Smith, "Managing Municipal Money," *Philadelphia Daily News*, March 18, 1993, p. 24.

13. Pennsylvania Intergovernmental Cooperation Authority, *Staff Report on the City of Philadelphia's Five Year Financial Plan for Fiscal Years 1994–98* (April 14, 1993), pp. 1–2.

14. "Rendell's Next Mission," *Philadelphia Inquirer*, May 6, 1993, p. A30.

# 8 ||| Deregulating State and Local Government: What Can Leaders Do?

## Richard P. Nathan

A FRIEND OF MINE who served as the head of a major state agency in two states contrasted the life of a leader in each. One, he said, has rigid personnel and labor management systems that make it extremely difficult to select and deploy top-quality associates and form a leadership team. Other barriers include elaborate regulations on purchasing, contracting, and ethics, rendering the systems user unfriendly for leaders. In the other state, rules for selecting, moving, and removing top agency personnel are much less stringent, and in other ways the life of a leader is far less rigid and rule bound. The point is that state and local governments in the United States vary greatly. This difference offers an ideal beginning for examining the degree to which different regulatory regimes affect the performance of government.

## The First Question

Why should government be deregulated? There are many possible reasons. One might believe, for example, that efficiency will be increased and money saved. Another motivation may be that government can be made more effective. There is also the matter of responsiveness; some reinventors of government would argue that the primary objective should be to make state and local government more entrepreneurial to satisfy the customers of government. I view

Frank J. Thompson provided suggestions for this chapter. A number of the ideas advanced here were influenced by colleagues on the National Commission on the State and Local Public Service; however, responsibility for the statements in this chapter is mine alone.

deregulation from the perspective of making it easier for leaders in
a democratic polity to be agents of change, to carry out the purposes of the body politic as they interpret them. It is on this basis
that they should be judged and reelected or turned out of office. In
this chapter, I focus on leadership in American state and local
government in relation to deregulation. Leadership can do three
things: operate better in less regulated environments; help reduce
regulatory barriers; and surmount those barriers that remain, since
government can never eliminate all of them.

My discussion of these connections between the leadership and
deregulation involves two biases, one in favor of the executive and
the second a belief that politicians are not villains. I am chagrinned
when colleagues disparage politicians as a class (I include both
elected and appointed officials and their helpers) and students pick
up this idea. Over the years, I have studied, worked with, and come
to admire hundreds of politicians, both in the executive and legislative branches, who have entered politics because they care about
their country and the issues they face and who continue to work
with dignity, decency, and skill in a difficult money-driven political
environment.

## The Setting

Americans do not like government. However, we have an awful
lot of it. The latest Census Bureau count shows 86,742 federal, state,
and local governments, all but 51 of them local governments—
cities, counties, towns, school districts, and special districts.[1] Of
course, not all the units classified as local governments are important or have significant powers and revenues. Some special districts
the Census Bureau includes as governments have taxing powers
but few staff members, or none (20,000 out of 30,000 have no
full-time employees). But even if one eliminates very small governments and special districts with a narrow scope and limited administrative functions and staff, a vast number remains.

Most domestic public services are provided by or through state
and local governments. And it is not easy to generalize about
administrative practices in such diversity. States vary greatly in the
way they charter and support local units. One common pattern is
fragmentation, with many general-purpose localities layered on top

158    RICHARD P. NATHAN

of one another. The functions and finances of local units of government both among and within states also vary widely.

Martha Derthick recently asked the right question: What is American federalism supposed to achieve? Citing the Supreme Court decision in *Gregory* v. *Ashcroft* (1991), she says that "perhaps the principal benefit of the federal system is that is constitutes a check on abuses of government power."[2] She adds that the Court discerned other important advantages of federalism—"sensitivity to the diverse needs of a heterogeneous society; increased opportunity for citizen involvement in democratic processes; more innovation and experimentation; and heightened responsiveness that results from competition among the states for a mobile citizenry." This is a good list. However, two hundred years after the Constitution was adopted, citizens have become discontented about inefficiency and fragmentation in this federal system and about gridlock in formulating and implementing important policies. At its roots, this frustration reflects the pluralism of U.S. government, which has two dimensions. One is horizontal, that is, among the three branches. The other is the vertical, among the federal, state, and local levels.

There is a special irony in this situation. Throughout the world, American-style pluralism has become a model as countries experiment with democratic institutions and devise new political systems. But pluralism is a luxury. It takes time and resources constantly to bargain and debate about the actions of the many state and local governments. Moreover, the more time spent bargaining about what governments should do, the less energy governments have to devote to actually doing things. Implementation is the short suit of American government.

In an age of increased international competition, frustrations about reduced U.S. economic prospects, the supposed inefficiencies of government, and its slowness or inability to act are often reflected in antibureaucracy diatribes and government bashing. This is wrong. We should be bashing ourselves. Government is cumbersome and often slow to act precisely because of the long tradition of pluralism. Although Americans call them special interests and often impugn their tactics, the idea that everyone should be heard in every state house and in tens of thousands of local communities is very American.

## The Greatest Need: Leadership

If forced to pick the reform most needed in state and local government I would choose leadership. What is needed is not just able and strong leaders, but leadership systems rooted in institutional reform. As Deborah Roberts has said,

> it is not enough to have a few dedicated, visionary, or inspiring individuals at the top. The other half of executive leadership is the *executive leadership system*, which supports democratically elected leaders in both effective governance and delivery of government services to the public. The executive leadership system encompasses not only governors, elected officials, and their appointed officials, but the system also reaches down to the level of careerists integrally linked with the creation and conduct of public policy.[3]

America needs to undertake institutional reforms that facilitate leadership and temper pluralism without destroying its basic nature or undermining personal and representational freedoms. This includes measures to deregulate government: the nation needs to unshackle its leaders and give them the tools to carry out the aims that express the public will and can win the confidence of the people.

Unfortunately, this prescription must deal with a difficult and widespread reality. Not long ago a former student of mine complained about a Catch-22 that shows how regulatory barriers can create a bad environment in government. A state government job she wanted was restricted to applicants who had experience in a lower job classification. But tests for the lower job are given infrequently; the last time had been five years ago. A new test would be conducted soon, but at the same time that a test for the higher-rated job she wanted was to be given. Then there would be another five-year hiatus. Even if the student qualified for the lower-grade position, she would have had to wait five years to take the test for the senior position for which she already had the necessary skills and qualifications. She decided not to work for the state.

It is not easy to attract talent and motivate workers in rigid test-dominated institutional settings like this. In June 1991 Joseph

M. Bress, director of the Governor's Office of Employee Relations in New York, criticized the state's civil service system, especially the "1-out-of-3 selection process," which requires that positions be filled by one of three people who have the highest scores on a written test. Bress said that such rigidity gives "a false perception of precision that only the top three have the ability or capability to perform a job."[4] He advocated changes similar to those made by other states and localities to loosen hiring and promotion rules.

New York represents an extreme. It is, according to Jonathan Walters, "the most constricted, calcified and complicated civil service system in the country."[5] But the combination of strong unions and rigid civil service rules are stultifying in many states and large local governments. The most rigid systems tend to be in the larger, older, and generally more liberal states.[6] Of course, the original goal of the civil service and public unionization was not so much to improve efficiency as to curb patronage and labor relations systems to protect the rights and interests of employees. Unfortunately, many state and large local governments have become so rule bound in the pursuit of these goals that managers must devote huge amounts of time and energy to circumventing the rules if they are to exert even a semblance of executive leadership.

States vary in the character and depth of the classified civil service; the number and type of appointed or exempt positions; the methods for recruiting, selecting, and deploying classified and exempt personnel; and the influence of unions over personnel decisionmaking. Although recognizing this variation, the National Commission on the State and Local Public Service in a recent report presented a program to overhaul state and local government management systems. The commission urged "(1) reforming the civil service, including reduced use of veterans preference and seniority; (2) streamlining the procurement process; and (3) making the budgeting process more flexible."[7]

The report continued,

> many state and local governments have created such rule-bound and complicated systems that merit is often the last value served. . . . How can merit be served when pay is determined mainly on the basis of time on the job? How is merit served when top performers can be "bumped" from their jobs by poor performers during downsizings?

Over the years, the basic purpose of the civil service system has been forgotten: To recruit the most talented among our citizens into government, not to employ legions of classification experts and personnel administrators who spend their days tracing bumping routes and rewriting job descriptions. State and local governments have a hard enough time as it is recruiting the best and the brightest without actively discouraging them. We must not be so hidebound in order to protect against failure that we quash the spirit of innovation.[8]

To bring these statements down to personal scale, it is useful here to quote former Houston mayor Kathy Whitmire, who spent fourteen years in city government in Houston. The excerpts are long, but they are telling comments by someone who has been there.

I found out that after I got to be mayor [of Houston], I had so many other duties of leading the community . . . that I had little time to spend on an executive leadership role. I still saw that as perhaps the most crucial part of my role as chief executive. . . .
   One of the biggest problems in getting good executive leaders is their concern about being able to manage their departments. In other words, if you have a city council that wants to micromanage the department, are you going to be able to attract good leadership? Strong leaders are going to want to make decisions, carry them out, and be held accountable—not have someone else do it. . . . We often find legislative bodies unsympathetic to the idea of performance compensation and rewarding employees for good work, but most top executives will want to reward employees for good work. If you have a city council that says no, that makes it very difficult. Or, if you have such a restrictive civil service system or collective bargaining agreement that the executive has very little latitude in managing the person, that too discourages the executive from taking a local government position. These are the impediments to attracting the type of executive talent that we want in government. These impediments need to be worked on. . . .
   Once it becomes established in a civil service system that a person will not get terminated, it becomes very difficult to get performance. When I was recruiting department directors, that was always high on my agenda in the interview whether they had

to terminate an employee in the civil service system. If they hadn't done it, because they did not want to, then I didn't hire them because it seemed to me that you had to have a basic willingness to try and make the civil service system work. But it is difficult. . . .

When it was time for promotion, the person would have to be promoted from within and would be based on a test score on a multiple choice test. That is the basis upon which folds are promoted to lieutenant, captain, deputy chief and so on. That is a difficult system to deal with because how can you appoint individuals who are going to begin a community policing program, or improve emergency medical services? That's the rule we are stuck with. We call it a mandate. The system needs reform.[9]

### Building an Executive Team

Even if administrative systems and formal structures are made more user-friendly and less rule bound, leadership will fail unless top managers have similar goals. Team building in government— where and how to do it—is a subject I have studied from two vantage points, the organization of the U.S. presidency and the management role of state and local executive branch officials. In 1976 I wrote about having served as an appointed budget and program official in the first Nixon administration:

The point of this book is not that elected chief executives should be managers in the sense of running the day-to-day affairs of government. Rather, it is that such officials should organize their office—appoint, assign, and motivate their principal appointees—in a way that penetrates the administrative process. The reason is that in a complex, technologically advanced society in which the role of government is pervasive, much of what we would define as policymaking is done through the execution of laws in the management process.[10]

I concluded that making the right appointment at the outset of a new government is one of the keys for a president in getting a managerial grip.

The experience of recent presidents suggests that the appointment of right people as cabinet members is fundamental to management control. The tempting and indeed customary approach to this task is to heal wounds and reach out to many groups and constituencies in order to form a cabinet and subcabinet that is balanced and broadly representative. The healing process may be good for the soul, but it is bad for the program.[11]

Recently, I extended this analysis to states and localities. The way top elected officials recruit, select, deploy, and support the heads of large public agencies has immense importance for domestic public programs, in which state governments now have a primary role. Unless the values that politicians stand for are reflected in the way state governments actually operate, all the new legislation in the world is for naught. When people vote for politicians, they have every right to believe that what those politicians promise to do is what they will do.

My preferred management model for state and local government is a strong elected executive supported by trusted agency heads who work well and closely with the executive as part of a team. The most important decisions for an elected executive should be about the budget, and these decisions should involve close and real consultation with agency heads. Other staff functions should be kept to a minimum to avoid intruding on the work of line agency managers. This is the "postbureaucratic model" described by Michael Barzelay and Babak J. Armajani, who challenge "the bureaucratic reform vision's presumption that the public interest is unambiguously served when staff agency employees use their expert knowledge to apply rules that regulate the administration decision of line agencies."[12] Barzelay and Armajani urge that personnel, procurement, legal, financial, and managerial functions should be decentralized. Staff groups should be advisory and supportive; they should be customer oriented to assist line agency managers rather than set up hoops for them to jump through, which can only frustrate and slow the progress of leaders in government who seek to be agents of change.

Unfortunately, the public holds elected officials at every level in federal government in low esteem for reasons that are not hard to find—negative campaigns, candidacies geared toward being telegenic rather than addressing issues, and reliance on spin doctors.

The public's willingness to limit terms, throw out incumbents, and cut government spending reflects a widespread feeling that politicians are toying with citizen's emotions, talking down to the public, and that they do not care about the way government operates. Bureaucratic top-heaviness and rigidity and the acceptance by many government workers that nothing can change, that every interest group will fight to keep what it has and prevent anyone else's gain, have fostered a spirit of resignation and time-serving.

### Appointed Officials

Many of the people who run public bureaucracies in the United States are appointed officials accountable to the politicians who selected them. In comparison with other countries, government here stands out because of the size of this corps of appointed officials. Their role in state government is especially crucial. Although the federal government provides financial support for many health care, education, welfare, and other programs, they cannot be micromanaged from Washington; predominant responsibility for them thus lies with the states, which administer these services directly or supervise their administration by local governments or nonprofit organizations.

Appointed agency heads in state government are major participants in all these programs and others. They can be professional politicians, but most are professionals in their field who come from other agencies, business, or nonprofit groups; many have moved up through the ranks. Elected officials need to give high priority to the role, salary, qualifications, performance, and tenure of these officials. Their jobs should offer excitement and a sense of fulfillment and service. And the potential is certainly there. The people who head large state and local public agencies direct armies of professionals, specialists, and line workers. They have an opportunity to make a mark in ways crucial to the well-being of their communities.

The disadvantages of taking on these management challenges, however, are formidable. Salaries and benefits for top managers have improved in some states but still fall short of what they can earn in the private sector. The politics that swirls around public agencies often makes these jobs frustrating and hastens managerial burnout. A manager's professional reputation can be severely compromised by attacks from politicians and journalists who seek scapegoats for the inability of government to deal with family poverty and dysfunction, child abuse, crime, drugs, homelessness, and other deep social problems. Finally, strict conflict-of-interest and financial disclosure laws may discourage candidates who have been successful in the private sector.

## Ten Lessons for Potential Active Leaders

My experience studying state and local elected and appointed executives suggests that leadership matters, that it can make a difference. Following are good practices for those who want to be agents of change at the state and local levels and in large nonprofit agencies.

—Strike while the iron is hot. Newly elected and appointed public officials should take advantage of their honeymoon period to create momentum by doing things early that are often much harder to do without the excitement of a new start.

—Institutions matter. Managers of public and nonprofit agencies who operate as agents of change have to think strategically about what they will leave behind—the organizational, personnel, and intergovernmental structures that can sustain the effects of their actions.

—People matter too. Good management depends on selecting good people. A public official can deal regularly with only a few people—maybe ten trusted (or at least pretty much trusted) associates. They have to be people the executive can talk to, can communicate quickly and clearly with in a way that is comfortable (and sometimes even fun). Picking this core group and forging relationships that make it work are vital to policy implementation and good management.

—Stick around. This fourth lesson is easier to state than to carry out. Public managers who care about putting a new policy or program in place need five years or more in a particular role or agency if they want their efforts to bear fruit not just for one season, but for many seasons.

—Set goals that can be used as the basis for rewards and punishments. Managers must reward and punish. But especially they should reward good performance. The rewards of public service in America are few, and leaders in high-visibility managerial positions can contribute to success simply by shining a spotlight on good performance.

—Avoid becoming mired in details. Good management in the complex world of government is not micromanagement. It requires trust in others. It requires delegating responsibility and in the process influencing and motivating people, especially in large organizations.

—Respect careerists but watch them. Civil service systems can be stultifying, and dealing with the results is as challenging as anything for people who want to exercise leadership. An appointed official cannot get very far without the trust and help of important people in the permanent bureaucracy. Smart agency heads show appreciation for the value of the career service, but this does not mean they should just defer to civil service procedures and requirements. They should use their best efforts and most finely honed political skills to move trusted people with shared values into crucial jobs. This calls for a high order of skill in selecting and deploying career personnel.

—Be shrewd about relations with the legislature. In the United States, legislative bodies are very powerful. The first article of the Constitution establishes Congress and enumerates its powers. Congress refers to itself as the first branch and acts accordingly. States have similar constitutions and their legislatures behave in like manner. Although public managers must be loyal to the officials who appointed them, often their goals cannot be achieved unless they also cultivate good relationships with the legislature.

—Do what has to be done. Leaders in state and local governments and nonprofit organizations who want to make changes cannot wait forever. Sometimes they must take decisive action even if it involves strong measures to discipline an uncooperative associate. Such actions can, of course, backfire and create an atmospl ere in which leadership is not possible. Nevertheless, firm action is often the right tactic for policy managers who want to make a difference. "Politics," said Mr. Dooley, "ain't beanbag!"[13]

## Reinventing Government

Fortunately, there is today a healthy new spirit, emanating from the presidency and involving many groups and experts, about reforming government. In *Reinventing Government* David Osborne and Ted Gaebler make a strong and well-received case for changing the style and spirit of government in domestic public affairs. They seek "a new framework for understanding government, a new way of thinking about government—in short, a new *paradigm.*"[14] They call for an entrepreneurial spirit in government and emphasize that like the private sector it should be customer oriented. Vice President Albert Gore's National Performance Review picked up many of these same themes.

But although their hearts are in the right place and their general emphasis is good, there are problems with customer orientation in government, as advanced by Osborne, Gaebler, and others. Many of the services provided by government are what economists call "public goods and services." They apply to everyone in society, including people who do not want them or at least do not want them in the form they are provided. This includes, for example, civil rights programs and protections; public education; residences for needy groups (drug addicts, foster children, the mentally ill, the homeless); the siting of waste treatment facilities, dumps, and transfer stations; national defense; and zoning laws. There are many groups of customers for government. They cannot all be satisfied. The constant bargaining that occurs is bound to be intense, and the more controversial the good or service, the greater the intensity. This situation limits the analogy between the public and private sectors. It places a premium on politically skillful, mission-oriented, executive leadership in government.

Regulatory barriers—internal and external—can be eased or skillfully navigated, but a tendency toward regulatory overload in government and controversies about public goods are givens. Because this is so, many government leaders are reactive, devoting little time or effort to creating and nurturing strong executive leadership systems and implementing public policies. Yet changes can be made in government that emphasize executive leadership, good performance, follow-up, and results.

## Deregulating State and Local Government

What kinds of barriers should be considered in addressing deregulation as a way to strengthen and reinforce leadership systems in state and local government? Two primary types of regulations impinge on leaders. Internal barriers include regulations that apply to the substance of a particular government function or activity. External barriers are universal regulations adopted for purposes larger than the operations of any particular government or agency. These include civil rights requirements, civil service rules, financial disclosure statements, affirmative action rules, environmental protection requirements, rules to ensure access for and fair treatment of disabled persons, occupational safety and product requirements, and so forth.

Often these external requirements are lumped together and complained about as "mandates" coming from sources unrelated to the governmental activity to which they apply. In the 1980s, with a conservative president in the White House and a liberal congressional majority, Congress often used mandates instead of money to force states and localities to carry out particular governmental purposes that would have few or no immediate budgetary effects. A 1992 report of the U.S. Advisory Commission on Intergovernmental Relations said that "the pace and breadth of federal preemptions of state and local authority have increased significantly since the late 1960s."[15] It went on to point out that more than half the significant federal preemption statutes passed since the country began in 1789 have been enacted by Congress since 1969.

The main source of most government regulations is not hard to identify. Like the line from the Pogo cartoon of the 1970s, "we have met the enemy and he is us." In 1977 Herbert Kaufman wrote, "red tape is everywhere and everywhere it is abhorred," but he cautioned that one person's burdensome mandate is another's cherished objective. Red tape, he continued, is "at the core of our institutions rather than an excrescence on them."[16] The fact that many rules inhibit the managerial and policy options of political executives who seek to be agents of change does not mean they are all bad and should be removed. This in a nutshell is the dilemma of deregulation in government.

In many situations, deregulation can be pivotal to an administrative strategy for a state or city. It can loosen civil service requirements for appointments, promotions, and placements and ease union rules. There are precedents for such efforts. Using a recent survey that focused on personnel systems, Jonathan Walters concluded that high-visibility civil service reforms are not as promising as more incremental, lower-key efforts, although both are hard to carry out.[17] In some states this issue has taken on very high visibility—notably in Florida where Governor Lawton Chiles made a media splash with a plan to subject the state's civil service system to sunset laws. But in contrast to the interpretation offered by Neal Peirce in this volume, Walters describes Chiles's efforts as "hyped-up" and "over-reaching." There has been little change, and although some good proposals have been advanced, they will cost money rather than save it.

Walters canvased other states and cities—California, Iowa, Minnesota, and Virginia, and Baltimore, Dallas, Indianapolis, and San Diego—that have smoothly carried out gradual reforms in ways that address many of the classic complaints about civil service. These governments adopted reforms such as moving away from the rule of choosing only from among the top three candidates for a job, reducing the number of job classifications, cutting management layers to increase the ratio of staff to supervisors, establishing new pay grades for technical and front-line staff, decentralizing personnel decisionmaking, and reforming central personnel offices into staff support units, "more as personnel consultants than as the gate through which all personnel decisions must pass."[18] Walters concludes that deregulation is best achieved in this incremental way: "In the real world of civil service reform, the tortoises are winning the race."[19]

## Gridlock and Leadership

The main ideas of my analysis should be clear. State and local governments need to unleash political executives not just as individuals but as members of institutionally reformed leadership systems to improve the performance of government. To some extent this objective can be achieved by deregulation. It can be achieved by surmounting regulatory barriers and by strengthening the leadership skills, motivation, and commitment of those elected and appointed to executive positions. This theme reflects both my preference for executive action and a corollary theme that legislative bodies should be less intrusive in administration.

An old axiom of American government associated with Woodrow Wilson is that there should be a demarcation between the responsibility of the legislature to make policy and the duty of the executive branch to carry it out. This is a false distinction. The line between policymaking and its execution, if there is one, is a blurry boundary with frequent border crossings. Policymaking involves both the legislative and executive branches, and it involves much more than passing a law. Once a law is passed, there are plenty of opportunities for its purposes and underlying values to be shaped in its execution. Members of Congress and the federal courts insert themselves in myriad ways in administrative processes, and this is also true at state and local levels. In addition, career civil service officials interpret laws and regulations in implementing them, and their actions often shape the meaning of the policies involved. Elected and appointed officials must be assertive in policy implementation. They have many opportunities to give meaning to policies—to translate ideas into realities in ways that reflect the purposes and values of a particular government. But this role is only as important as their willingness and ability to play it.

The possibility of legislative interference in administration is increased by the looseness of some statutes. Charles Lindbloom once said the best way to get legislation enacted in the American political system is to be vague about objectives.[20] The result is both a blessing and a curse for political executives. The blessing is that it gives them room to interpret policies. The curse is that legislators, courts, and civil servants can meddle with administrative decisions that give meaning to policies.

Various strategies have been advanced to curb the powers of legislatures. One that is now widely advocated is to limit the terms of legislators; fifteen states have recently adopted state legislative term limits. But the effects of term limits are uncertain.[21] They could strengthen the executive, which is the outcome I favor, but they could also increase the powers of legislative staffs.

There are other legislative reforms that could help strengthen executive leadership and allow more attention to policy implementation. One is to adopt mechanisms that get policy closure when legislators agree that action is needed but the decision process is gridlocked by competing entrenched interests. Additional reforms that could reduce the intrusiveness of legislators in matters affecting the implementation of policy are campaign finance reforms, which loosen ties to particular interests, and the rotation of legislative committee assignments, which could help achieve the same purpose. Such changes can be viewed as rebalancing the Madisonian system of checks and balances, or calibrating it, as a way to take account of the growth of government and the correspondingly larger and more difficult managerial roles of political executives and their appointees.

To sum up, the nation faces what has been called "a paradox of pluralism."[22] There are so many governments and government branches, and so many that have expanded their staffs and commitments, that it may be harder rather than easier to govern in many instances. Government is musclebound and besieged by interest groups. The real cause of gridlock and burnout is not bad government but very big government. We must now do things that can migrate these tendencies, which in large part are the result of good intentions gone awry.

## Governments of Acquaintances

In one important respect, leadership is easier to achieve at the state and local levels than at the federal level. Career patterns vary for public managers at different levels of government. In the federal government, people who are often amateurs in government typically stay for two or three years—too short a time—and then leave for more lucrative jobs outside government. The prevalence of this in-and-out pattern caused Hugh Heclo to give the title *Government of Strangers* to a book about high-level public servants in the federal government.[23] At the state and local levels, however, there are what Deborah Roberts calls "inners and arounders" in top management jobs. She writes not about a government of strangers, but about "a government of acquaintances," referring to the people who hold appointive jobs and when they finish a given assignment, move to a different branch or agency or to a related position in the same state, a different state, or a large city. They are in a sense professional political appointees.[24]

Research has borne this out. The median time of state service is twelve to fourteen years. The previous job of more than half the administrators has been in the same state, 33 percent in the same agency, and 21 percent in another agency in the same state. Sixteen percent have had immediately previous positions in national or local government.[25] On professionalism, Deil Wright concludes,

Among the clearest and most confirmed trend over the past three decades is better trained and better educated administrators. This conclusion derives from educational levels and specializations as well as from the career paths followed by the majority of state agency heads. Clearly, state government is not, if indeed it ever was, an administrative backwater.[26]

Unfortunately, many elected executives in state and local government tend to be preoccupied with responsibilities other than management and team building. Dealing with the press, interest groups, and the legislature often takes precedence over managerial tasks. In recent years, budget cuts have added problems in dealing with officials in the state executive branch and the legislature. The courts too have become managers, especially in social policy, and have increasingly involved themselves in administrative matters. Opponents of a given policy often go to court to prevent changes that agency managers seek in corrections, mental hospitals, education, and welfare. In some situations the courts are more influential than the other two branches of government. This is not to say that the public sector is necessarily more competitive and barrier ridden than some areas in the private sector. Nor is it to say that elected chief executives do not care about what happens inside government. There are many dedicated and caring elected political executives; their commitment, courage, and staying power is a critical ingredient of effectiveness in government.

## Conclusion

I have discussed three state and local management strategies. One is deregulation to loosen up management rules, which is especially critical where personnel and managerial systems are over-built. The second is executive leadership. The third is to cut back the influence of legislatures in administrative matters and to pursue methods to reduce legislative gridlock.

These ideas are in line with the now widespread reinvention movement in government. In effect, my formulation is broader than most in that it includes both executive and legislative reforms. It is also distinctive in spelling out deregulatory reforms and calling for changes in basic structures and structural relationships at the state and local levels.

The three strategies discussed in this chapter come together. Legislative reform and deregulation to reduce civil service and other barriers to action can aid strong executives. With the current hue and cry about gridlock (much of it justified), the strategies I have suggested can expedite government action in ways that are in keeping with American incremental political traditions and processes. Emphasizing executive leadership in this way is fully appropriate—indeed necessary—for modern democracies. During Franklin Roosevelt's administration, the report of the President's Committee on Administrative Management headed by management expert Louis Brownlow led, among other changes, to the creation of the Executive Office of the President. The report, warmly endorsed by the president, stressed the need for a strong executive: "A weak administration can neither advance nor retreat successfully—it can merely muddle. Those who waiver at the sight of needed power are false friends of modern democracy. Strong executive leadership is essential to democratic government today."[27]

## Notes

1. Bureau of the Census, *Census of Governments, 1992*, vol. 1, no. 1: *Governmental Organization* (Department of Commerce, 1992).

2. Martha Derthick, "Up to Date in Kansas City: Reflections on American Federalism," paper prepared for the 1992 annual conference of the American Political Science Association, p. 3.

3. Deborah D. Roberts, "The Governor as Leader: Strengthening Public Service through Executive Leadership," in Frank J. Thompson, ed., *Revitalizing State and Local Public Service* (San Francisco: Jossey-Bass, 1993), p. 42.

4. Joseph M. Bress, "The Public Service and the Future: Legal, Organization, and Other Issues," Albany, N.Y.: Nelson A. Rockefeller Institute of Government, 1991, p. 5.

5. Jonathan Walters, "How Not to Reform Civil Service," *Governing* (November 1992), p. 31.

6. Carolyn Ban and Norma Riccucci, "Personnel Systems and Labor Relations: Steps Toward a Quiet Revitalization," in Thompson, ed., *Revitalizing State and Local Public Service*, p. 72.

7. National Commission on the State and Local Public Service, *Hard Truths/Tough Choices: An Agenda for State and Local Reform* (Albany, N.Y.: Nelson A. Rockefeller Institute of Government, 1993), p. 11.

8. National Commission on the State and Local Public Service, *Hard Truths/Tough Choices*, pp. 24–25.

9. Kathy Whitmire, "Executive Leadership and Federal Mandates," regional hearing of the National Commission on the State and Local Public Service, Austin, Texas, March 25, 1992, pp. 20–22.

10. Richard P. Nathan, *The Administrative Presidency* (Macmillan, 1986), p. 82.

11. Ibid., p. 88.

12. Michael Barzelay and Babak J. Armajani, "Managing State Government Operations: Changing Visions of Staff Agencies," *Journal of Policy Analysis and Management*, vol. 9 (Summer 1990), p. 313.

13. Finley Peter Dunne, *Mr. Dooley in Peace and in War* (Boston: Small, Maynard and Company, 1898), p. xiii.

14. David Osborne and Ted Gaebler, *Reinventing Government: How the Entrepreneurial Spirit Is Transforming the Public Sector* (Addison-Wesley, 1992), p. 321.

15. U.S. Advisory Commission on Intergovernmental Relations, "Federal Statutory Preemption of State and Local Authority: History, Inventory, and Issues," report A-121, September 1992, p. iii.

16. Herbert Kaufman, *Red Tape: Its Origins, Uses, and Abuses* (Brookings, 1977), pp. 1, 3.

17. Jonathan Walters, "How Not to Reform Civil Service," p. 30.

18. Ibid., p. 34.

19. Ibid., p. 30.

20. Charles E. Lindbloom, *The Policy-Making Process*, 2d ed. (Prentice-Hall, 1980), p. 65.

21. Gerald Benjamin and Michael J. Malbin, eds., *Limiting Legislative Terms* (Washington: Congressional Quarterly Press, 1992), p. 3.

22. R. Scott Fosler, comment at the meeting of the National Commission on the State and Local Public Service, Albany, New York, December 6, 1992.

23. Hugh Heclo, *A Government of Strangers: Executive Politics in Washington* (Brookings, 1977).

24. Roberts, "Governor as Leader," p. 61.

25. Deil S. Wright, Jae-Won Yoo, and Jennifer Cohen, "The Evolving Profile of State Administrators," *State Government*, vol. 64 (January–March 1991), p. 4.

26. Ibid., p. 37.

27. President's Committee on Administrative Management, *Administrative Management in the Government of the United States* (January 1937), p. 47.

# 9 ||| Deregulating at the Boundaries of Government: Would It Help?

## Donald F. Kettl

ACADEMICS and public officials alike have sprouted scores of ideas to reform government. They have proposed deregulating, reinventing, downsizing, rightsizing, privatizing, reregulating, shrinking, and cutting back. They have suggested making government leaner, smaller, and larger. They have urged government to focus more on customers, results, and outputs, by engaging, enabling, empowering, investing, catalyzing, and collaborating. All the reforms have sought to root out the unholy trinity of waste, fraud, and abuse.

This broad movement has advanced on several fronts. Neoliberals, exemplified by David Osborne and Ted Gaebler, have argued the need for reinventing government.[1] Neoconservatives, led by spokespersons such as Jack Kemp, William Bennett, and James P. Pinkerton, have advocated a "new paradigm."[2] Even academics have joined the campaign.[3] In the aggregate these voices have built a brief for what can most generically be called a new governance, an effort to make government more effective and responsive. The brief argues that government is not working well, that the expectations of citizens exceed government's ability to provide satisfaction. It contends that government is too fragmented and pays far more attention to the pieces than to the whole.[4] Too often, critics agree, government employees and programs seem to be in business for themselves, or for special interests. The 1992 Ross Perot campaign for president drove home the message: citizens

I am grateful to the National Initiative on Rural America, which provided financial support for and reactions to ideas developed in this chapter.

175

believe government is often out of touch with them—and they pay the bills.

The underlying assumption of the movement's component voices is that government's usual way of business has become an impediment to performance and responsiveness. This impediment needs to be swept away; more flexibility, market incentives, and entrepreneurial activity (by both government employees and recipients of government services) need to replace existing behavior. The new governance argues, in short, that process must triumph over structure.

Given the obviousness of the problems and the attractiveness of the label, everyone has wanted to "reinvent" government. Immediately after the 1992 presidential election, virtually every reform plan was touted as some form of reinvention. In fact, of course, most of the proposals had at best fuzzy links with the Osborne and Gaebler book that coined the term. And many of the movement's leaders had strong disagreements with each other: the neoliberals with the neoconservatives over how strong a role the government ought to play in solving problems, and among the neoconservatives over whether fundamental social reforms had to occur before the government could be reinvented.

Two trends have, however, emerged. First, despite the many disputes among the reinventors, there are remarkable similarities in their pronouncements. In fact, they often have far more in common with each other than with the traditional elements in the Republican and Democratic parties. Second, despite the ideological firefights that have flashed around the movement, real results are emerging there. Osborne and Gaebler's ideas, in particular, resonate powerfully among government employees. Even though *reinventing* has now been applied to virtually any idea, new or old, it reflects an underlying belief that changes indeed are needed.

The new governance movement, moreover, has a close affinity with a broader and older impulse to deregulate government. Like the reinventors, the deregulators, who dominated discourse during the 1980s, contended that government's standard operating procedures had got in the way, that they too often became goals in themselves instead of ensuring efficient government performance. The deregulators differed from the newer movement, however, in the solutions. The reinventors have argued for an aggressive government to steer society in new directions (the neoliberals toward new public solutions to social problems, the neoconservatives toward stronger public support for individual liberties). The deregulators simply wanted to peel government back and get it out of the way.

On one level, it is impossible to argue with any of these positions. The neoconservatives have quite rightly pointed to the deterioration of the nation's moral fiber. The neoliberals have identified health and welfare reform and other problems that only government seems equipped to solve. The deregulators have agreed with both that pursuing solutions is difficult because government itself has become part of the problem. The other chapters in this book develop these arguments. My contention, however, is that no matter how successfully these strategies, any or all of them, are followed, they will leave untouched a critical and residual problem, the job of managing the boundaries of government, the interfaces between programs, agencies, and levels within agencies that all too frequently prove rife with conflict.

## The Boundaries of Government

The foundation of the residual problem of managing the boundaries lies in imprecise diagnosis by the deregulators and reinventors. If deregulating or reinventing government is the solution, what is the problem? One answer is obvious: in the minds of many observers, government performance and responsiveness is inadequate. But what has eroded performance and responsiveness? Employees who do not care? Rules that get in the way? A mismatch of public expectations and government resources? Poorly designed programs? Each of these explanations is part—but only part—of the problem. Reinventing government or simply sweeping bothersome procedures out of the way will not alter the critical underlying reality: in the past few decades, the boundaries across which government, its programs, and its officials must work have become far more numerous and infinitely more complicated.[5] The performance and responsiveness of government is troubled because managing that takes boundaries into account has become more difficult. The prescriptions of both the reinventing and the deregulating movements do not fully recognize this reality. And they cannot be successful without solving the problems that the proliferation of boundaries has created.

Consider an illustration. In January 1990 President George Bush launched the Presidential Initiative on Rural America. The plan aimed to encourage new partnerships, both intergovernmental and public-private, as a way of creating new strategies for rural development.[6] One piece of the initiative was the Monday Management Group, a coalition representing thirty-five federal agencies, operating out of the Department of Agriculture, to oversee the program and work toward solving problems that arose. At the state level, rural development councils were created to move different agencies doing related work into closer partnership.

When rural entrepreneurs in Kansas complained about "a mountain of application forms [from government agencies], all requiring the same basic information, but all using different formats," the state rural development council worked to create a single loan application form for seven different government programs. The Treasury Department helped the state council supplement the application form with an electronic loan application process. Meanwhile, Halstead, Kansas, began a $9.4 million project to control flooding on the Little Arkansas River. Local officials painstakingly assembled financing, acquired land, and let contracts. They were stopped, however, by conflicts about possible damage to a historic site. A delay clause in the contract threatened to cost $4,000 a day, and there was a danger that state support for the project might disappear.

The state rural development council intervened and called the parties involved to a conference. The council was able to resolve most of the problems, but council members ran up against a sixty-day waiting period mandated by the National Historic Preservation Act so that the value of a site could be reviewed. Only thirty days remained until the contract delay clause would trigger the penalty. Working with the National Advisory Council for Historic Preservation and members of Congress representing the area, the state council was able to conclude the review within thirty days. By beating the deadline the boundary spanning of the council saved Halstead $120,000, and the town was able to begin the project.[7]

Similar illustrations abound. Indeed, they represent the most important contribution of the new governance movement, and they share an implicit argument. Government's attack on public problems increasingly involves many programs and agencies, various levels of government, and complex public-private partnerships.

Each element has its own boundaries. Government's toughest problems, from finding common ground to winning the cooperation of disparate parties, increasingly occur at these boundaries. Problem resolution—and effective management of government itself—demands coordination. Solving the problems thus means developing new ways of spanning the boundaries.

Understanding the problems requires exploring the interconnections among three approaches: the new governance movement launched by people with hands-on experience of how government runs, the new institutionalist movement begun by political scientists, and the role that boundaries themselves play, as organization theorists have explained.

## The New Governance

From the left, the reinventors argue that government should be more customer centered and more results oriented. Government seems too much in business for itself; it should focus on the needs of its citizens. Government worries too much about increasing its budget; it should focus on what results taxes buy. Furthermore, the reinventors contend, government should concentrate on steering instead of rowing; it should worry far more about where it is going than on how it is getting there. In fact, government does not need to do the rowing. Private sector businesses, independently or in concert with government, could pull the oars.[8]

From the right, the new paradigmers contend that government needs to cope with changing realities. James Pinkerton aggressively argued that "we have to start by admitting to ourselves that we can't get there from here with the current methods."[9] Like the reinventors, the new paradigmers contend that government focuses too much on inputs instead of outputs, that it focuses too little on its fundamental mission, and that it insists too strongly on doing the job itself. It needs to decentralize its operations. But, the new paradigmers contend, government also needs to create a new system of rewards and incentives, to empower both citizens and bureaucrats to pursue those incentives, and to provide choice for those who receive services so as to enforce those incentives.[10]

It is both politically dangerous and wildly ambitious to seek middle ground between two groups that disagree fundamentally on how expansive the government's role should be. Distilled to the

180    DONALD F. KETTL

Figure 9–1.    Characteristics of New Governance

| Characteristics | New governance | Old bureaucratic orthodoxy |
|---|---|---|
| Contact with citizens | engage, enable | direct, announce |
| Goals | mission, value-driven | program-driven |
| Approach to problems | proactive; creative opportunities | reactive; solve individual problems |
| General behavior | decentralized, entrepreneurial, market driven through choice | centralized, hierarchical |
| Treatment of citizens | customers; government is customer-centered | clients; government is special-interest centered |
| Measures of success | results achieved | inputs spent |
| Spending | long-term benefits | short-term payoffs |
| Organizational linkages | horizontal alliances; collaboration with stakeholders | hierarchical; one size fits all |

Source: Derives from DeWitt John and others, "What Will New Governance Mean for the Federal Government?" *Public Administration Review* (forthcoming).

elements, however, the reinventors and new paradigmers have converged on a series of ideas quite different from previous orthodoxy. Figure 9-1 sketches these core ideas that focus on a customer-centered, results-oriented, competition-driven government.

The new ideas quickly proved the target of bitter attacks. Bush administration Budget Director Richard Darman pointedly engaged the neoconservatives with a speech warning about "neoneoism." The movement, he suggested, was nothing more than a fad, and he mocked it by asking, "Hey brother, can you paradigm?"[11] Academics attacked new governance ideas by arguing that citizens are government's owners, not its customers. Governments are not markets and exist in part because markets have failed to serve the public interest. Furthermore, government serves broader values, including equity, representativeness, and responsiveness, that would be lost if it modeled itself too much after the private sector. The Constitution, not competition, is the compass for the public sector. Finally, the academics contended, by focusing on steering instead of rowing, the movement tends to belittle the rowers who do the steady work of government and to ignore their critical role in setting the course.[12]

To some extent the critics of new governance are correct. The evidence for many of the movement's claims is based on individual cases and has certainly not been tested on a wide scale. And academics' arguments about the core values of government are ageless and most certainly true. Still, it is impossible to escape two crucial points. First, the enthusiasm that has supported the movement is a sign of genuine problems that government has not solved. Citizens' encounters with government are indeed too often confusing and off-putting, which is why Perot's promise to clean up waste in government and reduce its unresponsiveness was received so well. Second, even though citizens are indeed the owners of government, they also want to be treated like customers. General Motors stockholders may be owners of the company, but they surely want to be treated well when they enter a showroom. Critics may quibble over the prescriptions of the new governance movement, but it is difficult to deny that its supporters have tapped into something very real. And among the most enthusiastic supporters of the new concepts are bureaucrats who struggle every day to solve the problems the movement has highlighted.

## The New Institutionalism

The irony is that just as the new governance movement was sweeping aside institutions in the search for new procedures to reform government, many political scientists were rediscovering the critical importance of institutions.[13] In the 1960s and 1970s the behavioral movement had swept political science. It argued that understanding the behavior of key participants in the political process, from voters to elected officials, was far more important than studying the rules and procedures of the institutions, such as Congress, with which they worked. By the 1980s the behavioral movement had left many questions unanswered, and political scientists began reasserting that institutions mattered, that they created ground rules for behavior and patterns of interaction that influenced policy results.

Political scientists thus returned to the study of institutions just as many reformers saw institutional rules and structures as the very core of government's most critical problems. Proponents of the new governance from both the left and the right argued that government would work better if traditional control through authority were replaced with market incentives and entrepreneurial choice. The key, James Pinkerton argued, lies in recognizing that America is in the midst of a transformation from modernism, characterized most by bureaucracy, to postmodernism, characterized by lean and fast government agencies: "The Postal Service is modern," he explained. "Faxing and E-mailing are postmodern." Government does not work as well as it used to because it is a modern institution trapped in postmodern times. "Government can work, if it moves with the times."[14]

Pinkerton's challenge raises sharp questions for both the study of politics and for the task of reforming government programs. His argument, along with that of other new governance reformers, is that the problem lies in the processes of government and that reform requires creating new incentives for those who work in and encounter government. The new institutionalism of political science implies instead that the problem is structural and that understanding the behavior of institutions is the key to improving them. If the problem is institutional, how accurate are the claims of the new governance reformers that incentives matter most? And if the problem is incentives, what role do institutions play in shaping them?

One response is that the new governance reformers are following a fad. When the reinventing government movement encounters problems, the enthusiasm of its supporters will fade. Another possibility is that the new institutionalism is a reaction against the behavioral revolution. As more formal theories of bureaucracy that are based in economics come to dominate political science more, the new institutionalism will fade away. The truth lies in between. As public programs have become increasingly complex, it has become far harder for any organization, public or private, to manage any problem that truly matters. Government institutions create the bases from which public efforts are launched, but not the ultimate sources of controlling these efforts. The institutions, in turn, act most by interacting with others; in these interactions come the incentives for everyone involved.

Shared responsibility for common problems, rather than more clearly differentiated responsibility for separable problems, has therefore come to define American politics. Where responsibility is shared, moreover, what matters most is what happens at the boundaries of responsibility: how the federal, state, and local governments balance their respective roles; how government interacts with its private and nonprofit partners; and how these complex partnerships relate to citizens.

The changing functions of the federal government have further underlined the importance of boundaries. Government's role has, especially since World War II, gradually become that of a wholesaler and arranger of services instead of a retailer. With the notable exceptions of police and fire departments, criminal justice, and education, government at all levels has come to rely on partnerships with the private and nonprofit sectors for delivering its programs.[15] As Robert E. Rubin, a Clinton administration economic adviser, noted, "almost all issues have cross-agency ramifications."[16] Such partnerships, across government agencies, across levels of government, and between government and the private and nonprofit sectors, are scarcely new. They have, however, developed rapidly in number and complexity, in medicare and highway construction and social services delivery and job training programs.

Any effort to reform government without dealing with the complaints about bureaucratic inefficiency and unresponsiveness is doomed to fail. However, any effort to reform government bureaucracy by sweeping it aside and replacing it with private contractors is likewise doomed. The problem to which the new governance is the solution is not a failure of government institutions, which would require that the institutions be dismantled or side-stepped. Rather, it is that the complexity of problems and of the institutional interconnections that seek to solve them that have grown far faster than government's ability to manage them.

### Types of Boundaries

If government is not working well, the solution lies in discovering why before seeking to change institutions and their behavior. The why is the growing number and complexity of boundaries. Consider the boundaries that must be crossed in managing government programs.[17]

SECTORAL BOUNDARIES. Distinctions between things governmental and nongovernmental are the building blocks for institutions in society. Deciding what government ought to do, such as providing security and collecting taxes, and what ought to be left in private hands has always been the central problem for American government—indeed, for all governments. The American experience has been to debate endlessly where the boundaries ought to be drawn while pragmatically blurring them. American public policy, especially since World War II, has increasingly frustrated those seeking clean divisions between the public and private sectors. The government has come to rely on a vast network of private contractors to conduct basic programs. From national defense to environmental cleanup, complex partnerships between government and private contractors are how the government's business gets managed. In turn, private parties have become ever more dependent on the government's activity. From dealing with rural flooding to providing disaster relief, government has increasingly become the first, not the last, resort. And nonprofit organizations have become increasingly important partners in public social programs. The Department of Agriculture case cited earlier focused on bridging such boundaries.

INTERGOVERNMENTAL BOUNDARIES. Boundaries among the national, state, and local governments have also blurred. The Tenth Amendment to the Constitution, many of the founders thought, would draw the line clearly between national and state powers. The blurring of intergovernmental boundaries that set in almost immediately has continued, despite recurring campaigns to devolve more power to subnational governments. From health care to transportation, job training to social services, every domestic function depends on sometimes seamless intergovernmental partnerships. President Bush's Initiative on Rural America attempted to reach across intergovernmental boundaries to improve rural life. Integrating human services requires coordinating national goals with state and local initiatives managed typically through nonprofit service providers.

INTERAGENCY BOUNDARIES. American democracy provides multiple avenues for addressing any problem. And since political support often depends on building constituencies for their programs, few government agencies can resist the temptation to broaden their scope and their political base. It is scarcely surprising therefore that many agencies may work on the same policy problems and that clear responsibility for solving them is often elusive. When the Bush administration's Rural Development Initiative surveyed federal agencies for those whose programs affected rural areas, virtually every agency had had relevant programs. The Defense Department had military bases, the Department of Energy research and weapons programs, the Education Department reading programs. Finding a room big enough to hold the forty-five members of the initiative's Monday Management Group that met biweekly to discuss program coordination was a regular challenge.

INTERPROGRAM BOUNDARIES. Even within a single government agency, managers frequently find themselves running programs with overlapping missions and customers. The Department of Health and Human Services has many programs dealing with children and many others focusing on the aging. Each has its supporters, especially in Congress and among interest groups, so program managers must respect its integrity. At the same time, if managers do not look past the program's boundaries for opportunities to coordinate, the people who are supposed to receive services might well face a bewilderment of government forms and programs to navigate.

INTERLEVEL BOUNDARIES. Informal boundaries among levels of the bureaucracy also matter. Talcott Parsons contended that three functions tend to emerge within bureaucracies: technical, managerial, and institutional.[18] Cases as different as the explosion of the space shuttle *Challenger* and problems in managing the Environmental Protection Agency's toxic waste contracts demonstrate that these functions produce important effects.[19] In each one, frictions among levels of the bureaucracy led directly to bad management and costly failures. Different cultures at different levels of the bureaucracy produce different kinds of behavior. Negotiating across these boundaries often proves a daunting challenge for managers.

Boundaries affecting government, especially administrative, institutions are thus many, complex, and changing. What happens at these boundaries plays a critical role in shaping the performance of government and its programs.

### Why Institutions Matter

The fundamental strength of the new governance movement is to diagnose profound antigovernment feeling and to recognize innovative solutions devised by innovative government workers. It focuses on relationships and how they can be improved. Its fundamental flaw is its failure to recognize the critical role that government institutions must play in securing the public interest. Government cannot simply assign to private markets or market incentives problems for which it bears primary responsibility. Government is not just one participant among others in a lively market; it is the participant vested with intrinsic responsibility for pursuing the public interest. Institutions produce the results and structure the fundamental political interactions that produce these results.[20] Welfare programs, for example, flow from the way federal, state, and local programs interact and the face they present to welfare recipients.

Given the tools of modern government, there are lots of interactions. By focusing on the behavior of institutions, the new institutionalism provides insights into the interactions among them. Institutions matter because they structure the relationships at these boundaries. "If governance results from the joint interaction of many different parts," Hugh Heclo argued, "the appropriate unit of analysis is the cluster of interrelated parts that produces the results by which we are governed."[21] The critical questions are which boundaries matter and why, what happens at these boundaries, and what can be done to minimize problems and promote success?

## The Problems of Boundaries

Organizational theorists have long recognized the importance of boundaries. Boundaries define the organization, what lies within its jurisdiction and responsibilities and what is outside. Boundaries are where organizations exchange inputs (such as tax dollars) for outputs (such as public programs). Boundaries are the critical site for communication, where organizations have to learn about what is happening outside, interpret the information, and decide what to do.[22] Such matters have always been important. But as government has come to depend more on partnerships to deliver its goods and services, as it has moved from retailing to wholesaling, new boundary problems have developed. It has found itself but one participant in complex interorganizational networks, with important implications.[23]

### Blurred Boundaries

As the government's reliance on partnerships has increased, the responsibilities of the members of the partnerships have become more indistinct. When the *Challenger* space shuttle exploded, was it the contractor who built the solid fuel engine or NASA officials who pressed for a timely launch who were responsible? When radioactive residues contaminated the land surrounding nuclear weapons plants, were the contractors or the Department of Energy responsible? And when perhaps a dozen different agencies provide assistance to needy families—local schools, medicaid with its combination of state and federal funding, county probation authorities, nonprofit day care centers, federally funded job training programs operated through private contractors, among many others—who is responsible for overseeing the whole to ensure that the family's needs, not the individual program pieces, receive primary attention?

Most government agencies have naturally overlapping responsibilities. In Kansas, at least seven federal and state agencies manage loan programs for rural areas. That reflects the genius of governance in the United States, which provides multiple channels of access to government programs and thereby minimizes the chances that people in need will not be helped. However, this pluralism often creates a bewildering array of service providers. To whom should a person turn to solve a problem? Discovering which agency's program is the most appropriate one to deal with the situation can be a confusing task. Simply finding the program's office and then reaching it during business hours can be challenging. People care far more about having their problems solved than who serves them or where. Thus meshing programs effectively can often work better than creating new programs.

### Uncertainty of Goals

The new governance movement seeks to force government to focus more on results. But public goals are manifold, conflicting, and vague, and focusing on results is hard when the purpose is fuzzy. This inevitable fact of government life makes it difficult for officials to manage for results because no one can agree on what a good result would look like. Boundary-spanning programs make it difficult for government officials to control the pursuit of results because achieving them depends more than ever before on interorganizational partnerships in which the government has, at best only loose control over its partners. The tremendous complexity of programs, from preventing AIDS to curing poverty and joblessness, adds another layer of difficulty, for some goals are not fully achievable. The task then is to decide what level of achievement is satisfactory, and there can never be agreement on that.

When goals are fuzzy, organizational arrangements complex, and the problems daunting, the predictable reaction of officials is to retreat to bureaucratic procedures as surrogates for focusing on results. If it is difficult to equip unemployed workers with the skills needed for the modern work force, it is at least possible to count the number who go through training programs. The new governance argues the need to measure outcomes carefully, but this has long been one of government's most daunting challenges. What to do? If goals and outcomes are uncertain, the government can try to do good by following generally accepted rules.[24] That becomes all the more important because its information collection and assessment have been decimated through budget and personnel cuts.[25]

A preoccupation with rules and procedures is, of course, precisely what the new governance reformers complain about. In fact, Osborne and Gaebler torpedoed the two leading government processes for monitoring outcomes: "The only thing more destructive than a line item budget system is a personnel system built around civil service."[26] Osborne has since accepted that the United States does need a civil service system "to protect public employees against political manipulation." He has concluded, however, that it does not need "the kind of civil service system most jurisdictions use today." Instead, he has argued for a less complex classification system, more flexibility in pay, and an end to the bumping of more junior by more senior employees when layoffs occur.[27] Too much emphasis on internal rules, the reformers contend, makes government too inner directed. The emphasis, in turn, deflects attention from the needs of people.

Obeisance to rules and procedures, in fact, is the strongest evidence of why the reformers believe that government too often seems to be in business for itself. Human services programs are regularly criticized for forcing clients to meet providers' procedures instead of having service providers work to serve clients' needs. Critics of state driver's license bureaus, and the critics are legion, comment caustically that people frequently have to take time off from work to fit the convenience of the motor vehicles department. Organization for efficiency can sometimes seem like organization for its own sake.

The administrative networks on which the government increasingly relies for delivering its goods and services add another layer of complexity. Personnel, budgetary, and other standard management systems are premised on the assumption of direct service delivery. The networks upset the assumption. Moreover, the procurement procedures specifically developed to manage suppliers often do not serve the government well. Frequently there is a preoccupation with creating and rewarding competition and too little attention on what results the competition produces.[28]

That leads to a paradox. The harder it is for government to define and monitor its goals, the more it retreats to procedural safeguards. The more it focuses on procedures, the further it seems from focusing on results and the more distant it can appear from citizens and their concerns. The upshot is great uncertainty about what government actually accomplishes and enormous difficulty in discerning results.

### Risk-Averse Behavior

Patterns of monitoring tend to drive bureaucrats away from what is needed to manage boundaries effectively. Elected policymakers steer clear of specific definitions of goals. Clear goals make it harder to agree on what ought to be done to begin with and easier later to hold everyone accountable. Vague and ambitious goals drive managers to close partnerships with other organizations, public, private, and nonprofit, to shape programs. Uncertain objectives lead them to concentrate on procedures instead of outcomes, yet focusing on procedures makes it hard to determine what programs actually accomplish. The pattern, in short, is for each participant to try to minimize risks. Such minimization, however, tends to rigidify the boundaries that have to be crossed if the programs are to be effective.

James March and Herbert Simon once argued that "increased internalization of rules" can increase "rigidity of behavior."[29] The multiplication of boundaries that comes with growing reliance on organizational networks increases ambiguity, risk, and rule centeredness. This, in turn, drives organizations away from what is needed to reach effectively across those boundaries. In monitoring federal community development grant programs, with all the ambiguity over goals that accompanied them, federal investigators

tended to make sure the files were well organized instead of prob-
ing to see what the programs actually accomplished.[30]

## Increasing Conflict

Such interdependent, loosely coupled systems are inevitably
contentious. Boundaries create risks as well as opportunities.
They multiply the possibilities for conflicts over turf and resources. The more organizations must deal with factors outside
their boundaries, the less they have control over things that
matter to them and the more conflicting and competing demands
surface.[31] Perhaps the most extreme example is the Department
of Energy, which is little more than a loose administrative shell
struggling to manage a huge contracting empire. At one facility,
there were just 200 DOE employees to oversee 7,000 contractor
employees. At least 80 percent of the department's budget was
spent through contractors.[32] What it accomplished depended ultimately on how well the contractors performed. Such interdependent systems sometimes create situations in which everyone loses. The DOE faced tough technical problems with no sure
solutions. At the same time, strong interdependence may have
increased everyone's stakes in everyone else's behavior, just as
the incentives for cooperation shrank.

## Blurred Accountability

The more everyone's stakes in everyone else's behavior increase,
the harder it is to determine in the end who is responsible for
what.[33] In short, who is in charge when everyone is in charge?
Shared responsibility is an imperative of modern administration, for
no organization can hope to assemble the expertise necessary to
manage complex programs. The pragmatic realities of the modern
state, however, gravely weaken traditional concepts of accountability. The Department of Energy might properly be held accountable
for the behavior of its contractors, but how can it hold them accountable if it is so heavily dependent on them for its information?

Such questions of accountability have the fullest meaning at
organizational boundaries. It is at the boundaries between organizations that the balance of power is set. It is at the boundaries that

mutual influence is exerted. It is, finally, at the boundaries that organizations weigh control and discretion.

## Boundary Spanners

The new governance and new institutionalism movements at first glance seem to move in opposite directions: the new governance gravitating away from institutions toward processes, the new institutionalism away from processes toward institutions. A recognition of the importance of organizational boundaries, however, points to the critical common ground. Institutions matter because of the boundaries they create. In increasingly interdependent governmental programs, developing new procedures to span these boundaries is the key to more effective and responsive government. Even more important is developing incentives for government employees to reach across these boundaries, building bridges to other organizations with shared missions and common goals, and helping citizens negotiate the system. It is the key, as well, to helping traditional bureaucracies adjust to an increasingly changeable world.

Gatekeepers stationed at organizational boundaries are critical for successful coordination.[34] They seek information that matters to an organization and its mission. They work to assemble the resources—money, personnel, and political power—so that it can do its job. They assess competing demands on the agency. They develop feedback and cultivate allies.[35] Government organizations, in particular, have been slow to recognize the boundary problem or to develop effective boundary spanners. Cultivation of problem solvers, like the Rural Development Initiative's Monday Management Group, are an important innovation, but such advancements lag considerably behind the galloping pace of organizational change within government.

If developing the people who can reach across boundaries is the first problem, building a language to communicate is the second. When responsibility is shared, what matters most is results. Spanning boundaries effectively requires that government managers first find a way of understanding their common mission.

The traditional approach is to view management as a production function, with goals defined, resources applied, and results judged. The proper place for public participation is, then, at the beginning, to shape the objectives. From there on, the expertise of government agencies is to produce results consistent with the goals. The problem, of course, is that this description bears little resemblance to reality. Goals are not defined clearly at the beginning; they take shape in the execution of public programs. In the administration of programs, members of the public want to be involved because they sense the importance of the decisions and they demand that the decisions reflect their views. The production function model breaks down even more when organizational partners are added and their behavior conditions the outcome even more than the goals set at the beginning.

Boundary spanning requires citizens to work actively with government managers to define what ought to be done, structure how it ought to be done, and assess what has been done. If the process cannot a priori fix goals so that outcomes can be clearly measured, the alternative is to create a process acceptable and open to all comers, on every boundary, at every stage of development. The process can incrementally define what is to be done, how it is to be done, and what has been done. Such a dynamic process is the prerequisite for rebuilding public trust and confidence in government. It is, a DOE task force concluded, "the critical manifestation of the consent that lies at the heart of our declaration of independence."[36] If developing boundary spanners within organizations is the first part of the answer to improving government performance, developing an open and dynamic process is the second.

Government, especially at the federal level, has moved from being a direct provider of services to being the arranger of services produced by a vast network of public, private, and nonprofit partners. To be sure, even the federal government does still manage some operations—air traffic control, criminal justice, and so forth. (Even in air traffic control, however, the Federal Aviation Administration depends heavily on its relationship with computer suppliers, and contractors have begun managing prisons in the United States.) Although the business of government has changed, however, it still largely operates as if it were a retail operation. Making government work better requires adapting it to its transformed mission. More employees need to be hired for their skills in managing contracts and negotiating with other agencies, for example. They need to be rewarded for reaching out to other agencies with shared missions instead of defensively protecting their own agencies. Indeed, it will even require some deregulation and reinventing of their jobs. Deregulating or reinventing government without adapting it to its new function, however, would be like trying to reorganize General Motors without taking account of the foreign-made cars that have flooded the American market. New challenges require new solutions, but they first require recognizing what the new challenges are.

Managing this transition especially requires strong support from top policymakers. The boundary-spanning function is ultimately little more than good old-fashioned problem solving: identifying impediments to performance, seeking those who can remove the impediments, and working to get them out of the way. The deregulating and reinventing movements come even more clearly into focus here. Together they emphasize that results are more important than processes and that unproductive processes must be swept aside. Aggressive problem solving and boundary spanning by lower-level officials, however, requires top officials to provide political cover to permit variations from standard operating procedures, to explain behavior to outside overseers and the public. But they must ensure at the same time that the agency's mission is its focus. Coping at the boundaries of government thus imposes substantial and novel burdens on top officials as well.

## Conclusion

The changing tools, processes, and problems of government have increased the interaction among the widely varying parts of the system. In multiplying the participants—public, private, and nonprofit—the interactions have increased the importance of, and tension at, the boundaries between them. Eliminating the boundaries is no answer; the complexities of modern problems and their solutions demand intense organizational interdependence. Rather, organizations must develop people who can span boundaries and work to solve the problems boundaries can generate. In addition dynamic processes must be developed to allow those affected by the programs to have their voices heard. Public trust and confidence in the process, and the effectiveness and responsiveness of the results, depend on it.

The new governance movement, from its neoconservative to its neoliberal variants, seeks to replace the old bureaucratic paradigm with a new one. Deregulation has sought the same thing from a different starting point. All these movements are clear on some of the problems they are trying to solve: government is not working well and it has lost the confidence of the American people. At a deeper level, however, the problems are far less well understood. Garry Wills has put the issue squarely. "It is catch-up time in our history, when government must not be so much reinvented as relegitimized. What vision does it serve? What mission does it have?"[37] Relegitimizing government requires first recognizing the most critical problem: the multiple boundaries across which modern government must work. Second, it requires identifying how these boundaries can be effectively managed: by cultivating boundary spanners within public organizations to reach across and solve the problems and by bringing all those affected into the process at every stage. Finally, it requires transforming government management to deal better with the change from retail to wholesale operations. That, in turn, creates critical new burdens for political leaders.

At its core, the reinventors and deregulators have rediscovered anew the folly of attempting to separate politics from administration. Across the boundaries that shape governmental performance, politics is the fact of life. Reenergizing politics so that it drives the interdependent networks toward a new definition of the public interest is the ulitmate key to relegitimizing government.

## Notes

1. David Osborne and Ted Gaebler, *Reinventing Government: How the Entrepreneurial Spirit Is Transforming the Public Sector* (Addison-Wesley, 1992).

2. The label is most closely associated with James P. Pinkerton. See "General Schwarzkopf's New Paradigm: Domestic Lessons of Desert Storm," *Policy Review*, no. 57 (Summer 1991), pp. 22–26.

3. See, for example, Steven Kelman, "The Renewal of the Public Sector," *American Prospect*, no. 2 (Summer 1990), pp. 51–57; Christopher Hood, "A Public Management for All Seasons?" *Public Administration*, vol. 69 (Spring 1991), pp. 3–19; and Michael Barzelay with Babak J. Armajani, *Breaking through Bureaucracy: A New Vision for Managing in Government* (University of California Press, 1992).

4. See DeWitt John and others, "What Will New Governance Mean for the Federal Government?" *Public Administration Review* (forthcoming).

5. I am indebted to a conversation with Brett Hammond for developing this idea.

6. Presidential Rural Development Initiative, Monday Management Group Expansion Task Force, *Reference Guide for State Rural Development Councils: The Initial Milestones* (Department of Agriculture, 1992).

7. National Rural Economic Development Institute, "Kansas Council Clears the Way for Rural Development Agency," University of Wisconsin-Extension/Madison, February 1993.

8. See Osborne and Gaebler, *Reinventing Government.*

9. Pinkerton, "General Schwarzkopf's New Paradigm," p. 22.

10. James P. Pinkerton, "Post-Modern Politics: The Search for a New Paradigm," speech to the Illinois New Paradigm Society, September 16, 1991.

11. For an analysis, see Jason Deparle, "How Jack Kemp Lost the War on Poverty," *New York Times Magazine,* February 28, 1993, especially pp. 48, 56.

12. See, for example, H. George Frederickson, "Painting Bull's-Eyes around Bullet Holes," *Governing,* vol. 6 (October 1992), p. 13; H. George Frederickson, "The City Manager Who Could Steer But Not Row," *PA Times,* vol. 16 (February 1, 1993), pp. 9, 12; Frank P. Sherwood, "Reinventing Government and Public Personnel," *PA Times,* vol. 15 (July 1, 1992), p. 5; and Charles T. Goodsell, "Reinvent Government or Rediscover It?" *Public Administration Review,* vol. 53 (January–February 1993), pp. 85–87.

13. Most notably, see Stephen Skowronek, *Building a New American State: The Expansion of National Administrative Capacities, 1877–1920* (Cambridge University Press, 1982); James G. March and Johan P. Olsen, "The New Institutionalism: Organizational Factors in Political Life," *American Political Science Review,* vol. 78 (September 1984), pp. 734–49; and March and Olsen, *Rediscovering Institutions: The Organizational Basis of Politics* (Free Press, 1989).

14. Pinkerton, "Post-Modern Politics."

15. See Murray L. Weidenbaum, *The Modern Public Sector: New Ways of Doing the Government's Business* (Basic Books, 1969); especially pp. 3–5; Frederick C. Mosher, "The Changing Responsibilities and Tactics of the Federal Government," *Public Administration Review,* vol. 40 (November–December 1980), pp. 541–48; Lester M. Salamon, "Rethinking Public Management: Third-Party Government and the Changing Forms of Government Action," *Public Policy,* vol. 29 (Summer 1981), pp. 255–75; Donald F. Kettl, *Government by Proxy: (Mis?)Managing Federal Programs* (Washington: Congressional Quarterly Press, 1988); and Kettl, *Sharing Power: Public Governance and Private Markets* (Brookings, 1993).

16. Gwen Ifill, "The Economic Czar behind the Economic Czars," *New York Times,* March 7, 1993, sec. 1., p. 22.

17. Examination of these issues began with Frederick C. Mosher, *The GAO: The Quest for Accountability in American Government* (Boulder, Colo.: Westview Press, 1979), pp. 236–37.

18. Talcott Parsons, *Structure and Process in Modern Societies* (Free Press, 1960), pp. 59–65.

19. See, for example, Barbara S. Romzek and Melvin J. Dubnick, "Accountability in the Public Sector: Lessons from the *Challenger* Tragedy," *Public Administra-*

*tion Review*, vol. 47 (May–June 1987), pp. 227–38; and Kettl, *Sharing Power*, especially chaps. 5, 6.

20. March and Olsen, *Rediscovering Institutions*, pp. 16–19.

21. Hugh Heclo, "An Executive's Success Can Have Costs," in Lester M. Salamon and Michael S. Lund, eds., *The Reagan Presidency and the Governing of America* (Washington: Urban Institute Press, 1985), p. 374.

22. See, for example, James G. March and Herbert A. Simon, *Organizations* (John Wiley, 1958), especially pp. 161–71; Parsons, *Structure and Process in Modern Societies*, pp. 18, 74–78; and Michael L. Tushman, "Special Boundary Roles in the Innovation Process," *Administrative Science Quarterly*, vol. 22 (December 1977), pp. 587–605.

23. On interorganizational networks in general, see Howard E. Aldrich, *Organizations and Environments* (Prentice-Hall, 1979), chaps. 8–12. On the specific implications for public management, see H. Brinton Milward, Keith G. Provan, and Barbara Else, "What Does the Hollow State Look Like?" in Barry Bozeman, ed., *Public Management Theory: The State of the Art* (San Francisco: Jossey-Bass, 1993).

24. For an examination of different kinds of accountability, see Barbara S. Romzek and Melvin J. Dubnick, "Issues of Accountability in Flexible Personnel Systems," in Patricia W. Ingraham and Barbara S. Romzek, *Governance and the Public Service: Rethinking Change in Public Organizations* (San Francisco: Jossey-Bass, forthcoming).

25. General Accounting Office, *Federal Evaluation: Fewer Units, Reduced Resources, Different Studies from 1980*, PEMD-87-9 (January 1987).

26. Osborne and Gaebler, *Reinventing Government*, p. 124.

27. David Osborne, "Civil Service Reform: Is It Really That Complicated?" *Governing*, vol. 6 (April 1993), p. 80.

28. See Kettl, *Sharing Power*; and John D. Donahue, *The Privatization Decision: Public Ends, Private Means* (Basic Books, 1989).

29. March and Simon, *Organizations*, p. 39. See also Paul Shrivastava and Susan Schneider, "Organizational Frames of Reference," *Human Relations*, vol. 37 (October 1984), pp. 801–04.

30. Donald F. Kettl, *The Regulation of American Federalism* (Louisiana State University Press, 1983).

31. Jeffrey Pfeffer and Gerald R. Salancik, *The External Control of Organizations: A Resource Dependence Perspective* (Harper and Row, 1978), p. 37.

32. Senate Committee on Governmental Affairs, *Oversight of the Structure and Management of the Department of Energy: Staff Report*, 96 Cong. 2 sess. (December 1980), p. 310.

33. Mosher, *GAO*, p. 237.

34. Tushman, "Special Boundary Roles in the Innovation Process," pp. 591–92; and Richard L. Daft and George P. Huber, "How Organizations Learn: A Communication Framework," *Research in the Sociology of Organizations*, vol. 5 (1987), pp. 5–6.

35. Gary L. Wamsley and Mayer N. Zald, *The Political Economy of Public Organizations: A Critique and Approach to the Study of Public Administration* (Lexington, Mass.: Lexington Books, 1973), p. 59.

36. Secretary of Energy Advisory Board Task Force on Radioactive Waste Management, *Earning Public Trust and Confidence: Requisites for Managing Radioactive Waste* (June 1993), p. 2.

37. Garry Wills, "Can Clinton Close the Vision Gap?" *New York Times*, November 8, 1992, sec. 4, p. 17.

# 10 | Policing: Deregulating or Redefining Accountability?

Mark H. Moore

OVER the past decade, many of the nation's leading law enforcement practitioners and analysts have come to support the general ideas of community-based policing, and scores of jurisdictions have tried some form of it. Yet, despite the widespread enthusiasm, community-based policing remains more an aspiration than a reality. One major but often overlooked reason is that it requires changes in administrative ideas and operations that are inherently difficult to make and incredibly hard to sustain. Community-based policing means at least two things: bringing police officers and citizens into working partnerships at the neighborhood level and giving the police responsibility for identifying and solving neighborhood problems even if they are not conventional law enforcement matters. Thus traditional command-and-control forms of police organization must give way to forms that are less centralized, less rule-oriented, and less regulation-bound. Deregulation may well be the key to community-based policing.

In the analysis that follows, I will not dwell on community-based policing itself. Rather, my account of the administrative evolution of police bureaucracies will provide a window on deregulation and other reform strategies. Deregulation is a key to the development of community-based or kindred forms of policing, but only if deregulation means not merely mechanical changes in personnel and procurement procedures, flattened hierarchies, and the like, but also fundamental, discretion-enhancing changes in how police and other public servants define and act upon their accountability to the public. This vision of deregulation extends not only to police and other bureaucrats who interact directly and personally with the public but also to technical personnel, senior officials, and other office-bound bureaucrats who have minimal direct and personal interaction with the public. I am relatively optimistic that deregulation in the service of fostering community-based policing is both desirable and possible. But there are no easy answers: this kind of policing demands a major shift not only in conventional ideas about law enforcement but also in conventional ideas about public bureaucracy.

## Public Administration and Police Management

Long ago Max Weber observed that the essential, defining quality of a state was its monopoly over the legitimate use of force.[1] In doing so, he put police administration at the center of public administration, for it is through the operations of the police that the state enacts this defining quality.[2] The badge, the nightstick, and the gun are both the symbols and the tools of state authority, and it is municipal police departments that are supplied such instruments.

Because police administration is so closely tied to the defining purposes of the state, it follows that if there is something distinctive about public administration, it will show up in the theory and practice of police administration.[3] Police administration will necessarily have to express those special qualities, and so, I think, it does.

Because police use state authority so extensively, police departments are under enormous pressure to be accountable, to explain and justify their actions to citizens and their representatives. The police do so partly by making practical and instrumental arguments: they point to the urgency of controlling crime, their success in doing so, and the crucial role that state authority plays in helping them.

But the police must also justify their actions by making principled claims about the fairness and propriety with which they operate. They must be able to show that they enforce laws fairly and impartially as well as effectively and that they use their substantial powers to detain, investigate, and subdue properly, that is, only when warranted and only to the degree necessary.

Finally, because police can restrain freedom, intrude into private life, damage reputations, and even injure and kill in pursuit of their law enforcement objectives, and because they often must act in ambiguous circumstances without the benefit of supervision, counsel, or time to think, an enormous premium is placed on avoiding errors. They, more than many other public employees, must live up to a standard of "zero tolerance."

The persistent demands that the police be accountable for achieving important social results, operate fairly and properly, and avoid mistakes have caused police managers to adopt particular practices long viewed as the most effective devices for controlling officers and the aggregate performance of their organizations. These management doctrines were originally prescribed by Max Weber and then defended and further developed by Frederick Taylor.[4]

At their core is the claim that managers can achieve efficiency, fairness, and high degrees of perfection in operations by developing extensive written rules to control the behavior of operating-level officials.[5] To ensure efficiency and effectiveness, the rules should be based on the best available technical knowledge in the field. To ensure control and fairness, the rules should be complete and comprehensive, covering all situations that the officials can be expected to encounter.

Of course, these theorists knew that the rules were not self-executing. To ensure that the rules would be followed consistently, managers were instructed to establish clear lines of authority and accountability. In addition, narrow spans of control would ensure close supervision of operating-level officials. Extensive investment in training, ideally before officials began their jobs, would be necessary to equip and motivate them to do their jobs properly and effectively. And there would be strict accountability and punishment for any wrongdoing or corruption.

To avoid corruption, it was also important to organize operations to prevent low-level officials from getting too close to their clients lest they develop personal relationships that would bias their handling of individual cases. For the police, technology was enlisted to support the goals of reducing personal contact, ensuring equal access, and providing close supervision. By building an elaborate communication system that linked citizens to police officers through telephones and radio-controlled dispatching, police managers broke the close links between individual beat officers and citizens that had characterized the early days of policing (and fostered no small amount of favoritism and corruption). These arrangements also allowed all citizens to have immediate access to the police department and enabled those at the center of the department to monitor the activities of individual patrol officers.

Thus police departments were initially conceived, and subsequently developed, as classic bureaucracies. They took this form partly to achieve effectiveness in accomplishing their mission. Just as important was ensuring that police exercised public authority uniformly, fairly, and impersonally—the defining attributes of public enterprises. It is in the field of police administration, then, that one should expect to find the strongest commitment to traditional theories of public administration and management and the greatest resistance to change. And, to some degree, that is the case.

What makes consideration of police administration so important to any exploration of the case for deregulating the public service and adopting alternative approaches is that the revolution in managerial thought is beginning to make inroads even in this most traditional of public bureaucracies. If, as Melvin Dubnick argues in chapter 12, deregulation and other contemporary approaches to reform share the goal of dethroning King Bureaucracy, then to reform police bureaucracies is to effect a coup against one of the oldest and mightiest kings of all.

In policing, as in other fields of public administration, there are compelling reasons to be interested in "deregulating the public service," developing a "customer service" orientation, or "reinventing" government organizations. And these pressures have begun to spawn important managerial changes in police departments. Partly it is the pursuit for increased effectiveness that motivates the changes. As the police have been held accountable for achieving substantive results as well as merely enforcing the law as fairly and impartially as they can, and as research has revealed the weakness of some of their methods, managers have attempted to change both the ends and means of their organizations.[6]

But an important source of change is also increasing doubt about the success of the traditional methods for producing disciplined, high-quality organizations. It is no longer clear that police organizations can be free of error, corruption, and brutality by applying tighter rules, closer supervision, and stricter penalties for misconduct. Indeed, this bureaucratic apparatus increasingly looks like an expensive way to produce the form but not the substance of a disciplined, effective force.[7] Thus the changes in police administration mark the depth of the discontent with the traditional models of public administration.

It is by no means clear yet where the current revolution in policing will go. Nor is it clear that the new forms of organization and control will be more effective than those of the past. Yet it does seem clear that those interested in public management might learn a great deal about the limits and possibilities of new forms of public administration by looking closely at the changes now sweeping through policing. More important, this might reveal why deregulation, customer service, and reinvention are, at best, imperfect slogans for identifying the true nature of the managerial work that must be done to improve the performance and credibility of public sector organizations.

Specifically, my research on police management suggests that to deregulate the public service makes sense only if the concept of deregulation encompasses working to change the terms under which public sector organizations and workers are held accountable.[8] The demand for accountability in public organizations will continue to be strong, and managers' abilities to satisfy that demand will be an important mark of their talents. But what is needed is a wider recognition of the role that senior managers of public enterprises can and should play in shaping the terms of their own accountability. As James Q. Wilson argues in chapter 3, managers ought to be authorized to take the initiative in negotiating the terms of their accountability with their political overseers and in introducing important innovations into their organization. What I have in mind is not mechanical deregulation (fewer rules, more flexible procedures, less procurement hassles). Rather, it is better conceived as changing the *form* that the continued regulation takes.

My research also leads me to the view that the "customers" of the police organization are not simply the "clients" who call on the organization for services or are exposed to its efforts to impose public responsibilities on individuals. The customers are also taxpayers and their representatives who may be seen as having a collective view of what the organization ought to be producing and what particular features of the organization's performance would indicate quality.[9] These overseers, evaluating organizations in terms of whether they embody some idealized general conception of how they should operate, are in many ways the most important customers.

These observations do not apply only to police organizations. Although policing may be an extreme case in terms of the prominence with which public authority is used, the police are similar to all public organizations in at least one crucial respect: by definition, *all* public enterprises rely on the use of public authority.[10] This is most obvious in the case of the police and other similar organizations such as regulatory and tax-collecting agencies that impose obligations on citizens rather than provide services. But even public organizations such as welfare or public health agencies that provide services to their clients do so with the benefit of public authority. After all, public authority was used to raise the money to support their operations and provide the benefits they dispense. To the extent that special concerns for propriety and fairness attach to any use of public resources, then, these organizations too will have something important in common with police departments.

## The Classic Theory of Police Administration

For the past two generations, a well-developed, coherent concept that defined important ends, programs, and administrative arrangements has guided the management of police organizations.[11] The concept is so powerful that it has produced a remarkable degree of homogeneity among municipal police departments despite the fact that 17,000 independent departments now exist across the country.[12]

### Professional Law Enforcement

In the traditional conception the fundamental purpose of municipal police departments is to enforce the law and to do so in a professional way. What *professional* means in this context is using the best available technical practices and doing so in accord with the laws of the society.[13] Of course, there has always been some ambiguity about what particular laws are to be enforced.

When municipal police departments were developed at the turn of the century, there were a great many laws on the books. Some were traditional common law prohibitions against murder, rape, robbery, and burglary, but others were municipal ordinances prohibiting "offenses against public order" such as swearing, spitting, and littering. Initially, municipal police departments accepted the responsibility for enforcing all these laws. Gradually, however, the police narrowed their focus to enforcing the most important criminal laws.[14] They did so for three reasons.

First, it seemed economical to give the highest priority to the most serious crimes. The pressures on police forces to provide adequate security to urban residents grew rapidly throughout the 1950s and 1960s, but resources did not keep pace, so something had to give. The natural response was to deemphasize the offenses against public order to conserve resources to deal with crimes that caused serious victimization.

Second, enforcement efforts focused on offenses against public order had always enjoyed less legitimacy and public support than efforts against the common law street crimes. Many had doubted the wisdom of using criminal laws and scarce criminal justice resources to regulate minor disorders and "crimes without victims."[15] And to enforce these laws the police often had to act proactively.[16] This left room for police biases to be expressed. Police statistics showed that the poor and the ethnic minorities bore the brunt of such enforcement efforts. The enforcement of public morality laws also led to corruption.[17] Thus in reducing their emphasis on offenses against order, the police could not only save resources but avoid a great deal of unwanted criticism.

Third, the development of the Federal Bureau of Investigation's unified crime reports had the unintended consequence of encouraging concentration on common law crimes. The reports required local police departments to record crimes in categories that cut across the diverse criminal codes of the different states and defined different kinds of crime in a consistent way. The aim of the system was to aggregate these individual reports into an overall picture of the crime problem confronting the nation.[18] Seven crimes were singled out as part I offenses: murder, rape, robbery, aggravated assault, burglary, car theft, and arson. All the other offenses (including many offenses against public order) were relegated to the status of part II offenses. Eventually, the reports, particularly changes in the frequency of part I offenses, began to be used to measure the performance of police departments as well as to portray the national crime problem. Inevitably, these evaluations focused the attention of police managers and police officers on the common law crimes.

As the municipal police function developed, so did a body of law that sought to regulate the conduct of the police as well as that of citizens. This body emerged from interpretations by the Supreme Court of what constitutional protections against unwarranted search and seizure or cruel and unusual punishment actually meant in the operational context of policing.[19] The police were ordered, for example, to abandon coercive methods for gaining confessions, to obtain warrants for conducting certain kinds of searches, and to warn those arrested of their constitutional rights.[20] When the judiciary became dissatisfied with police compliance with the laws regulating searches, they made illegally obtained evidence inadmissible in court.[21] More recently, citizens have used civil laws to hold police officers liable for violations of civil liberties when they overstep constitutional limits regulating their use of authority.[22]

Predictably, the police have never embraced this body of law as enthusiastically as the laws that regulate the conduct of others. Yet law enforcement agencies are duty-bound to enforce it both in principle and in practice. And agencies inside and outside police departments bring these laws to bear on individual officers.[23]

Thus although police organizations like to describe themselves as law enforcement organizations, the particular laws they are committed to enforcing are not all the laws, but a fairly narrow set—those that prohibit common law crimes. The laws that regulate conduct in public locations have been deemphasized as less important and more difficult to enforce. The laws regulating police conduct have tended to be viewed as constraints that handcuff police efforts to accomplish their real mission: enforcing criminal law. Thus the goal of the police is not, strictly speaking, law enforcement, but using the criminal law to control crime and punish serious criminal offenders.

## Patrol, Rapid Response, and Retrospective Investigation

To control crime, the police have developed three primary tactics: patrol, rapid response, and retrospective investigation of crimes.[24]

From the very beginning, police in Anglo-Saxon countries relied extensively on patrol.[25] The basic idea was that if they could field a lookout force, offenders would be deterred from committing crimes, crimes in progress would be thwarted, and criminal offenders would be caught quickly and brought to justice. In the early days this function was performed by constables, night watchmen, and foot patrol officers. The advent of motorized vehicles, however, greatly increased the enthusiasm for patrol. Police theorists hoped that the new mobility would create a sense of omnipresence that would dramatically improve the deterrent value of patrol.[26] Modern police began patrolling city streets in automobiles and on motorcycles.

Much of this patrol was random, one virtue of which was that unpredictable patterns would allow the police to magnify their deterrent impact. Randomness also ensured a kind of equity, or at least the absence of a bias, in the allocation of patrol efforts. Everyone would have an equal chance of having a patrol car pass by.

Gradually, however, randomness gave way to an interest in directed patrol. At the most general level, this was reflected in the development of hazard systems that recorded when and where crimes occurred or calls from service were originated. These were used to define the geographic sectors that needed intensive patrol and to shape police work schedules.[27] More particularly, directed patrol allowed officers to concentrate in very small areas where crimes seemed particularly likely to occur. Most commonly, these patrols were directed toward particular times and places, but occasionally they were focused on individuals who were thought particularly likely to commit offenses.[28]

Rapid response emerged from the development of motorized patrol and of dense modern communication systems. Once citizens could be linked to police headquarters through telephones and headquarters could communicate with individual officers through two-way radios, a mobile police patrol suddenly became capable of responding quickly to citizens' calls for service. The apotheosis of these developments has been the citywide 911 systems and the computer-aided dispatch systems, which together have made it possible for a police car to arrive at virtually any location in any city in less than five minutes after receiving a call.

This capability, like the patrol capability, was thought to be particularly valuable in deterring criminal offenders, thwarting crimes, and allowing the police to identify and apprehend offenders.[29] Indeed, it extended the potential reach of police from public locations that they could see from their cars to private spaces being monitored by ordinary citizens. Heavy investments were made in rapid response capability because it seemed sure to be effective in controlling crime and producing arrests.

Retrospective investigation of crimes, like patrol, had long been part of the basic operational repertoire of the police. Once a crime had been committed, it was important to identify the offender and develop evidence to support the prosecution. The basic tools of criminal investigation had always included such procedures as interviewing victims and witnesses to help identify the offender and examining physical evidence associated with the crime. Fingerprint identification and extensive information systems that identified offenders and their favorite methods of operation gradually evolved to support criminal investigation.

To a great degree, it was detectives and the prospects for ever more sophisticated methods of solving crime that came to be the focus of policing's aspirations for a technical kind of professionalism. There were some important technical features of patrol, including the development of sophisticated communications equipment, and there was an emerging interest in traffic management that brought analytic methods to bear on preventing traffic accidents. But it was in criminal investigation that most of the technical, professional aspirations of the police lay. It was there that science could best be applied to making arrests and bringing offenders to justice.

### Bureaucratic Mechanisms of Control

The organizational structures and bureaucratic systems established to support these operational tactics have several important and distinctive characteristics. First, from the outset, the police were organized in highly centralized, paramilitary structures with a well-defined and highly visible chain of command. Police officers were distributed across formally defined ranks. Those in higher ranks were authorized to direct the activities of those in lower ranks. Uniforms displayed the rank of the officers so that everyone would know who could give an order and who had to obey.

The paramilitary form may have been adopted for policing for no deeper reason than that it was available to copy. But it also seemed to be consistent with some important functions the police had to perform. Although most police work is undertaken by relatively small units operating independently, sometimes the police do have to form up into larger units to accomplish their goals. This was particularly important in the early days of policing when they were called upon to handle large-scale disturbances.[30] It remains important today not only to deal with such disturbances but also to coordinate other complex tasks such as managing high-speed pursuits or responding to floods, earthquakes, and other civil emergencies.

The paramilitary form also seemed to ensure effective control over the conduct of officers and thereby to guarantee a consistent response to individual cases. Fixing accountability and providing for intensive, close supervision enhanced the prospects for discipline and fairness. The aim was to reduce individual discretion by making everyone in the organization nothing more than an expression of the will of the person at the top. The will of that person was expressed in the organization's general orders, policies, and procedures.

A second feature of the structures used to manage police departments was functional rather than geographic subdivisions. In the early days of policing, departments were often organized on a geographic basis, with the different functions, such as patrol and investigation, subordinated to geographically defined units. Because all the police functions reported to local precinct commanders, they became the functional equivalent of police chiefs for their local areas. This, in turn, fostered close relationships with locally based political machines, economic elites, and gangsters who could go to the local captain to get what they needed. That, in turn, fostered uneven law enforcement and corruption.[31]

To break the power of the local political machines and ensure a more uniform enforcement of the laws across a city, police departments gradually evolved into functional organizations. Now municipal departments are typically divided into a patrol force, a detective unit, and an administrative support unit.[32] The patrol force is usually divided into geographic areas, but the detective and administrative units have citywide jurisdictions.

The result of these changes is that local groups can no longer manipulate all the police resources operating in their areas. If they want the police force as a whole to help them out, they must speak to the chief rather than just to the precinct commander. The chief, in turn, can resist their demands by talking to them about the overall policies and needs of the city as a whole.

Functional organization also aligns with the professional aspirations of the police: functional specialties recognize, and allow the development of, technical expertise. Detective and administrative divisions house many units that require special training and qualifications to join. This also helps create career tracks inside police departments that allow aspiring officers to move out of uniformed patrol and enjoy the greater discretion and prestige that go with the department's more specialized operations.

A third bureaucratic characteristic is that because police departments are centralized, hierarchical, and obsessed with maintaining control over the activities of the officers, an enormous amount of paperwork must be done to document the organization's activities. Reports must be filed every time the police respond to an incident, every time an arrest is made or evidence seized, and every time an officer fires or even unholsters a gun. This extensive demand for paper is judged necessary to maintain effective internal discipline, support the processing of cases in the rest of the criminal justice system, and make police operations transparent to the outside world.

A fourth bureaucratic characteristic is a sustained effort over the past several decades to raise the eligibility standards for recruits and increase the amount of training they receive before they hit the streets. In earlier days the police were recruited from the ranks of the uneducated and the less industrious. Indeed, a third of the London police force was dismissed for drunkenness or sleeping on the job in the first few years of its operation.[33] But as recognition of the importance and complexity of the police job has increased and as the technical requirements of the job have grown, the police have sought to set the standards for recruitment much higher and to provide more training.[34] All departments now require that applicants have a high school diploma and a clean arrest record. Many require some college education. Similarly, most departments now provide a minimum of nine weeks of training before officers go onto the street.[35] The training focuses on understanding the law and mastering some of the technical arts of policing such as handling a radio, high-speed driving, and learning when and how to use a service revolver.

### Bureaucratic Systems, Values, and Behaviors

Reflection on the way the police have defined their mission, developed their core technologies, and administered their organizations suggests the values that have guided the development of police departments and some important tensions among them.

It is surprising to many to see how greatly the police have been shaped by the concern for embodying legal virtues such as economizing on the use of the criminal law, preserving privacy, and ensuring consistency and fairness in law enforcement. This is perhaps most evident in modern policing's reliance on patrol, rapid response, and retrospective investigation. What is remarkable about these particular tactics is how superficial and reactive they are. Patrol skims over the surface of social life, regulating only public spaces. The police may probe more deeply into social affairs when circumstances or citizens invite them in and warrant their scrutiny. But it is only when citizens call, or only when a crime has been discovered, that the police really intervene and look closely into individuals and their activities. Vast areas of private life are thus shielded from public scrutiny.

Concern for protecting legal values is also evident in extensive efforts to ensure precision and consistency in the police department's response to individual circumstances. That is what fuels the interest in written policies, in hierarchies and close supervision, and in training. Respect for fairness and equity is also evident in the development of citywide 911 systems and the use of hazard formulas to allocate police resources. All this helps a department claim that it is equally available to all and that it polices a city equitably as well as effectively.

Of course, many of these features could also be justified by their contribution to economy and effectiveness as well as fairness. It is economical as well as protective of privacy to wait until a crime occurs before responding to it; otherwise police would waste a great deal of effort on situations that would not become criminal offenses. Hierarchies are efficient because they ensure that everyone in the department uses the best available knowledge for dealing with problems. Allocating patrol forces to places where trouble occurs is effective as well as consistent with the principle of allocating to need rather than wealth or status.

However, any fair reading of the development of policing would have to recognize that police departments have been powerfully shaped by the demand for propriety and fairness as well as for economy and effectiveness. Even though the police often talk as though their only important objective was controlling crime and they chafe against legal restrictions, it is clear that they are a legal as well as an instrumental enterprise.

A sharper and less easily resolved tension in the organization and operation of police departments concerns the status of individual police officers. On one hand, administrative arrangements reflect a determined effort to dampen the initiative and discretion of individual patrol officers, to turn them into neutral functionaries who administer the law in a technically sophisticated but completely neutral and unbiased way. On the other hand, there is a trend toward recognizing the independent, professional stature of officers, which is apparent in the efforts to raise eligibility standards, insist on more education, and recognize different kinds of expertise in the functional organization of the departments.

In the past, police control systems have blunted professional aspirations, and limited progress has been made in increasing entry standards and educational efforts. To many both inside and outside the profession, policing remains—in its organizational form and its recruiting patterns—a blue-collar occupation. Yet research is gradually revealing what common sense has long held true: much about the actual practice of policing requires a high degree of professionalism. The tasks police encounter are technically complex.[36] The decisions they make are critical to the lives of citizens. And, despite the strenuous effort to keep them under close supervision, they do most of their work unsupervised. That is particularly true when it comes to their most consequential decisions—to pursue or not, arrest or not, shoot or not.[37] In these respects, then, society depends on the professionalism of the individual officers. It is also clear that the officers aspire to professionalism. For a generation, they have sought to increase their own professional standing, partly by working hard to increase the technical content of the jobs and partly by increasing the educational standards for admission to the force.

Whether the balance in attitudes toward police officers should continue to be struck as it has in the past is one of the crucial questions facing today's police managers. What has been true, however, is that police managers, acting with the encouragement of the broader society, have tended to view police officers as having more potential to cause trouble than to make significant contributions on their own.

## Toward a New Strategy of Policing

A different way of thinking about the police has recently emerged, mainly but not solely in connection with the community-based policing movement.[38] This conception is guided less by principles of law and more by concepts designed to help managers maximize their organizations' value to local communities.[39] These new ideas about policing are based on both a general theory of public sector management and a particular application to the field of policing.

### Strategic Management: A New Theory

The general theory of public sector management adapts the concept of private sector corporate strategy to the special environment of the public sector.[40] The idea is that the management of a public enterprise should be guided by an overall strategic concept, and that for a particular strategic idea to be useful and valuable, it must meet three conditions.[41]

First, the strategy must define a mission, or a set of goals and objectives, that is plausibly valuable to the public. There must be a rationale that explains why society should launch or maintain the enterprise. A claim that some people will benefit must include an explanation of why those people are particularly deserving. Perhaps the organization exists to solve a problem that society perceives as pressing and important, or to erase some kind of inequity, or to exploit an opportunity for public benefit. There must be something that citizens of a society could reasonably value.

Second, the goals and objectives that define the mission of the organization (and therefore the value that the enterprise seeks to produce) must be able to summon support and enjoy legitimacy from citizens and their representatives who oversee the organization's operations. This includes those elected to the executive and legislative branches of government and the media, interest groups, and professional associations that influence these groups. It also includes the clients and customers of the organization.[42] The articulated goals of the enterprise must meet not only a theoretical, substantive test of public value but also a practical, political test.

Third, for a given strategy to be useful, the enterprise must have (or be able to develop) the operational capabilities to achieve the desired objectives. This does not imply that all the capacity to produce the result must exist within the boundaries of the organization charged with implementing the strategy. That would be rare in the public sector, for the success of public enterprises often depends on many individuals and organizations outside the boundaries of a given organization. For example, children cannot be taught to read if parents do not help; rivers cannot be cleaned if companies do not participate in cleaning up; and the streets cannot be made safe if communities do not help defend themselves.

At some level, this concept of an organizational strategy is a fairly trivial idea. All it says is that to be valuable, public enterprises must pursue valuable purposes that are widely supported and can be achieved. What could be more obvious? Several considerations make this idea useful and important despite its self-evident quality, however.

First, it focuses managers' attention on the problem of making sure that *all* these different conditions are, in fact, met. This is important because it is tempting for managers to think that they can succeed if they have lined up one or two of the required conditions. If only they have the right objective, the rightness of their cause will ensure their success. Or, if there is broad political support for a goal, they are safe because the technical means for accomplishing the goal will surely come to hand.

The stern reality, however, is that managers must touch all three bases if they are going to succeed. Imagine what happens when one is missing one of the key elements of the strategy. If one has an attractive goal and political support for it, one can still fail if it is impossible to achieve the goal. And if one has an attractive goal and the capacity to achieve it, but no one supports the goal anymore, the enterprise will also fail.

Most public managers will testify that it is very difficult to meet these three conditions. It is even harder to sustain the effort long enough to make the investments in operational capacities that are necessary for success. Thus the idea is less than trivial because it forces a hard-nosed evaluation of circumstances and establishes a rigorous test that disciplines managerial aspirations.

This simple strategic concept is also a reminder that ideas about what would be worth doing can come from various places.[43] The traditional theory of public administration assumes that public enterprises operate with legislative mandates that define the specific public purposes to be achieved and provide the authority and money to do the job. In such a world, all the manager must do is deploy the resources provided in the most efficient and effective ways: two parts of the strategic triangle (gaining legitimacy and support and defining purposes) can be safely ignored. The manager's attention can be focused downward on the operational management of the enterprise, rather than upward to the political environment that authorizes the organization to continue or outward to visions of the value that could be created or the opportunities that could be exploited.

If one takes the concept of strategy in the public sector seriously, however, one must recognize that ideas about what would be worth doing could be initiated by managers, who could receive them from many different places. For example, the organization's own experience in trying to do its work could reveal an unexpected problem that needs to be dealt with, an unexpected limitation in the organization's methods, or an opportunity that could be exploited. The manager might nominate those ideas for new action to those who authorize the enterprise. Or parts of the organization's political environment could become alarmed that the organization was sacrificing some important value and might insist that it change its operations. For example, the police, although effective in controlling crime, might be perceived as becoming corrupt. The manager could respond creatively to this emergent problem.

Perhaps the most interesting case, however, would be one in which the manager of a public enterprise notices that the organization has developed a capacity that is valuable in a use other than the organization's original purpose and that it would be relatively easy to adapt the organization to this new use. Thus, for example, a library might turn out to be valuable in caring for latchkey children, or a drug abuse treatment program helpful in controlling crime, or the U.S. Marine Corps useful in training delinquent youth to be accountable and responsible. The manager might propose this new use of the organization to its political overseers.

This response is particularly interesting because it is much closer to the way private managers think than the way public managers do.[44] Because public managers have mandates that define their purposes and provide them with resources, there is little incentive to work outside the boundaries of their mission. Indeed, it would be a distraction. Public sector managers are constrained as to ends and accountable for finding efficient means. Private sector managers think differently. They are free to pursue any enterprise that seems valuable. Consequently, they often begin by looking at the capabilities of their organizations and then ask what of value could be produced. Private sector managers are constrained as to means and free to define their ends.

There are other interesting features of the idea of strategy in the public sector, but it is enough for now to have introduced these four: managers in the public sector should try to manage their organizations by thinking about an overall strategy; the strategy should define a mission or purpose that is publicly valuable, politically sustainable, and operationally achievable; these three conditions must all be met concretely for the strategy to be useful and valuable; and a manager can begin thinking about what is worth doing from any of the three perspectives. This strategic conception can be used to contrast traditional and emerging strategies of policing.

### Limitations of the Traditional Strategy

The traditional conception of policing has served as an enormously powerful and successful strategic concept. It has earned the police widespread public support.[45] It has carried policing from ridicule, incompetence, and corruption to an image (and, to a considerable degree, the reality) of discipline and professionalism. Yet some cracks are now appearing in this formidable pillar of police administration.

First, it is no longer clear that this strategy can succeed in eliminating police misconduct and corruption. Recent beatings by police in Los Angeles and Detroit testify to the limited success of the current administrative tools for preventing the misuse of force.[46] The reemergence of corruption in the New York City Police Department, despite the department's aggressive administrative efforts to minimize bribery, suggests the limitations of the traditional methods of controlling corruption.[47]

A second weakness is that the strategy has done less to control crime and still citizens' fears than was initially hoped. Levels of violent crime have continued to increase as this strategy was being adopted and implemented across the United States. Fear seems to have increased even more sharply.[48]

Third, to the extent that the popularity of the traditional strategy of policing rests on the claim that the police alone can succeed in reducing crime and fear, it has been founded on a dubious claim. Decades ago, experiments revealed that motorized patrol was essentially ineffective in reducing crime or reassuring citizens. When patrols in an area were doubled or halved, neither criminals nor citizens could seem to tell the difference. Both crimes and citizens' fears remained at the same level. Studies of directed patrol operations—some directed at locations, others at people—produced the same results: minimal or no effects on crime or levels of fear.[49]

Fourth, numerous studies have undermined confidence in the value of rapid response. It had always been assumed (not at all unreasonably) that getting calls for service more quickly would allow the police to thwart crimes in progress, catch offenders, and help establish a sense of omnipresence that would deter offenders and reassure citizens. Studies of rapid response have revealed, however, that this capacity, too, seems ineffective in reducing crime, increasing apprehensions, or reassuring citizens.[50]

The studies have also revealed the reasons. The overall response time is composed of several components, including the interval between the time when the crime occurs and when it is reported, as well as the interval between when the crime is reported and when the police arrive on the scene.[51] The studies showed that the police have become very successful in arriving soon after they receive the call. But the crucial time interval is the one between the crime's occurrence and the reception of the call. Many crimes occur out of the sight of witnesses. Even when they are within sight, witnesses often do not recognize that a crime is occurring until after the fact or they hesitate to call. The victims are too busy being victimized to call. Indeed, their first call often goes to a friend or relative with whom they can share their pain. The result is that the police rush to crime scenes not to thwart the crime or apprehend the offender but to hold the hand of the victim. That may also be important, but it is not the result the police intend.

The fifth blow to traditional policing strategy came when studies focusing on the investigative function indicated that the police could usually solve crimes only when witnesses and victims told them who committed the offense.[52] The sophisticated forensic methods have proved more valuable in nailing down a case for prosecution than in actually identifying the offenders.

Some observers have interpreted these accumulating studies as indicating that the core police programs for controlling crime have been ineffective. A more accurate view, however, would be that the effectiveness of traditional policing strategies depends on the amount of trust and cooperation the police receive from citizens. The police know this, of course. Even in the 1950s they were mounting campaigns that urged citizens to "support your local police."

But the police have probably not been aware of just how dependent they are on citizens. Nor have they focused attention on how to ensure that support would be available when they need it. They have simply assumed that citizens are interested in ensuring justice and crime control and that they will turn to the police to help them accomplish that result. This assumption has proved right in some parts of the community, but wrong in general and particularly wrong in minority areas of cities, where the support is critically needed.

The failure of the police to focus enough attention on increasing their contact with and support from citizens has produced a sixth major limitation of the traditional strategy of policing: public policing has not been able to keep its market share in the security industry. One of the reasons police felt comfortable with the traditional strategy of policing was that they thought they had no competition. There would always have to be a public police department. Enthusiasm for controlling crime would ensure that the public police would survive and flourish and would blunt any effective criticism of their efforts. As experts in the field, they could decide what their department should do.

This complacent view ignored the fact that the public police did face competition. In the field of public policing they were clearly monopolists. But in the broader market, citizens can buy private security as well as public. They can join together to hire private guard services or to patrol their own communities. They can purchase locks, guns, and dogs to help protect themselves and their property. And they can stay at home to avoid being victimized. Gradually, these private responses to crime have grown at the expense of the public responses. There are now more than twice as many private security guards as public police officers in the United States.[53]

Of course, there is much of value in these private responses to crime. Insofar as they are successful in reducing fears and risks of victimization, they contribute to overall social objectives. Yet there is also something worrisome, and not just for the bureaucratic interests of the public police. To the extent that security is privately provided, it will go to those who are most able to pay or most able to produce it rather than to those who are most in need, and the rights of ordinary citizens to travel freely through a city or have certain protections even when they are accused of crimes may be circumscribed.

But the fact that private security has been growing relative to public policing clearly indicates that something is wrong with the traditional strategy of policing. The public police continue to be popular as an abstract entity, but when the time comes to shell out money for security, citizens are increasingly turning to private suppliers.

## Community-based Policing as a New Corporate Strategy

These increasingly evident limitations in the traditional strategy of policing have caused some pioneering police executives to begin searching for an alternative strategy of policing.[54] That search is by no means complete. It is being guided, however, by several important new ideas.

### Improving Community Relations

The first axiom is that the quality of the relationship between police and the community is of paramount importance, both for the legitimacy of the police and for their operational effectiveness. If the police are not closely linked to the community, it is impossible for them to do their job. It follows, as a corollary, that the police should make a concerted effort to improve the quality of their services to support that relationship. A good relationship with the community is something the police can influence, and, given its importance, they should not rely only on a good public relations office or a community relations division. The task of earning a strong, supportive link to the community must be built into the day-to-day operations of the department. To achieve this purpose, several important changes have been made in the way the police are organized and seek to operate.

First, they have tried to reestablish and strengthen local geographic accountability. They have redefined precinct and sector boundaries to coincide with naturally occurring communities, established mini–police stations and storefronts to give them a physical presence in local communities, decentralized initiative and accountability to precinct commanders and beat cops, gathered detailed information about local areas and compiled them in "beat books" to link day and night shift operations, and reconfigured their dispatching systems to give lower priority to minimizing citywide response times and higher priority to maintaining a car in a given geographic area to allow continuity in who responds to calls for service.[55] Some departments have even begun decentralizing specialized functions to local patrol commanders for use as they see fit. All this helps to change the focus of policing from a citywide perspective to a local one, to build detailed knowledge of local communities, and to foster a sense of responsibility for and accountability to the local areas.

The police have also sought to rely increasingly on methods of policing that get them out of their cars and into closer, more sustained contact with residents. In the old style of policing, it was assumed that high-quality service consisted of a quick response to a call. This idea survives in the minds of many citizens, overseers, and police executives.[56] Yet there is an important paradox associated with the aim of producing a rapid response to calls that is perfectly symbolized by a common usage in policing. When a police officer arrives at the location to which he or she has been dispatched, the officer radios the dispatcher and announces that he or she is now going "out of service." After meeting with the citizen and dealing with the problem, the officer gets back in the car, radios the dispatcher, and announces that he or she is now back "in service." This usage declares that the time spent with the citizen is *not* service, while the time spent in the car waiting for the next call *is* service.

This is more than a semantic point. If the challenge to the police is to make rapid responses to calls for service and always have some cars available for emergency calls, then the task of the police is to be ready, rather than to supply the service to the citizen. The goal is to minimize the amount of time police spend with citizens so they can get back in service to be available to rush to the next call, which can then be cut short to get ready for the next one, and so on. Moreover, to minimize citywide response times, the dispatching system tends to use the entire patrol force as a resource, which results in cars being dispatched across the city, far from their originally assigned territories. That reduces the knowledge and interest that the officers have in responding to any particular call for service. Thus by focusing on the speed of the response as the only important attribute of service quality, the police lose other aspects of quality, such as the sense among citizens that their problems are taken seriously or the prospect that the officer who arrives at the scene is someone the citizens know and trust.

The value of some of these other attributes of service quality has been demonstrated. Experiments with foot patrol, for example, have shown that citizens greatly value familiar, daily, face-to-face contacts with officers. They can tell when levels of foot patrol have been increased or decreased, unlike motorized patrol. Foot patrol turns out to be effective in reducing fears, and is also a more satisfying experience for officers.[57] On foot patrol, the officers have an entirely different experience with the communities. When they spend their days responding to calls for service, they see the community at its worst. They go only to places where people are dangerous or pathetic. Once they spend their days walking, they learn that there are responsible and resourceful people in the community.

Obviously, foot patrol is not feasible in many parts of the country or in all parts of cities. But the enduring lesson of the foot patrol experiments has been that devices that promote frequent, continuing, personal encounters between officers and citizens are extremely valuable, and that anything that can be done to promote these will improve the quality of police-community relations. This insight has justified not only foot patrol and "park and walk" programs but also the creation of decentralized police stations, greater use of surveys conducted by officers to make contact with citizens, and the use of motorcycles, scooters, and bicycles to help officers get around without reducing their contact with citizens, as cars seem to do.

The third important change designed to rebuild strong community relations is a reconsideration of how to handle the volume of calls for service. A huge increase in the overall volume of calls—

many calls concerning situations that are neither crime related nor particularly urgent—is one of the consequences of linking police officers to citizens through the 911 systems.[58] The reason the police get these calls, of course, is that they are the only governmental agency that is open twenty-four hours a day, seven days a week, and can be reached by a phone call. Apparently, the police are valuable to citizens for many purposes other than responding to crimes. In traditional policing, the nonurgent, noncrime calls have been viewed as a useless claim on police resources that distracts them from their primary purposes and reduces their overall effectiveness in controlling crime. The goal has been to get rid of these calls as quickly as possible.

The eagerness to reduce the burden of the calls without permanently alienating citizens spawned some important experiments in call management and differential police response.[59] Through these experiments, the police, like many service providers in the private sector, have learned important ways of managing citizens' expectations. They can prioritize their calls: not every call has to receive the same class of service. Citizens will accept slower service if they are given an accurate estimate of how long their wait will be. And citizens will often be satisfied with nothing more than a conversation on the phone with a police representative. Although these experiments were initiated to protect the police from being swamped by calls for service, it soon became apparent that the methods could be used to free up patrol time for other activities.

The strategy of community-based policing would approve of these experiments in call management as a way to improve service to citizens and increase the patrol time available for being present in the community. But the new paradigm goes further than call management in reinterpreting the potential value of "nuisance calls." Instead of viewing the noncrime calls as nuisances, the new strategy views them as an important opportunity to produce value for citizens. Far from being a distraction from crime fighting, the calls help support this key function because the community relationship is considered an essential crime-fighting asset.

The police can also view the nonurgent, noncrime calls as a potential opportunity for crime prevention. Many calls are about situations that could easily escalate into emergencies: a noisy argument could quickly become an aggravated assault or a homicide; rowdy youth could start a gang fight; a minor traffic accident could become an assault if the citizens involved are forced to wait a long time for a response. Thus good responses to minor incidents might actually prevent crime.

Finally, the police can view the response to noncrime calls as valuable even if it makes little contribution to fighting crime. It is not a waste to do something useful for citizens that is outside one's primary mission so long as mission performance is not badly compromised.

### Using Police as Problem Solvers

A second axiom guiding the development of the corporate strategy is that the police should think less in terms of responding to incidents and more in terms of responding to the underlying problems.[60] This is not to suggest that the police should pay more attention to the roots of crime or that they should become social workers. It is, instead, a recognition that they are frequently called to the same situation over and over. Research has shown that a very small number of addresses and locations, dubbed "hot spots," accounts for a very large proportion of all the calls for service.[61] The challenge before the police is not to respond mindlessly but to learn more about what is causing the problem and what could be done to handle it more effectively. A few examples are useful to give the flavor of this important operational change.

In New South Wales, Australia, a patrol officer noticed that she was being dispatched to a particular location every Friday night at 11:00 in response to calls from a community of elderly people that they were being frightened by bands of marauding teenagers. By the time she got there, the area usually seemed quiet and secure, but the calls kept coming in at the predictable time. Instead of continuing to respond to the calls, she went to the area on a Friday night before the calls came in to see what was occurring. Sure enough, at 11:00 large numbers of teenagers suddenly appeared on the streets. She got out of the car and asked some of them what was going on. They explained that there was a roller skating rink nearby, and the owner routinely provided a bus to a group of teenagers from another part of the city to bring them to the rink for the evening. The rink closed at 11:00 and the teenagers were walking home. The shortest route passed through the elderly people's neighborhood. The obvious solution was for the officer to persuade the owner of the skating rink to provide a bus home as well as to the rink. The calls stopped.

In Baltimore Country, Maryland, the police were summoned several times to deal with fights that broke out at a bus stop. A little investigation revealed that the bus stop was being used by students from a predominantly white private school and a predominantly black public school. The fights were nasty disputes fueled by school rivalries as well as racial prejudice. The police dealt with the problem first by creating two bus stops so that the groups would not come into close contact. Then, because that seemed to leave the racial attitudes unaddressed, they joined with the schools in teaching a program of racial tolerance, linked to the particular problems at the bus stop. When the bus stops were put close together again, the fighting did not resume.

These may seem like trivial ideas, but in the context of police work they are potentially revolutionary. In some deep way, problem solving changes the basic unit of work in a police department.[62] In the traditional strategy of policing, the basic unit of work is the "incident." The important question is whether a crime has been committed and, if so, who is the probable offender. The job of the police is to make this determination accurately and to identify and arrest the offender. If no crime has been committed, the police lose interest.

In the community-based strategy, the police are encouraged to look through the incident to see what lies behind it.[63] The crucial analytic work that goes into determining the police response is not simply whether a crime has been committed, but what seems to be causing the problem. The response that the police can make is wider than simply making an arrest; it can include resolving disputes or mobilizing other agencies like the skating rink and the schools to help the police deal with the problem.

Of course, problem-solving activities have always been part of police work. Indeed, if one presents these examples to experienced police officers, they are astonished to discover that this is considered new. However, if one then asks them whether they engage in such activities with the official sanction and encouragement of the department's administrative systems, their answer is no. All such activity, which they understand and recognize as good police work, occurs despite rather than because of the administrative systems of the department.[64] As an official enterprise, problem solving is new to modern policing.

How to recognize and support problem-solving activities in the administrative systems of police departments is no trivial problem. The simple way, of course, is to divide the police department into one unit that does community problem solving and one that does rapid response policing.[65] This solution at least ensures that some of the police will engage in proactive problem solving. However, it also creates a potentially divisive conflict in the organization over which kind of policing is real policing and whose job is better. Moreover, this solution still leaves the problem of how to guide, account for, and control the activities of the problem-solving unit. One solution is to establish some formal system in which problems would be treated as cases are treated in detective bureaus. Each problem would have a file, and efforts and progress in dealing with it would be recorded. Quality in identifying and solving problems could be ensured through supervisory or peer review of the efforts that are made.

Some important issues remain unresolved, however. One is that problems come in many different sizes. Some require substantial resources, take lots of time, and make heavy claims on specialized capacities or the assistance of higher-level commanders in contacting other organizations. Other problems are much smaller. How to accommodate this variability and have the right distribution of differently sized problems is an important question.

Another issue concerns what qualifies a problem to be taken seriously. To a degree, of course, problems can be identified through the examination of information available to the police from their operations, such as calls for service or levels of reported crime. And the officers will have their own views based on their experience with the local communities. But it might also be important to create mechanisms for individuals or small groups within the community to nominate problems for the officers' attention. This is consistent with the goal of promoting community relations as well as solving problems. Because the idea of problem solving is open-ended, the police can accommodate the many different kinds of problems that communities can and do nominate, ranging from street-level drug dealing to abandoned cars.[66]

A third matter is how to evaluate the success of problem-solving efforts. This is partly a technical problem of defining indicators that should be measured and monitored. But it is also a conceptual difficulty in that some problems never get solved; they just get improved.[67] And others get solved by being moved to a different location (often with some corresponding reduction in level or intensity).

By far the most difficult issue, however, is how to promote problem-solving activities beyond the boundaries of a special unit. The reasons for doing this are to avoid the divisiveness that inevitably attends the creation of special units, to extend the reach and scope of problem solving beyond what could be done by a special unit, and to encourage the synergy that is possible when the problem-solving efforts of the police are informed by experience with the calls for service from the same geographic area.

Whatever the reason, there are serious management challenges involved in making problem solving part of the dominant culture and operational style of an entire police organization. One is how to create both the time and psychological room to get off the treadmill of responding to 911 calls. Call management systems and additional resources for the department can create additional time for problem solving, but some way of recognizing administratively and accounting for the organizationwide problem-solving efforts is also needed. The techniques developed for managing this work in special units can, of course, be extended to the wider organization. But ordinary patrol officers must be able to bring problems they would like to solve to the attention of their managers. They must also be able to be temporarily relieved of some or all of their rapid response responsibilities to work on these problems. The officers will need a great deal of training and information to do this job well, and that is difficult to get when one is not part of a special unit.

Probably the greatest difficulty, however, comes from the radical change in the overall conception of how the organization works and where the locus of initiative and creativity should be. Under the traditional strategy of policing, police organizations are structured as production line organizations. Although there are many different products associated with the heterogeneous tasks they perform, there is a standardized way of producing them that is laid out in the organization's extensive rules. In the new strategy, police organizations may come to be seen more as job shops. They will face heterogeneous problems that require customized responses. Thus some of the brains and initiative of the organization must move from the top of the organization to operational levels and from staff operations to line managers and patrol operations. The organization must be made flexible enough to allow it to form teams of different sizes to deal with varied problems, and officers should be encouraged to take the initiative in nominating problems and proposing solutions. This usually means organizations that are much less hierarchical than those in the traditional model of policing.

### Making Police Professionals

These requirements lead to the third axiom that is now guiding police managers: if the police are going to give high-quality service to their clients and participate in creative problem-solving efforts initiated by operational officers, police organizations must recognize and value officers' discretion, prepare them to exercise it well, and hold them accountable for their performance after the fact. In short, police officers must become true professionals and be controlled through the methods that are used to control professionals. It is not enough to deregulate the bureaucratic structures of traditional policing; the norms and values of public accountability that motivate deregulation must be internalized by the officers themselves.

This point can best be illustrated by drawing an analogy to the concept of a commissioned officer in the military.[68] The distinction between commissioned officers and enlisted men is a very old one. One important and continuous difference has been how enlisted men and commissioned officers are armed. When the fighting was done without firearms, the enlisted men were armed with longbows, crossbows and pikes; the commissioned officers had swords and daggers. Later, the enlisted men were armed with rifles, machine guns, and bazookas; the officers were equipped with pistols. In each case, the enlisted men's weapons could reach the enemy and the commissioned officers' could not. The officers' weapons were designed to help them reach their own men. The fundamental job of the commissioned officer was to make sure that the enlisted men stood and fought rather than ran.

But what caused the officers to stand and fight? Maybe it was easier when the enlisted men were between the officers and the enemy. But the more appealing answer was that this was what the commission was for. Commissioned officers could be counted on to do the right thing because they completely identified with the highest values of the society and would fight for honor rather than out of fear. Enlisted men, without the same stake in the society, the same sense of honor, or the same training, had to be coerced into doing the right thing by the commissioned officer's weapon.

This analysis poses rather sharply the question of who is commissioned in modern police departments. One answer is only the chief. He is the only one who can be trusted and therefore the only one who is really accountable for the performance of the organization. It is the chief's vision, skills, and virtue (honed by tradition) that infuse the organization's policies and procedures. And because the policies have all been thought out, the only task for the officers is to be obedient to those rules. That is essentially the answer that traditional policing gives.

A quite different answer is that all police officers are commissioned by the public. When they put on a badge and take up their gun and nightstick, they are expected to act as officers of the society and its laws. They are trusted to do the right thing not only because they have the proper technical skills and character, but also because their values and commitments are sound and appropriate. In short, they are professionals.

It is not simply technical skills that justify commissioning people as officers. Technical skills are important and necessary features of becoming a doctor, a lawyer, or a commissioned officer. But society expects more of commissioned officers and professionals who are authorized to act on behalf of others. Such people must also commit themselves to using their talents to advance important social values.

The drive for improving the professionalism of policing has gone astray in this regard. Advances in professionalism can never be made solely by honing the technical skills. Advances also depend on the development and inculcation of proper values, and it is here that the police have worked less assiduously than they might. By continuing to base their legitimacy and standing on their technical effectiveness in fighting crime and by signaling their resistance to some of society's important values by opposing many laws that seek to regulate their own conduct, they have raised suspicions about whether they can be trusted (that is, commissioned) to use their substantial powers without someone who can be trusted—a judge, a prosecutor, a superior officer—looking over their shoulder.

This is also one of the important reasons that those who are experimenting with new strategies of policing are trying to manage by articulating primary values to which officers should make commitments rather than by developing detailed rules and regulations.[69] This is also why police administrators are experimenting with training and evaluation by peer reviews of officers' work rather than trying to avoid any mistakes by insisting that officers get prior approval of their actions. Such measures are not only consistent with the professional aspirations of the police; they are also consistent with the operational realities of policing where most of the time, and for the most important decisions, the officers work alone without close supervision.

## Conclusion: Leadership and the Risks of Reform

These axioms point toward a new strategic vision of policing. That vision includes the following elements.

—The goals of the police would be expanded to include preventing crime, maintaining order, reducing fear, and responding satisfactorily to social emergencies of various kinds in addition to controlling crime and regulating traffic.

—The legitimacy of the police would be based not only on their ability to enforce the law fairly and equitably and to control crime, but also on the responsiveness of their operations to the large and small concerns of the communities they police.

—The operational capacities of the police would include problem solving as well as the ability to patrol, respond rapidly to calls for service, and conduct investigations. Mobilizing community groups and other government agencies might become as important to police operations as making sound arrests.

—To support such operational capacities, police organizations would probably have to have fewer layers of bureaucracy and become more decentralized. Officers might advance by adding to their specialist knowledge rather than rising through the ranks.

There is no guarantee that such reforms will occur or will be successful. Yet someone must explore these new opportunities because the problems of spiraling crime and pervasive fear are urgent and the current answers unsatisfactory.

To take advantage of the opportunities means society needs to rethink its relationship to its public managers. In traditional doctrines of public administration, public managers are accountable for means, not ends. And they are supposed to know answers, not have ideas about what might be valuable. Exploration of new possibilities is supposed to be left to elected representatives or officials in the legislative and executive branches of government. But as examples of community policing show, it is enormously valuable to have the public engaged in the search for better ways to accomplish a public organization's purposes and use its capabilities. It is the police executives who see most clearly the limitations of their current strategies, and it is they who are groping their way toward better ones. They, and other public managers, need to be supported in their search for public value, not viewed as self-serving empire builders.

Still, when society sees public executives embarking on changes as large and significant as those now occurring within policing, and changes that could produce bad results as well as good, it is not enough to simply deregulate the managers and send them on their way. Nor is it enough to offer bland assurances that the customers of the organization will be happier and more satisfied. Democratic accountability demands more than this. These executives must continue to satisfy their overseers as well as their customers. Indeed, because they are using public resources to produce public results, their overseers are their most important customers.

The need to satisfy overseers imposes two demanding burdens. First, managers must engage them in an intelligent discussion about what is publicly valuable to do. They must help the conflict-laden, fluid political process that defines and evaluates their work become articulate about what is worth doing and then help sustain the political agreement long enough to allow them to meet the operational demands of the mandate they helped develop. Second, they must create a flow of information about their organization's activities. That is what makes them accountable and earns them the support they need to do their jobs. The need to be accountable, particularly when one is engaged in a strategic innovation, cannot be wished away. Managers must remain accountable to political expectations they encounter at the reporting end of their organization as well as to the customers they meet at the operational end.

Obviously, this accountability places burdens on managers and may blunt their initiative. Yet managers who engage in the hard political work of getting their efforts authorized and making them accountable to overseers may be rewarded by discovering that their ability to make their organizations work is improved. Accountability to overseers may give managers the leverage that allows them to ask their organizations to do things that are hard but ultimately valuable to the public. In the case of policing, for example, it may be impossible for police managers to control corruption and brutality without making themselves accountable to external agencies.

Similarly, the process of mobilizing support for reforming organizations may also enlist citizens to help managers reach their goals. In policing, for example, one way of rousing the community to action is to explain over and over again to anyone who will listen that the police must rely on citizens to be the first line of defense in controlling crime and increasing security.

Finally, the success of public enterprises depends not only on the skills of the leaders but also on those of the front-line workers. If public employees can be counted on to do the right thing, performance improves and administrative costs fall. If they must be intensively supervised, performance deteriorates and administrative costs rise. This suggests that much more needs to be done to attract, develop, and retain high-quality personnel. It reinforces the lesson stated by Paul A. Volcker and William F. Winter in the introduction to this volume: high-quality people languish or leave when they are forced to operate within bureaucratic structures that do not reward public-spirited performance. It also suggests a need to reconsider the devices now used to control public sector employees. For example, more frequent use of after-the-fact peer evaluations, rather than before-the-fact approvals by supervisors, is probably called for. Whether such devices can satisfy the demand for accountability and instill the determination in public employees to do things right remains to be seen. But in evaluating these methods of control, the right comparison is with the level of control that is really (rather than theoretically) delivered by the existing systems of control.

Policing is just one frontier on which creative public managers are exploring the possibilities of a deregulated, postbureaucratic public sector. With any luck, they will produce a new and better vision of policing. They will also produce important lessons about public management, for there is no organization that feels the tug of the traditional models of public administration more strongly than the police. The methods police executives invent to escape from these powerful gravitational fields will almost certainly help other managers who wish to make the same journey.

The example of policing shows that there is enormous utility in having police executives actively searching for better ways to police cities. It is they who have begun to develop the promising new strategies. And it is they who will have to act to realize their potential. Yet society remains enormously ambivalent about the kind of leadership it wants from public executives. It may not tolerate gambling with public resources to find better ways to do a job. Thus it is not clear that police executives will be allowed to develop the potential of the new strategies.

Perhaps the answer to this dilemma is for police executives to recognize that they will never be granted carte blanche to experiment. The public will always demand that the executives and their officers remain accountable. The way to innovate, then, is not to plead for deregulation but to negotiate the terms of their accountability with their overseers. The important deregulation that may be required is for the overseers to encourage the executives to become innovative and to enter into a negotiation with them about what can be done. Included in their ideas for the future should be risky new ventures as well as continued operations.

## Notes

1. Max Weber, *From Max Weber: Essays in Sociology,* translated by H. H. Gerth and C. Wright Mills (Oxford University Press, 1958), p. 78.

2. Egon Bittner, *The Functions of the Police in Modern Society: A Review of Background Factors, Current Practices, and Possible Role Models,* (Cambridge, Mass.: Oelgeschlager, Gunn, and Hain, 1980).

3. Graham T. Allison, "Private and Public Management: Are They Fundamentally Alike in All Unimportant Respects?" in Jay M. Schafritz and Albert C. Hyde, eds., *Classics of Public Administration* (Chicago: Dorsey Press, 1987), pp. 510–29.

4. Frederick W. Taylor, "Scientific Management," in Schafritz and Hyde, eds., *Classics of Public Administration,* pp. 29–37.

5. Ibid. See also Herbert Kaufman, *Red Tape: Its Origins, Uses, and Abuses* (Brookings, 1977); and James Q. Wilson, *Bureaucracy: What Government Agencies Do and Why They Do It* (Basic Books, 1989).

6. Malcolm Sparrow, Mark H. Moore, and David Kennedy, *Beyond 911: A New Era for Policing* (Basic Books, 1990).

7. Mark H. Moore and Darell W. Stephens, *Beyond Command and Control: The Strategic Management of Police Departments* (Washington: Police Executive Research Forum, 1991).

232    MARK H. MOORE

8. Mark H. Moore, "Police Leadership: The Impossible Dream?" in Erwin C. Hargrove and John C. Glidewell, eds., *Impossible Jobs in Public Management* (University Press of Kansas, 1990), pp. 72–102.

9. Mark H. Moore, *Creating Public Value: Strategic Management in the Public Sector* (Harvard University Press, forthcoming), chap. 2.

10. Ibid.

11. George L. Kelling and Mark H. Moore, "The Evolving Strategy of Policing," *Perspectives on Policing*, no. 4 (November 1988).

12. Mark Harrison Moore, "Problem Solving and Community Policing," in Michael Tonry and Norval Morris, eds., *Modern Policing* (University of Chicago Press, 1992), p. 107.

13. Ibid., pp. 107–10.

14. Erik Monkkonen, "History of Urban Police," in Tonry and Morris, eds., *Modern Policing*, pp. 547–80.

15. Edwin Schur, *Crimes without Victims: Deviant Behavior and Public Policy: Abortion, Homosexuality, Drug Addiction* (Prentice-Hall, 1965). See also Jerome H. Skolnick, *Justice without Trial: Law Enforcement in a Democratic Society*, 2d ed. (Wiley, 1975).

16. Skolnick, *Justice without Trial.*

17. Donald Black, *The Manners and Customs of the Police* (Academic Press, 1980); and Skolnick, *Justice without Trial.* See also Allan N. Kornblum, *The Moral Hazards of Police Strategies for Honest and Ethical Behavior* (Lexington, Mass.: Lexington Books, 1976).

18. Dennis W. Banas and Robert C. Trojanowicz, *Uniform Crime Reporting and Community Policing: A Historical Perspective*, Community Policing Series, no. 5 (Michigan State University, 1985).

19. John Kaplan, Jerome H. Skolnick, and Malcolm M. Feely, *Criminal Justice: Introductory Cases and Materials* (Westbury, Conn.: Foundation Press, 1991).

20. Ibid.

21. Steven R. Schlesinger, "Criminal Procedure in the Courtroom," in James Q. Wilson, ed., *Crime and Public Policy* (San Francisco: ICS Press, 1983), pp. 183–202.

22. For a discussion of civil liability and its effects on policing, see W. W. Schmidt, "Recent Developments in Civil Liability," *Journal of Police Science and Administration*, vol. 4 (June 1976), pp. 197–202. See also Candace McCoy, "Lawsuits against the Police: What Impact Do They Really Have?" in James J. Frye, ed., *Police Management Today: Issues and Case Studies* (Washington: International City Management Assoc., 1985), pp. 55–64.

23. S. Walker and V. W. Bumps, "Civilian Review of the Police: A National Survey of the 50 Largest Cities," *Criminal Justice Policy*, vol. 91, no. 3 (1991).

24. Sparrow, Moore, and Kennedy, *Beyond 911.*

25. Leon Radzinowicz, *A History of English Criminal Law and Its Administration from 1750*, vols. 1-5 (London: Stevens and Sons, 1948–86).

26. Orlando W. Wilson and Roy C. McLaren, *Police Administration*, 4th ed. (McGraw-Hill, 1977), p. 320.

27. Ibid.; see also Richard C. Larson, *Urban Patrol Analysis* (MIT Press, 1972).

28. Tony Pate, Robert A. Bowers, and Ron Parks, *Three Approaches to Criminal Apprehension in Kansas City: An Evaluation Report* (Washington: Police Foundation, 1976).

29. The President's Commission on Law Enforcement and Administration of Justice, *Task Force Report: The Police* (Washington: Government Printing Office, 1967).

30. Allan Silver, "The Demand for Order in Civil Society: A Review of Some Themes in the History of Urban Crime, Police and Riot," in David J. Bordua, ed., *The Police: Six Sociological Essays* (Wiley, 1969), pp. 1–24.

31. Robert Fogelson, *Big City Police* (Harvard University Press, 1977).

32. Moore, "Problem Solving."

33. Radzinowicz, *History of English Criminal Law.*

34. David L. Carter, Allen D. Sapp, and Darryl W. Stephens, *The State of Police Education: Policy Directions for the 21st Century* (Washington: Police Executive Research Forum, 1989).

35. Ibid.

36. Herman Goldstein, *Policing a Free Society* (Cambridge, Mass.: Ballinger, 1977); for a more anecdotal presentation, see Jonathan Rubinstein, *City Police* (Farrar, Strauss, and Giroux, 1973).

37. Bittner, *Functions of the Police in Modern Society;* see also Richard Elmore, "Organizational Models," *Public Policy*, vol. 26 (Spring 1978), pp. 185–228.

38. Sparrow, Moore, and Kennedy, *Beyond 911;* see also Moore and Stephens, *Beyond Command and Control.*

39. Moore, *Creating Public Value.*

40. Kenneth R. Andres, *The Concept of Corporate Strategy*, rev. ed. (Homewood, Ill.: R. D. Irwin, 1980); Michael E. Porter, *Competitive Strategy: Techniques for Analyzing Industries and Competitors* (Free Press, 1980); and David A. Lax and James K. Sebenius, *The Manager as Negotiator: Bargaining for Cooperation and Competitive Gain* (Free Press, 1986).

41. Moore and Stephens, *Beyond Command and Control*, p. 16.

42. Moore, *Creating Public Value.*

43. Ibid.

44. Ibid.

45. Bureau of Justice Statistics, *Sourcebook of Criminal Justice Statistics 1981* (Department of Justice, 1982).

46. Gail Diane Cox, "Christopher Commission Talks about the Verdict," *National Law Journal*, vol. 14 (May 18, 1992), p. 32; see also "Panel in Beating Said to Avoid Issue of Fault," *New York Times,* July 9, 1991, p. A17.

47. David Kocieniewski, "The Wrong Place for Peanuts," *New York Newsday*, November 13, 1991, p. 4; Leonard Levitt, "DA's Need Cops Too Much to Charge Them, Critics Say," *New York Newsday*, November 15, 1991, p. 7; Leonard Levitt and David Kocieniewski, "Did Cops Impede Current DA Probe?" *New York Newsday*, November 17, 1991, p. 19; and Mike McAlary, "New Serpico Did His Duty, Now He Takes the Heat," *New York Post*, November 17, 1992.

234 MARK H. MOORE

48. Bureau of Justice Statistics, *Report to the Nation on Crime and Justice*, 2d ed. (Department of Justice, 1988).

49. George L. Kelling and others, *The Kansas City Preventative Patrol Experiment: A Technical Report* (Washington: Police Foundation, 1974); and Pate, Bowers, and Parks, *Three Approaches to Criminal Apprehension*.

50. William G. Spelman and Dale K. Brown, *Calling the Police: Citizen Reporting of Serious Crime* (Washington: National Institute of Justice, 1984).

51. Ibid.

52. Peter W. Greenwood, Jan M. Chaiken, and Joan Petersilia, *The Criminal Investigation Process* (Lexington, Mass.: D. C. Heath, 1977).

53. William C. Cunningham and Todd H. Taylor, *The Hallcrest Report: Private Security and Police in America* (Portland, Ore.: Chancellor, 1985), p. 112.

54. Sparrow, Moore, and Kennedy, *Beyond 911*.

55. Lee P. Brown, *Interim Report on the Plan of Action* (Houston: Houston Police Department, 1984); David C. Couper and Sabine H. Lobitz, *Quality Policing: The Madison Experience* (Washington: Police Executive Research Forum, 1991); personal communication and presentation from Patrick Colgan, Vera Institute of Justice, March 1993; and David M. Kennedy, *Computer-Aided Police Dispatching in Houston, Texas*, John F. Kennedy School of Government case #C16-90-985.0 (Harvard University, 1990).

56. Bill Evans, "The False Choice between Preventing and Solving Crime," *Governing*, vol. 5 (February 1992), p. 11.

57. Police Foundation, *The Newark Foot Patrol Experiment* (Washington, 1981); and Robert Trojanowicz, *An Evaluation of the Neighborhood Foot Patrol in Flint, Michigan* (Michigan State University, 1982).

58. Mary Ann Wycoff, *The Role of the Municipal Police: Research as a Prelude to Changing It: Executive Summary* (Washington: Police Foundation, 1982).

59. Michael T. Farmer, Raymond Sumrall, and Jane Roberts, *Differential Police Response Strategies* (Washington: Police Executive Research Forum, 1981), p. 40.

60. Herman Goldstein, *Problem-Oriented Policing* (Temple University Press, 1990).

61. Laurence W. Sherman, P. R. Garten, and M. E. Buerger, "Hot Spots of Predatory Crime: Routing Activities and the Criminology of Place," *Criminology*, vol. 27 (February 1989), pp. 27–55; and Lawrence W. Sherman, *Repeat Calls to Police in Minneapolis* (Washington: Crime Control Institute, 1987).

62. I am indebted to Malcolm Sparrow for making this point in a personal communication.

63. Goldstein, *Problem-Oriented Policing*. For examples see Raymond W. Kelly, *Problem-Solving Annual: Disorderly Groups* (New York City Police Department, 1993).

64. Sparrow, Moore, and Kennedy, *Beyond 911*.

65. Lee P. Brown, "Community Policing: A Practical Guide for Police Officials," *Perspectives on Policing*, no. 12 (September 1989).

66. Sparrow, Moore, and Kennedy, *Beyond 911*.

67. Personal communication from Patrick Colgan.

68.  John Keegan, *The Face of Battle* (Viking Press, 1976).

69.  Robert Wasserman and Mark H. Moore, "Values in Policing," *Perspectives on Policing*, no. 8 (November 1988).

# 11 ||| Mass Transit Agencies: Deregulating Where the Rubber Meets the Road?

## Mark Alan Hughes

CITIES ARE bewildering places. Traveling within them can demand feats of memory, patience, stamina, and courage. Systems develop to bring order to density and to make life sustainable. Some systems, such as time, become so internalized as to be unexamined abstractions. Others create a more tangible tyranny. I cannot forget my first trip from my small hometown in the Ozark Mountains to New York City. Dazzled by the sights along the sidewalk, I found myself standing beneath one of the seemingly endless traffic regulation signs. It read, "NO STANDING." Suddenly realizing that I had, in fact, been standing on that spot for several seconds, I quickly moved along. Relieved that I had avoided arrest, I determined to learn the apparently many rules of urban life as quickly as possible.

Of course, the greater naiveté of that story is that I could ever think that movement in cities is so well managed that pedestrians are segregated from waiting bus riders so as not to confuse a bus driver into making an unneeded stop. (I continued to struggle with a rationale for the sign for some time.) In fact mass transit (defined here as the public provision of shared transportation in vehicles with carrying capacity greater than automobiles) is a clear example of a system in which goals are many, vague, contradictory, and constantly changing, and in which the mission is strictly constrained by external realities. In this chapter I will review these external restrictions from the perspective of deregulating the government.

*Deregulation* is useful in that it balances other perspectives on public service, including privatization and the idea of "reinventing" government, that emphasize internal constraints on innovation and efficiency. Mass transit has had intensive recent experience with both these reform agendas. Privatization of transportation services was a major initiative of the Department of Transportation during the Reagan administration. And the idea of running mass transit more like a business, though often heard in current debates, hardly constitutes a reinvention because most mass transit was a business—a bankrupt business—less than a generation ago. Such an agenda seems more a case of amnesia than a mandate for change.

This is not to say that internal dynamics are irrelevant to operating inefficiencies in mass transit. One such dynamic is the selection of risk-avoiding leadership. Public intolerance of government failure reduces transit managers' incentives to experiment—failure being an inherent component of bold, persistent experimentation. With the risks of experimenting so high (news media exposés often seem incapable of distinguishing failed experiments from waste, fraud, and abuse), transit managers often stand pat. Better to listen to routine gripes about graffiti on subway cars than to institute antigraffiti measures, paint all the cars pure white, and risk a visible failure if the graffiti returns. The result can be an internal culture of coping rather than of innovation.

But internal dynamics have been thoroughly explored by the proponents of privatization and reinvention.[1] My focus will be on the external regulations that burden public managers. I review the many forms that overregulation takes in relation to mass transit, discuss the accumulation of these restrictions for post–World War II transit, and examine examples of the regulatory pressures facing mass transit managers.

## The Foundations of Overregulation in Mass Transit

In chapter 2 John DiIulio and Gerald Garvey summarize the many challenges public managers face. One of the most difficult for mass transit managers is the way in which transit systems' mission has been informed by vague, contradictory, and changing goals, especially those imposed by the federal government:

Transit has been expected to revitalize central cities and create jobs; reduce congestion and air pollution and save energy; improve transportation for carless households, the elderly, and persons with disabilities; and protect the working conditions of transit employees—and to accomplish these goals while providing safe and reliable service. Each set of expectations brought new rules and regulations with which transit managers had to comply. And each set has been cumulative. Most of the regulations contained in the [Urban Mass Transportation] Act of 1964 still apply.[2]

Government expectations for the universal benefits of mass transit have a long history, one that began with the debates over internal improvements during the first years of the republic. In 1808 Albert Gallatin, President Jefferson's secretary of the Treasury, defended road and canal construction, stating that "no other single operation, within the power of the Government, can more effectually tend to strengthen and perpetuate the Union which secures external independence, domestic peace, and internal liberty."[3] Quite an expectation.

It is no wonder, then, that in the late nineteenth century the Progressives turned much of their energy to reforming transportation. Their reforms of public service were based on the theory that expertise should be encouraged among managers. A telling example of Progressive optimism about expert management in transportation comes from E. W. Scripps, the newspaper magnate, who wrote in 1909 to Logan W. Page, director of the federal Office of Public Roads, commenting, "In all this great nation there are perhaps no other two men who have better opportunities to serve their country and who are making better use of them than are you and [conservationist Gifford] Pinchot. Despite the fact that neither of you have any high sounding titles or official positions which in themselves would give you great distinction—perhaps just because of that fact, you are epoch-makers."[4] Page had the decisive role in shaping the first federal highway policy, but his career illustrates the seduction of policy by expertise and the resulting tensions. These tensions, in turn, led to many of the regulations that confine contemporary public managers of mass transit.

It is possible . . . to see highways as the perfect reform and Page as the perfect Progressive, for he combined the age's emphasis on efficiency through an apparently disinterested professionalism with its idealistic and crusading efforts. . . . Yet the ease with which experts carried their arguments, thanks to the legitimacy granted by their expertise, undercut the democratic goals they claimed to be advancing. The greater significance, however, may lie in the failure of most Americans to recognize that disinterested expertise involved far more complex and ambiguous issues than initially met the eye. Highway reform was one result of the Progressive combination of efficiency, altruism, and idealism; however, it also involved advocacy and more sophisticated political manipulation than the political machines that the experts were intended to replace.[5]

The bureaucrat in effect became policy adviser and interest broker. Interest brokering is especially relevant to mass transit because transit agencies are often the only significant regional entities in metropolitan areas, which are otherwise characterized by parochial political jurisdictions. And decisions about service and fares and procurement can greatly favor certain localities over others. During the New Deal and later, growing public awareness of policy advising and interest adjusting by agencies helps explain efforts by Congress and the courts to impose controls on the bureaucracy.

## Mass Transit Regulation, 1945 to 1990

The primary development in transportation policy after World War II was the massive investment in roads required by the ascendance of the automobile. The construction of the Pennsylvania Turnpike in 1939–40 demonstrated public willingness to pay, even through direct tolls, for high-quality, high-speed roads. By 1953 nearly 2,000 miles of toll roads were open or under construction. And in 1954 President Eisenhower inaugurated the modern era of U.S. transportation policy by signing the Federal Defense Highway Act, which created the present interstate highway system. The act authorized a twelve-year outlay of $25 billion financed through gas and tire taxes paid into a new highway trust fund.

Federal involvement in mass transit began in reaction to a resulting crisis.[6] With the inauguration of the interstate highway program, passenger rail systems, along with streetcars, omnibuses, subway trains, and commuter railroads, had come to be regarded as archaic.[7] They also represented a declining private industry for which there was no justified federal intervention. Indeed, the Federal Transportation Act of 1958 made it easier for the nation's struggling railroads to divest themselves of passenger service. Before this act, a railroad had to receive approval from state authorities to discontinue passenger service. The new law allowed a railroad company to suspend service with thirty days' notice, subject to investigation by the Interstate Commerce Commission. So great was the desire to shed passenger service, especially on commuter routes, that the day Eisenhower signed the act the New York Central announced service cuts:

> The New York Central Railroad posted notices announcing that it would discontinue its West Shore Ferry Service (the ferry linked Manhattan with New York Central's commuter railway operation on the west side of the Hudson River). . . . The I.C.C. did not investigate the action proposed by the New York Central, and thirty days later the ferry boats stopped running. . . . West shore commuters, needless to say, soon found other ways to get to New York. The New York Central was soon able to completely justify removing the rail service because of the ensuing lack of patronage.[8]

Mass transit use declined precipitously from 17.2 billion passengers in 1950 to 11.5 billion in 1955 to 9.3 billion in 1960, and the industry faced collapse.[9] The transit-dependent cities of the East became alarmed by the prospect of discontinuation of all commuter rail service.[10] Under the leadership of Mayor Richardson Dilworth of Philadelphia, a coalition of big-city mayors and railroad company presidents began to lobby actively for mass transit interests.

Concern for mass transit revived significantly in President Kennedy's proposed Urban Mass Transportation Act of 1962. This bill reflected a fundamental change in the direction of U.S. transportation policy. Previous postwar federal programs had been devoted exclusively to highway construction, and a balanced transportation policy was considered one that mixed 50 percent asphalt with 50 percent concrete. The proposed legislation signaled the beginning of a more meaningfully balanced federal policy.[11] The rationale, in Kennedy's words, was to provide "good urban transportation, with the properly balanced use of private vehicles and modern mass transport to help shape as well as serve urban growth."[12]

Although the bill was defeated, the coalition that had supported it grew stronger and succeeded in passing what has become the key piece of federal mass transit legislation, the Urban Mass Transportation Act of 1964. President Johnson's legislative prowess was crucial to the passage of the act, but so too was the support of organized labor, which had opposed the 1962 legislation. More than 95 percent of mass transit was privately owned,[13] and despite executive order 10988, issued by President Kennedy in 1961, which had authorized collective bargaining by federal civil servants, labor was concerned that substantial government funding of mass transit would expose private sector transit jobs to municipal takeover with resulting restrictions on the right to strike. The quid pro quo for labor's support is embodied in section 13(c) of the 1964 act. It requires that capital grants (under section 9 of the act) and discretionary funding (under section 5, from which after 1974 grants for operating aid were derived) receive the approval of local transit unions. This has proved a powerful weapon in the hands of labor, since more than 80 percent of the transit work force is governed by collective bargaining, and three-quarters of transit operating costs are employee salaries, wages, and benefits.[14]

In the remainder of the 1960s, gains represented in the 1964 act were consolidated. In 1966 the Department of Transportation was established, and in 1968 the Urban Transportation Administration moved to it from the Department of Housing and Urban Development and was renamed the Urban Mass Transportation Administration (it was renamed the Federal Transit Administration in the Intermodal Surface Transportation Efficiency Act of 1991). The move to the Department of Transportation placed the transit administration's fifty-eight employees in the considerable shadow of the Federal Highway Administration's 6,000.

The move raised a fundamental issue. The original location of the agency responsible for transit policy was within the department responsible for housing and urban policy. Although this arrangement had ultimately been a matter of convenience, it had several advantages. To formulate transportation policy, especially mass transit policy, in isolation from urban or housing or land-use policy, dooms the policy to failed or at best muted outcomes. Mass transit policy only makes sense in a broader context: as a way of conserving resources expended by the automobile and the suburb or as a strategy for aiding those without automobiles and those who live in cities. It may be that many or all of the intergovernmental and interagency conflicts, and even many of the labor-management conflicts, described later are unavoidable or unimportant when compared to mass transit's basic task to serve postwar urban America with a technology that is in direct competition with the private automobile.

That task has grown more complicated with each decade as urban systems have become more strained and as the effects of overregulation have grown burdensome. In 1970 environmental protection was added to mass transit's mission. In 1974 energy conservation was made a major part of reauthorizing legislation. And in 1978 provisions were added for accommodating disabled transit riders. Each of these pieces of legislation, and a host of accompanying administrative regulations and judicial interpretations, was crafted with considerable faith in transit's capacity to improve urban life. These years have been dubbed the idealistic period in transit policy.[15] The period was short-lived, but the loss of faith in transit's capacity to solve urban problems was not accompanied by an end of its mandate to try.

The 1980s marked the beginning of the cost-effective period in transit policy.[16] Budgets submitted by President Reagan proposed a phased end to transit operating subsidies. The attacks on transit budgets were bolstered by a 1981 General Accounting Office study that estimated that subsidies transit needed from all levels of government would rise from $2.2 billion in 1978 to $6 billion in less than a decade.[17] A long and loud debate began over the future of public transportation.

> Public financial support of transit—regardless of the level of government—was expensive, productivity had been falling, and transit had not achieved many of the things hoped for. Yet transit was essential—or at least essential enough to warrant federal capital expenditures. Transit had not achieved . . . downtown rejuvenation and control of pollution and fuel use, or increased safety—either because it was passé and couldn't achieve much under the best of conditions or because there had been insufficient money spent on it; which position is taken depends on the eye and attitude of the beholder. Transit management . . . was either good and doing the best it could under the circumstances, or it lacked the professionalism to do the job and consisted largely of political hacks. . . . It should be obvious that transit could not attain many of its hoped-for results because there was no government policy offering rational, long-range goals or ob-

jectives integrated with other policies affecting the urban fabric and urban life.[18]

## Current Overregulation in Mass Transit

The 1990s began with legislation called "the first of the postinterstate era" by its principal architect, Senator Daniel Patrick Moynihan.[19] As James Q. Wilson suggests in chapter 3, the Intermodal Surface Transportation Efficiency Act has become one of the clearest examples of legislative micromanagement. The law as passed is 300 pages long. It establishes as U.S. policy the development of "a national intermodal transportation system that is economically efficient, environmentally sound, provides the foundation for the nation to compete in the global economy, and will move people and goods in an energy-efficient manner."[20] The law contains many exacting requirements and does nothing to relieve mass transit providers of the accumulated requirements of previous federal law.[21] Indeed, the 1964 legislation authorizing the Federal Transit Administration still governs the life of mass transit managers. First, section 13(c) remains in force, and labor unions retain the power to delay all federal operating and capital grants. In addition, section 5(i) requires public hearings for all changes in fares and services, and section 15 requires extensive data collection. Both provisions have contributed to the expansion of administrative staff to 9 percent of the mass transit work force.[22] The FTA authorization also contains "buy America" provisions that increase paperwork through, for example, preaward audits in addition to potentially increasing the cost of procurement. Finally, FTA regulations prohibit mass transit agencies from supplementing revenue by providing charter or school bus services—a sort of counterprivatization provision.

Beyond specific FTA provisions, mass transit providers who operate both transit and commuter rail operations must negotiate ambiguities and contradictions between FTA and Federal Railroad Administration regulations. For example, the FTA, the FRA, and their parent Department of Transportation have different regulations regarding drug and alcohol testing, so management must attend to different rules depending on whether a driver runs a subway train or a commuter train. Again, railroad workers and transit workers have different retirement packages (railroad pensions are of higher cost and lower quality than transit pensions) and managers cannot broker these differences.

Of course, beyond the Department of Transportation there are the general federal provisions discussed elsewhere in this volume. The Davis-Bacon Act requires all federally assisted construction projects to pay the prevailing union wage. Federal procurement rules require the selection of the low bidder and cost-only consideration for all federally assisted contracts. Environmental impact statements slow all major capital projects. And Office of Management and Budget provisions, particularly those in circular A-102, require compliance with detailed project management practices.

In addition to federal provisions, mass transit agencies must abide by state and local regulations. Consider the Southeastern Pennsylvania Transportation Authority (SEPTA). The State of Pennsylvania requires that it practice competitive bidding for procurements and sets limits even lower than those of the federal government. This means significant paperwork on very small projects. And inconsistent standards and priorities can also make SEPTA subject to two masters. The Pennsylvania Utility Commission requires hearings on bridge repair and replacement projects, which often causes substantial delay and uncertainty. The commission also shares jurisdiction over grade crossings with the Federal Transit Administration. Local provisions can be even more frustrating. Local jurisdictions often make changes in street ordinances with no regard to their impact on transit routes and schedules. And the local permit process allows each municipality to treat SEPTA like a private developer. Thus projects such as changes to stations may be delayed until the agency agrees to contribute to local improvements such as landscaping, sidewalks, and so forth.[23]

But an even more onerous burden than federal authorizing legislation, regulatory guidelines, and intergovernmental inconsistencies are mandates for which there is no funding. For example, the Clean Air Act of 1990 requires reduced emissions from buses and possible future conversion to alternative fuels. It also requires agencies to convert their nonrevenue fleets to alternative fuels. And it will create substantial new demands on transit systems because of employer trip-reduction actions. New business sounds good, but since mass transit operates with a subsidy, meeting this demand will require increased subsidies unless the demand occurs at points in the transit system where there is excess capacity, which is unlikely because most increases occur in intrasuburban commuting where new service is already needed.

The most far-reaching unfunded mandate is the Americans with Disabilities Act of 1990. Among other things it requires that new fixed-route buses, rapid-rail or light-rail vehicles, or other vehicles purchased, leased, or solicited for public transportation, be readily accessible to and usable by people with disabilities, including those who use wheelchairs. As soon as is practicable but no later than five years after enactment, at least one car on every train with two or more cars in light-rail and rapid-rail systems must be accessible by wheelchairs. If a public entity operates a fixed-route public transportation system, it must also provide transit to people with physical or mental impairments (including vision impairment) who are unable to board, ride, or exit a regular vehicle or to those whose conditions prevent them from traveling to a boarding location or from a disembarking location on a fixed-route system. Of course, new stations and other transit facilities must be readily accessible by those with disabilities. Finally, within three years of enactment all stations in intercity rail systems and major stations in light-rail and rapid-rail systems must be accessible to those with disabilities.

These kinds of overregulation impinge on managers' activities in hundreds of ways. For example, in the 1960s and 1970s the Southeastern Pennsylvania Transit Authority took over the Philadelphia Transportation Company, the Philadelphia Suburban Transportation Company, and the Schuylkill Valley Lines. One of the many anachronisms it inherited was the provision of special service for school students. Sixty-five thousand public and parochial students use SEPTA vehicles each weekday. Many use regularly scheduled, tariffed routes: buses and subways used by the public at large. However, by 1989, more than one hundred buses were being used to provide service for students only. These nontariffed routes often overlapped with regular routes but were available only to student riders, and many of their stops were unmarked by SEPTA transit signs. Furthermore, the electronic destination signs on the buses displayed "Chartered" or "Not in Service," and most of the routes operated without published schedules.[24]

The inspector general of the Department of Transportation audited SEPTA in 1989 and determined that the agency's dedicated school services violated provisions of the Urban Mass Transportation Act of 1964 and federal regulations (49 CFR 605). Federally funded vehicles (many of the "school" buses were acquired from the formerly private Philadelphia Transportation Company but had been rehabilitated with federal dollars) must be operated in ways that encourage public use. But effective school service, such as stopping on school grounds or discouraging nonstudents from riding during peak school hours, are at odds with that mandate.

SEPTA's local political masters insisted that the service to public and parochial schools in the city and the suburbs continue undisrupted. But the federal Urban Mass Transit Authority gave SEPTA eight months to bring the service into compliance with the 1964 act. SEPTA immediately changed instructions to drivers to emphasize that trips were available to the general public and that drivers were to display appropriate destination signs. Temporary cardboard windshield signs were printed and placed in the buses and photocopied public schedules with route maps were distributed.

After these measures, a comprehensive review was conducted. Where possible, schools were served by adding turn backs to nearby regular routes. For schools that were too far from regular routes, SEPTA formalized service into so-called 400 routes. Eighty-six such routes had to be created to maintain the level of school service. The required hearings were held in which public access was emphasized and schools were never mentioned. Instead, the routes were treated as analogous to those designed to meet the off-peak demands of factory shift changes. Nearly 1,000 bus signs had to be placed or changed. Finally, public timetables and schedules, again avoiding the word *school*, were designed and printed.

The most difficult hurdle facing SEPTA was to devise new policy regarding loading on school grounds. Buses on campus pose traffic problems and generate safety problems for students (riders and nonriders) and for the public. The transit agency ended the campus service where possible. Where it was maintained, signs were posted at the edge of the school grounds. In a perfect expression of the tightrope SEPTA was forced to walk, the signs both invited the public to board the buses at the school stop and warned them that they would do so at their own risk.

During the first weeks of the new operation, a few drivers were disciplined for continuing to exhibit "not in service" displays or failing to stop for nonstudents. The inspector general cited SEPTA for poor employee commitment, and drivers were prodded into compliance by messages attached to pay envelopes.

After two years of operation, less than 10 percent of the riders on 400 routes are not students (most are school employees). But to retain federal operating assistance, SEPTA has had to retrain drivers, discipline some employees, design scores of new routes, signs, and schedules, and hold public hearings and private negotiations with county and church officials. And it had to fulfill this mandate in a few months under threat of sanction.

## Taking the Brakes Off Deregulation

SEPTA's difficulties illustrate the dilemmas facing many providers of mass transportation. Operating under heavy regulation, they must answer to the demands of many masters. They are confronted by contradictory requirements, all of which they are forced to attempt to meet. Many providers perform this balancing act with aplomb. But a deregulation perspective helps illuminate the constraints they face. They are asked to solve problems as diverse as air pollution, urban sprawl, and providing mobility to students, the elderly, and the disabled. Perhaps inherently, these responsibilities generate regulations. Perhaps the only way to relieve some of the regulatory pressure is to reduce the number of responsibilities. But rather than hold public managers hostage to the public's ability to impose missions, it may be more helpful to focus on more proximate solutions. That is the potential of the deregulation perspective and the job facing future research.

## Notes

1. On privatization, see Stephen Hanke, ed., "Prospects for Privatization," *Proceedings of the Academy of Political Science*, vol. 36, no. 3 (1987). On entrepreneurialism, see David Osborne and Ted Gaebler, *Reinventing Government: How the Entrepreneurial Spirit Is Transforming the Public Sector* (Addison-Wesley, 1992).

2. Gordon J. Fielding, *Managing Public Transit Strategically* (San Francisco: Jossey-Bass, 1987), p. 34.

3. Albert Gallatin, *Report on Roads and Canals*, quoted in Bruce Seely, "A Republic Bound Together," *Wilson Quarterly*, vol. 17 (Winter 1993), p. 21.

4. Quoted in Bruce E. Seely, *Building the American Highway System: Engineers as Policy Makers* (Temple University Press, 1987), p. 36.

5. Ibid., pp. 44–45.

6. George M. Smerk, *The Federal Role in Urban Mass Transportation* (Indiana University Press, 1991), chap. 5.

7. This succession was contentious and heavily political. See Paul Barrett, *The Automobile and Urban Transit: The Formation of Public Policy in Chicago, 1900–1930* (Temple University Press, 1983).

8. Smerk, *Federal Role*, pp. 60–61.

9. American Public Transit Association, *1987 Transit Fact Book* (Washington, 1987), p. 32.

10. Michael N. Danielson, *Federal-Metropolitan Politics and the Commuter Crisis* (Columbia University Press, 1965). Danielson has exhaustively documented the effects of the Federal Transportation Act of 1958 on commuter rail service for large cities.

11. Fielding, *Managing Public Transit*, p. 18.

12. *The Transportation System of Our Nation*, message from the president of the United States, H. Doc. 384, 87 Cong. 2 sess. (1962), pp. 9–10.

13. Smerk, *Federal Role*, p. 91.

14. Fielding, *Managing Public Transit*, pp. 171–73.

15. Ibid., p. 22.

16. Ibid., pp. 31–35.

17. General Accounting Office, *Soaring Transit Subsidies Must Be Controlled*, CED-81-28 (February 26, 1981).

18. Smerk, *Federal Role*, pp. 201–02.

19. *Congressional Quarterly* (November 30, 1991), p. 3518.

20. *Congressional Quarterly* (December 21, 1991), p. 3737.

21. It should be noted that the act contains many worthy elements, including provisions that increase the spending options available to local decisionmakers. In particular, up to 54 percent of the federal highway program may be allocated to mass transit at the discretion of state and local officials. But I will focus here on the law's strictures.

22. Fielding, *Managing Public Transit*, p. 34.

23. I gratefully acknowledge the assistance of SEPTA's leadership, particularly Robert Wooten, the assistant general manager for public affairs, in compiling this information.

24. Van Wilkins, "Operating Special Services According to Regulations," *Mass Transit* (January–February 1993), pp. 26–29.

# 12 || A Coup against King Bureaucracy?

## Melvin J. Dubnick

OFFICIALS at a state university, authorized to lease space for off-campus programs in a nearby city, find it is more cost-effective to purchase the site outright. They take the initiative and arrange for the purchase using funds set aside for the lease.

Administrators at a county hospital in California grow increasingly concerned with the lack of prenatal care available to needy local residents. They develop a program to provide comprehensive care through improved use of existing resources and mobilization of public and private resources, volunteers, and grants.

Faced with the need to encourage recycling, a Minnesota municipality develops a high-technology solution to the problem. Using hand-held computers to scan bar-code stickers on recycling bins, the town monitors residential use of recycling and adjusts trash collection bills accordingly—the more recycling, the lower the bill.

Iowa was having a problem finding a market for recyclable waste generated by local business. The solution was to establish a by-product and waste search service, through which state administrators play matchmaker between generators of recyclable waste and potential users.

These cases might be dismissed as mere isolated innovative actions by government administrators.[1] But stories like these pepper the specialized journals that focus on the work of state and local governments. Recent issues of *Governing* magazine, for example, have highlighted innovations in property acquisition and leasing, responding to community challenges to waste disposal plans, reducing paperwork burdens, lowering the costs of computer maintenance contracts, increasing the power of local human service agencies, building facilities that turn waste into energy, and reclaiming abandoned industrial sites for productive uses. Competitive awards celebrating innovative excellence in state and local governments have not lacked for nominations, and university centers devoted to improving government productivity have been busy providing support to officials requesting help with new projects.

For American public administration, in short, necessity has become the spur of change and innovation. Stirred to action by budget cuts attributable to tax revolts and economic downturns, government administrators have responded with creative solutions that challenge the stereotypical image of the recalcitrant bureaucrat. Administrators have begun breaking free of the constraints that have characterized their jobs. Insofar as they have loosened those binds, they have engaged in deregulating government. In doing so, they have forged ahead of political leaders, academics, and the "good government" reformers who have traditionally led the charge for changes in public administration.

Recently, the nation has witnessed the conversion of this ad hoc process into a consolidated reform movement, a version of the so-called management revolution that spread throughout corporate America in the 1980s.[2] That revolution also began when managers broke through well-established organizational constraints and market barriers. It first came to the public's attention through Tom Peters and Robert Waterman's *In Search of Excellence*, a study built on observations of what successful companies were doing that made them stand out during a business decline.[3] Even the jargon of that private sector movement, from *total quality management* and *entrepreneurialism* to *liberation management* and *learning organizations*, has become common wherever public officials meet to discuss reforming government.

The similarities do not end there, for just as a private sector revolution has generated a variety of managerial reforms, deregulating government is but one reform to emerge in response to what is taking place in the public sector. In what ways does this impulse resemble other reform efforts that have gained support in recent years? What are the prospects for significant and sustainable change under deregulation or its alternatives?

## A New Movement toward Reform

Change in government has been promoted by rekindled public interest in administrative reform.[4] The increase in innovative government actions has been one product of this renewed focus. Another has been the development of relevant administrative theories that—separately or together—might provide an intellectual framework for reform.

### Theories of Reform

The question of whether government administrators' actions preceded administrative theories in the development of reform initiatives or vice versa might be important for historians, but for purposes here it is enough to think of the two as having emerged simultaneously. The conditions that launched the innovative actions in the United States and abroad—economic recession and stagflation, tight energy resources, awareness of environmental degradation, the failure of domestic social and economic policies— also stimulated rethinking about what government is and how it should work. Among the products of that rethinking were three theories of government administration:

—the minimal state theory, closely associated with the administrative strategies used by the Reagan administration;

—deregulating government, which has found favor among some academics and leaders in public administration, including members of the Volcker and Winter commissions; and

—reinventing government, which has received considerable attention in the news media and has attracted a following among public sector professionals and politicians.

The label of minimal statism can be applied to similar schools of thought that have roots in the work of Frederick A. Hayek and Milton Friedman and draw intellectual sustenance from the work of William A. Niskanen, Gordon Tullock, Nobel laureate James M. Buchanan, and other members of the "public choice" school.[5] Robert Nozick, a leading advocate of the perspective, calls for a government with limited functions: "protecting all citizens against violence, theft, and fraud, and . . . [guaranteeing] the enforcement of contracts."[6] To the extent that an administrative theory emerges

from this outlook (I shall call its adherents minimalists), it is anti-
bureaucratic and focuses on adapting the practices of corporate
management to the public sector. This managerialism involves forcing agency heads to contend with a competitive rather than merely
administrative environment.

> In a competitive situation, they had to meet prevailing expecta-
> tions outside their control. They had to keep on their toes. They
> could not afford to relax; otherwise somebody else might steal a
> march on them. They could never feel completely secure. They
> had to keep running just to stay in the same place. To advance,
> they had to be better and do better. They had to keep up with
> improvements and, more importantly, they had to try to be first
> with improvements. They had every incentive to police them-
> selves, improve their own functioning and adjust to changing
> conditions.[7]

During the Reagan administration, minimalism was implemented
through various means that sought diminished expectations of government; budgetary restraints and centralized decisionmaking; a
leaner and more responsive political establishment; and a focus on
a few objectives of overriding national importance.[8] Administration
officials also used management techniques aimed at minimizing the
number and importance of career federal administrators: "President
Reagan's essentially negative view of government intervention included an equally negative view of the public service."[9]

In contrast to the minimalist position, the views reflected in this
volume, especially in James Q. Wilson's call for deregulating government, contend that too many controls and constraints harry
public servants.[10] Addressing the need for better performance
among federal agencies, the 1989 report of the National Commission on the Public Service (the Volcker commission) urges that

> once presidential choices are made . . . the decisions should be
> implemented in the federal departments and agencies where the
> President's own appointees and government's top career manag-
> ers must have both authority and responsibility. The jobs will be
> done well or poorly depending on their competence, morale, and
> commitment, not on the rules and reporting requirements im-

posed by the White House staff, Office of Management and Budget (OMB) and Office of Personnel Management (OPM).[11]

Disentangling government agencies from overintrusive White House control is only one problem adherents of deregulation seek to redress. They have been equally critical of congressional micromanagement and judicial interference.[12] Wilson observes that among all advanced nations the United States seems to have the most rule-bound bureaucracies. This he attributes to the American character and public mores as well as to the distinctive institutional context within which U.S. government agencies must operate.[13] Although no deregulator advocates a relaxation of all constraints, they all regard the elimination of some and loosening of others as critical to improving government performance.

The third theory, reinventing government, lacks the academic underpinnings of the others and in fact cites authors from the other approaches approvingly.[14] But although they draw rationalizations from the advocates of minimal statism and deregulating government, the reinventors take their true inspiration from the experience of practitioners. From such a composite of theory and practice, a journalist, David Osborne, and a former city manager, Ted Gaebler, coauthored the bible of this approach, *Reinventing Government*. The popularity of this book and similar works was one of the most visible signs that this movement was widespread and had gained momentum.[15] Given its dozens of case studies drawn from state and local governments, the work found a receptive audience among administrators at those levels. As Jonathan Walters reports, "lots of state and local officials are getting plenty done, [and] 'reinvention,' by whatever name is going on all over the country."[16]

Ideas posited by Osborne and Gaebler had the enthusiastic endorsement of Bill Clinton, and many appeared as major planks in his 1992 presidential platform. Clinton followed through on those platform promises by creating a National Performance Review task force headed by Vice President Al Gore. The theme of "reinventing" was preeminent in the work of the task force, and when the group's 168-page formal report was unveiled on September 7, 1993, the inside-the-beltway media attributed principal authorship to "reinventing government guru and NPR consultant David Osborne."[17]

## Differences among the Theories

In many respects, these three theories of government reform would seem better described as ideological alternatives than as the basis for a single political movement. The minimalist position is clearly antigovernment. William A. Niskanen, the premier theorist of minimal bureaucracy and an important economic advisor to the Reagan and Bush administrations, portrayed this perspective best when presenting his "dream that Washington might once again be a quiet southern town with several major shrines and minor universities and where everyone, other than tourists, had the good sense to leave town in the summer."[18] In contrast, the advocates of reinventing show no reluctance in touting the virtues of greater reliance on government, once it is reconfigured into reinvented forms. The deregulators tend to be more centrist, advocating the effective government where it can be most appropriately used.

Differences among the three are just as evident in the strategies each would employ to promote reform. In general terms they offer three distinct strategic options: push, release, and pull. The minimalists regard a forceful push into the abyss of budget and personnel cuts as the only effective means to bring needed changes. Bureaucrats, they contend, thrive in times of plenty, but in the face of significant budget cuts they would develop creative means of using whatever resources they have. The result will be a leaner government. For proof the minimalists point to startling innovations made by administrators at all levels of government under the budget limitations of the 1970s and 1980s.

The deregulators want to release administrators from increasingly binding constraints. Greater flexibility is their call to arms: let administrators do what they can do best is the underlying theme.[19] And if, operating free of arbitrary binds, they do not deliver, the failure may signal that government should not be involved in a particular activity.[20]

The reinventors are more traditional. Reform is to be accomplished by example and through political means. Their pull orientation provides the rationale for energizing a politically effective movement. To focus that energy, they call for revolutionizing how the nation thinks about government and the way things get done. Innovative actions of public officials represent "nothing less than a shift in the basic model of governance used in America."

This shift is under way all around us, but because we are not looking for it—because we assume that all governments have to be big, centralized, and bureaucratic—we seldom see it. We are blind to the new realities because they do not fit our preconceptions. . . . What we need most if this revolution is to succeed . . . is a new framework for understanding government, a new way of thinking about government.[21]

Thus what the reinventing government approach lacks in theoretical originality is made up for with a firm belief in the ability to institute comprehensive improvements through rethinking government and taking advantage of a political situation in which all the conditions for reform are present.[22]

### Strange Bedfellows, One Blanket

In spite of the ideological and strategic differences among the strands of the reform movement, there is a common theme: the urge to debureaucratize government administration. Debureaucratization is an idea neither new nor restricted to critics of American government. Frustration among political leaders and others at what they perceive as the more pernicious effects of big government has been endemic worldwide for decades.[23] In the British Commonwealth, administrative reforms such as the new public management have emerged in New Zealand, Australia, and the United Kingdom. Scandinavian nations have embarked on programs to renew their national administrative systems, and even the highly centralized French government adopted a plan that would endow the provinces with greater importance.[24]

Nor would advocates of debureaucratization have to search far for the domestic roots of the impulse. Innovative public programs that have broken free of the constraints of bureaucratic procedures have been common. "America is constantly inventing itself," observed Bruce Smith a decade ago, "and the capacity to invent new ways of accomplishing the public's business has been a great strength."[25] The working technology of public action greatly expanded between the 1930s and 1960s.[26] Government contracting and other strategies were adopted at all levels of American government. The responses to the challenges of the times received little

attention,[27] but they established a practical legacy for the debureaucratization movement.

If the diverse debureaucratization approaches coalesce to form
an effective political movement, it will not be the first time. The
movement that created the administrative structure so vehemently
challenged by the debureaucratizing coalition was itself the product
of a coalition that developed after the Civil War when middle-class
reformers sought to end political corruption and adopt more businesslike approaches to government administration. By the early
1900s the coalition had found common ground with both the Progressive movement and the scientific management school.[28] The
resulting archetype for government, regarded at the time as a significant improvement, is now itself the target of reform common to the
minimalist, deregulating, and reinventing focus.

### The Bureaucratic Challenge

Unlike earlier reform movements in which the focus was the
corruption of public officials and the inefficiencies of government,
the advocates of debureaucratization are focused on the logic that
has defined the work of the public sector and public administration
for nearly half a century.[29] Each takes aim at the bureaucratized
public sector. Although few would question the significant role
played by the bureaucratized public sector in the development of
the modern state, it has rarely lacked for critics. Bureaucratization is
credited by both friends and foes with having redesigned the social
world.[30] Thus when approaching the problems of bureaucratization, the new reformers address problems that go beyond the hierarchical forms of public organizations or the creation of bureaucratic personalities. Too much attention to structures, they contend,
leads to mere tinkering rather than substantial change, and attack-
ing the behavior of bureaucrats is akin to blaming the victim.[31]
Instead, they focus on the way bureaucratization distorts government and the way it operates.

Bureaucratization can accomplish three closely related tasks. It
can reduce uncertainty; it can impose order; and, through appropriate designs, it can constrain and guide the very power its orderliness
unleashes. These are desirable functions, but each also generates a
challenge to effective governance. Reducing uncertainty means
minimizing disruptive forces from outside (competition, for exam-

ple) and from within the organization (as with innovativeness). Orderliness, brought about primarily through hierarchical structures, has similar stifling consequences and can separate an organization from reality. These negative results have often been reinforced through restrictions that were mostly designed with other dangers in mind.

Redressing these results demands rethinking bureaucratic logic. For many of the new reformers, debureaucratizing requires transformation of ideas, a revolution that changes the model of governance.

For the minimalists, bureaucratization manifests itself in big, expanding government agencies administered (as opposed to managed) for the benefit of the agencies and those that support them. Beyond proselytizing for smaller government, minimalists want to push remaining agencies into more competitive, market-based circumstances. Under such conditions, they argue, the urge to survive will generate less bureaucratic behavior. But to accomplish this will require a radically different formulation in the logic that structures and operates government. Thus America must adopt a more democratic paradigm based on a theory of public goods: "When the central problem in public administration is viewed as the provision of public goods and services, alternative forms of organization may be available for the performance of [public service] . . . functions apart from an extension and perfection of bureaucratic structures."[32]

Promoting debureaucratization through paradigmatic change is also the focus of those who advocate reinventing government. They scrutinize beliefs "embedded in the bureaucratic paradigm," including the definitive delegation of hierarchical authority, the uniform application of rules and procedures, the reliance on experts to carry out both line and staff functions, a narrow definition of primary responsibilities, and the efficiency of having the centralized staff exercise "unilateral control over line agencies' administrative actions."[33] Michael Barzelay provides a systematic articulation of the bureaucratic paradigm by elaborating a point-by-point comparison with an emerging postbureaucratic paradigm. The bureaucratic paradigm, he contends, focuses on

—the public interest as opposed to "results citizens value,"
—efficiency as opposed to "quality and value,"
—administration as opposed to "production,"

—control as opposed to "winning adherence to norms,"

—specifying functions, authority, and structure as opposed to stressing mission, services, customers, and outcomes,

—justifying costs as opposed to delivering value,

—enforcing responsibility as opposed to building accountability,

—following rules and procedures as opposed to a more norms-based, problem-solving approach, and

—operating administrative systems as opposed to organization strategies based on a continuous process of developing and strengthening appropriate norms and incentives.[34]

Osborne and Gaebler's view of the bureaucratic paradigm is best captured in what governments would replace by adopting the principles of reinventing:

—bureaucratic commitment to deliver services ("rowing") must be replaced by a commitment to ensure the provision of such services ("steering");

—bureaucratic "ownership and control" of programs ("serving") must be replaced by community-based ownership ("empowerment");

—bureaucratic propensity for monopolization must be replaced by competition among potential service providers;

—bureaucratic rule-driven organizations must be replaced by mission-driven organizations;

—bureaucratic preoccupation with costs must be replaced by concern for results;

—bureaucratic self-interest and parochialism must be replaced by focus on meeting the needs of the consumer;

—bureaucratic stress on spending must be replaced by an emphasis on earning;

—bureaucratic urge to focus on cures must be replaced by a preventive orientation;

—bureaucratic hierarchicalism must be replaced by more participatory approaches; and

—bureaucratic aversion to the market must be replaced by an embrace of market principles.[35]

The deregulators are much less likely to label what they are confronting bureaucracy; rather they focus on factors that cause otherwise well-intentioned and well-functioning bureaucracies to adopt pathological behaviors. The problem is not bureaucracy per se, but overbureaucratization, which renders the beneficial elements of agency operations dysfunctional and counterproductive.[36] The primary cause of overbureaucratization is the urge to take administrative control too far. Bureaucracies must balance the pressures to achieve goals with the constraints imposed by policymakers and a public fearful of waste, fraud, and abuse. "Talented, strongly motivated people usually will find ways of making rule-ridden systems work," James Q. Wilson has commented, but not every agency is blessed with such personnel, and the result may be overbureaucratization that will start at the top of an agency and reach to the lowest levels.[37] More tempered reforms—ones that build on greater public trust of administrators—are required if America is to avoid the consequences of too much bureaucratization.

## Obstacles to Reform

With debureaucratization as a common theme, the coalition of minimalists, deregulators, and reinventors seems to have the potential to amass the theoretical and strategic resources needed to launch a reform movement.[38] Launching a movement and succeeding, however, are not the same. To succeed, they must do three things: offer a viable agenda for reform, which means they must get their theory in order; establish the movement as a credible political force; and move cultural and institutional biases away from supporting the dominant bureaucratic paradigm.

### Lack of a Consistent and Coherent Agenda

Exactly what do the members of the debureaucratization coalition want? To say that they seek a less bureaucratized government administration is not enough. Obviously, specific proposals are needed if they are going to get beyond rhetoric: an agenda to act on, one that can be explained to policymakers and the public and packaged as actions for legislators, executives, or managers. To create such an agenda, the three schools must develop a reasonably coherent theoretical structure for their alternative to the bureaucratic paradigm. This will not be easy.

First, the schools vary greatly in the sophistication of their theories, and this variation may prove disruptive if they turn out to be unredeemably incompatible. If they do not, the minimalists have a clear advantage, for their roots are in the writings of neoclassical and public-choice scholars whose primary concern was building and articulating theory. In contrast the reinventors offer little theoretical underpinning, relying on anecdotal evidence and theory borrowed from others. The deregulators have a clear sense of theory, but it has yet to be formally explicated and instead must be culled from scattered statements made by its advocates.

A sophisticated theory, however, does not necessarily translate into a viable agenda for reform. Reform requires public understanding and support, and all too often it has been the more vacuous theories that have worked best before mass audiences. Furthermore, prescriptions engendered by a well-articulated theory might prove politically and technically infeasible. The objective should be a theory satisfactory to all three schools that can generate a realistic agenda.

The second difficulty with developing a theoretical base for debureaucratization is in the ideological and strategic differences among the three schools. These political differences can erupt at any time and counteract efforts to develop a synthesis of theory. A common enemy—the overly bureaucratized public sector—may not be enough to keep a theory-centered coalition together. To the extent it does, a viable theory might develop and will, in turn, complement the efforts to sustain a credible political effort. However, that intellectual common ground may not be enough, in which case the foundation for theory-building efforts might be provided by those leading the political charge.

The consequences of abandoning the effort to construct a theory and allowing the political agenda to proceed on its own was amply demonstrated by the steps taken early in the Clinton administration to launch its program for reforming government. Lacking a coherent theory, the reinventors had not presented a useful agenda for President Clinton to act on.[39] As a result the administration's initial steps, under the banner of reinventing government, were a hodgepodge of initiatives, many of them based on questionable assumptions.[40]

What are the theoretical underpinnings of the debureaucratizing schools? For present purposes, I will compare the three along four dimensions: purpose, personnel, organization, and management procedures. These dimensions address the questions of why, who, what, and how public administration ought to be conducted.[41] This

Figure 12-1. Characteristics of the Bureaucratic Paradigm and Three Reform Approaches

| Characteristics | Bureaucratic paradigm | Minimal state | Reinventing government | Deregulating government |
|---|---|---|---|---|
| Purpose of government | Execution of the will of the state | Provision of public goods and services | Meet citizen expectations | Solve "public" problems |
| Nature of public servants | Neutrally competent | Rational, self-interested budget maximizers | Entrepreneurs | Public-regarding |
| Organization of work | Tightly structured hierarchy | Competitive, multiorgan- izational marketlike setting | "Appropriate" organizational form | Loosely structured hierarchy |
| Management approach | Close supervision, Standard Operating Procedures | Cost-minimizing, consumer- oriented management | Facilitative management; total quality management | Mediation management; balancing control and flexibility |

summary is accomplished, of course, at the risk of oversimplification. Nevertheless, even a general overview can provide a sense of the potential for and content of a debureaucratizing agenda (see figure 12-1).

PURPOSE. What is the primary purpose of government administration? Frank J. Goodnow's "execution of the will of the state" stands as the classic expression of purpose for the bureaucratic paradigm.[42] The phrase is often preceded with qualifiers—*efficient, effective, equitable*. Drawing the qualifiers together is the instrumental view of public administration implied in Goodnow's statement of purpose.[43]

Minimalists adhere with considerable consistency to the vision of the minimal state: the purpose of government should be limited to the provision of public goods and services, that is, those goods and services with characteristics such that they cannot be produced or distributed through the private sector. Under the best of circumstances, all goods and services could be classified as either private or public. Most, according to the minimalists, could be produced and distributed through market mechanisms and must be so offered. Others would be provided by the public sector. For mixed goods and services—those that have some divisible and some indivisible characteristics—the minimalist bias would be against relying on the public sector because nonmarket mechanisms are, by definition, less efficient than market mechanisms. Where nonmarket means must be used, the minimalists would impose tight fiscal controls to keep costs and inefficiencies down.

For reinventors the primary function of government is to meet citizens' expectations by providing what they value.[44] The government is a consumer-driven organization. Osborne and Gaebler stress government as catalyst rather than provider of value, which adds another feature unique to the reinventors' theory. In this regard they cite New York Governor Mario Cuomo's statement that "it is not government's obligation to provide services . . . but to see that they're provided."[45]

Deregulators emphasize still another view of the purpose of government: solving public problems. Unlike the minimalists, their definition of what is public is not a technical matter, but a political matter decided by the nation's policymakers. In this sense the deregulators take a traditional view of the purpose of public administration. But they strongly imply that the details should be left to the competent administrators of government programs. Greater freedom for line managers and workers is a constant theme: public and policymakers will be well served by allowing public sector workers to develop solutions to the problems they have been asked to deal with.

PERSONNEL. The bureaucratic paradigm regards the issue of who will best serve the public as a complicated problem reflecting the desire to guarantee that bureaucrats are both competent and nonpartisan. Such criteria are the foundations for the merit system as originally designed. In contrast to this neutrally competent standard, the minimalists assume the type of person one actually finds in bureaucratic positions is a rational, self-interested budget maximizer.[46] The reinventors focus on the entrepreneurial personality within public sector workers. And the deregulators see submerged in overbureaucratized agencies public-regarding persons who act much differently when provided the right incentives.

ORGANIZATION. The bureaucratic paradigm tends to rely on tightly controlled, unified, and centralized hierarchies. The minimalists would create a multiorganizational situation in which market or marketlike interactions (that is, competition) could be maximized. The reinventors are even more relaxed, advocating the use of whatever structural arrangements would work to help meet citizen expectations. Finally, the deregulators remain committed to the traditional bureaucratic forms but with much looser structures, rules, and regulations.

MANAGEMENT PROCEDURES. In the bureaucratic paradigm the ideal form of management is based on close supervision of employees or at the least management through standard operating procedures and regulations. For the minimalists, those who manage public agencies in a competitive context will, by necessity, have to be cost conscious and more consumer oriented because their jobs depend on it. The reinventors are more facilitative, taking their ideas from the total quality management movement and the work of Tom Peters and his colleagues.[47] The deregulators regard managers as mediators who must balance the demands for control and guidance with the needs of those on the line trying to solve the public's problems.[48]

AN AGENDA WITHOUT ASSUMPTIONS. Figure 12-1 provides an overview of these positions. There is no doubt that all three schools have an aversion to the traditional bureaucratic paradigm. But it is also striking how little they overlap in their assumptions about government and what it takes to improve it. Developing an agenda that will satisfy all three in detail does not seem feasible (or logically possible) given their differences. Thus two options seem open. The first is to develop a synthesis reflecting their common ground. The second is to adopt an agenda based on the most feasible of the three approaches.

A synthesis of the schools is not out of the question. For example, all three question the traditional assumption that the purpose of government is to serve some abstract entity (the state or the public interest), and all believe that government should deal with more technical ends (public goods and services) or empirical ends (citizen values, specific problems). To the extent that reinventors and deregulators can agree that public problems are defined by what citizens value and expect, there is hope for synthesis at least between those two schools.[49] Satisfying the minimalists is more difficult, however, for their reliance on the technical definition of what is or is not public does not leave much room for flexibility. But there have been attempts among minimalists to move beyond this view.

Charles Murray, for example, has argued that government should foster the pursuit of happiness for its citizenry; and although he maintains that this is best accomplished through very limited government, his approach might create some room for a useful synthesis on this very significant point.[50]

A synthesis might also emerge on other points. The entrepreneurial public servant does form a bridge between the self-interested and public-regarding extremes, and the reinventors' pragmatic approach toward organizational forms offers an inviting basis for synthesis.[51] The synthesis in the management approach is the idea of a results-oriented method of running government.

Once a general synthesis of theory is worked out, action can be more effectively organized. Although the synthesis might emerge on its own, a more timely elaboration is likely to require the energy generated by political activity.

An alternative approach to developing an agenda would be to take the route of least political and administrative resistance by building the movement around the reforms most likely to sell politically and generate the least opposition from those most directly affected. Questions of politics and implementation are extremely important. Historically, the American constitutional system has been more likely to favor gradual transformations than radical reforms. Thus although the Pendleton Act of 1883 was a watershed in the history of administrative reform, its initial effects were insignificant; not until forty years later could reformers claim that most of their agenda had been adopted.[52]

Gradual reform will favor the agenda of the deregulators. Deregulating government does not pose a radical challenge to the status quo, which both the minimalists and the reinventors have promised in their statements. As described by the Volcker and Winter commissions, the agenda of the deregulators focuses on changes that many regard as both necessary and feasible. This is especially true for public personnel policy; people representing all shades of the political spectrum have urged greater flexibility in hiring and promotions. But taking this path has its costs, especially for purists who regard deregulators as tinkers whose ideas will not lead to the needed transformation of government administration. Still, the history of administrative reform in America is filled with examples of progress made through political expediency.

## Need for a Politically Credible Force

What does it take for an administrative reform movement to be taken seriously in the American political arena? Despite the constant concern with administrative reform in contemporary American politics, successful movements can be counted on one hand. If the measure of a successful reform is defined as the establishment of a new administrative culture, then success has occurred only twice since 1787: the institutionalization of the spoils system (1820s–80s) and its replacement by the bureaucratic paradigm associated with the Progressive Era.[53] The two cases differ in indications of what constitutes credible politics for promoting a reform movement. The first was tied to a partisan political program; the second evolved over several decades, relying on a variety of organizational and political strategies.

But one can broaden the number of relevant models by considering other movements in American history. Neil J. Smelser provides such an analysis in his study of movements that seek to restore, protect, modify, or create social norms. The various cases have one characteristic distinguishing them from other forms of collective action: "mobilization to organize and push through a program [of norm-oriented reform] takes a long time—a longer time than is generally required for the mobilization phases of panics, crazes, and hostile outbursts. For this reason, the mobilization phase of a norm-oriented movement is likely to be very complicated; it has to adapt to the exigencies of maintaining an organization over long periods."[54]

A crucial factor in a mobilization effort is leadership, and several roles can emerge during a movement. Leaders in developing the beliefs upon which the movement is based (Smelser calls these leaders "formulators") are important, as are those who mobilize members ("promoters"). To the extent that the movement has an organized component, it will need organizational leaders ("bureaucrats") who will be concerned with the stability, growth, and tactics of the group. Political leaders ("power seekers") will also arise within the movement to represent factions that might have strategical or ideological differences with other factions. Even "prestige seekers," leaders "engaged in maintaining the prestige of the organization or movement in the public eye," are needed.[55]

As a political force, debureaucratization has not developed so far as to need a formal organization, although it has from time to time and place to place been associated with other organizations (for instance, the minimalists' links with the Republican party under Reagan and Bush and the reinventors' links with the Democratic party under Clinton). There are leaders who can be labeled formulators, but their contribution has been limited to writing books and articles, giving speeches, and providing advice, formally or informally, to policymakers. What is missing is a mobilizing leader, someone who can bring the diverse elements of the movement together into some organizational form. For now, these leaders have met with limited success.

The problem faced by potential mobilizing leaders is that administrative reform does not have the appeal of other issues. This was brought out most clearly by what Clinton campaign officials called the "Speech He Never Gave."

> It was the one on "reinventing government," or "entrepreneurial government," or the "New Paradigm," depending on the buzz phrase you choose to describe the theory. . . . It's not that Clinton wasn't itching to talk about the subject. . . . What held Clinton back was the fear of putting audiences to sleep with an arcane discussion of applying ideas of management gurus . . . to federal institutions. So he kept his discussions about the specifics of reinventing government private.[56]

Without a mobilizing leader or some other force to get the agenda in front of the public, the debureaucratizing movement will remain in the "incipient phase" of its development. With effective leadership it would achieve "enthusiastic mobilization," which would then be followed by a "period of institutionalization and organization."[57]

As the example of the Progressive reformers demonstrates, however, although mobilizing leaders like Theodore Roosevelt or Robert LaFollette are needed, a credible movement can still develop without a unified organizational base. For the Progressives there were various jurisdictions (local, state, and national) and institutional contexts (electoral systems, legislature, executive branch, and even judiciary) through which to affect reform. As Neil Smelser observes, "the history of any given movement—its ebbs and flows, its switches, its bursts of enthusiasm—can be written in large part as a pattern of abandoning one method which appears to be losing effectiveness and adopting some new, more promising method."[58]

Still, the political success of debureaucratization will depend heavily on the development of mobilizing leadership. This can be a role President Clinton or even a leader of the partisan opposition such as Jack Kemp might play. But tying the reform agenda to either party does not bode well for long-term success. It would be more fruitful if the leadership of both parties supported the movement, a cooperation that worked well for the Progressive reformers. Short of that, the support of the party in power will have to suffice. The minimalist reformers were in such a position during the Reagan-Bush years, but through most of the 1980s they stood alone. With Clinton in the White House, the advantage now is to the reinventors who can take the lead. Whether they will remains to be seen.[59]

The deregulators have, consciously or not, taken a decidedly different approach. Deregulating government was the principle theme underlying the work of the Volcker and Winter commissions. The two chairpersons have provided energetic and articulate voices for the recommendations of their respective groups. The bipartisan and diverse membership of each group further enhances the value of having used national commissions. The main question is whether a collective form of mobilizing leadership can be effective and sustainable. If so, the advantage once again goes to the deregulators.

### Problems of Dethroning King Bureaucracy

A viable agenda and political clout are necessary, but little reform will be achieved in the long run without addressing the dominance of the bureaucratic paradigm. There are other obstacles to be side-stepped or overcome, but the bureaucratic orthodoxy must be dethroned: "if the dogma survives," Robert Golembiewski has commented, "any successful innovative arrangements will be regarded as but exceptions to good practice."[60] Do the reformers possess enough intellectual and political power to unseat the orthodoxy? Perhaps, but the bureaucratic model is strong. It has intellectual roots that link it with the academic study of public administration, it has the ability to generate solutions to administrative problems that are feasible and workable, and it is compatible with the political culture and institutional context of contemporary government.

268     MELVIN J. DUBNICK

THE BIRTH OF A FIELD AND A PARADIGM. Part of the problem facing reformers is that the emergence of public administration as a field of study was closely linked to the efforts of Progressive reformers to establish the bureaucratic paradigm as the dominant model of governance for the United States. Most histories trace the academic roots to Woodrow Wilson's 1887 essay, "The Study of Administration," which urged systematic investigation of the business side of government.[61] The goal was to discover principles that could be applied to promote efficient government operations. At the same time, Wilson implicitly outlined the bureaucratic paradigm. Besides the classic separation of administration from politics, a pervasive premise was his assumption that administration must be rooted in a centralized and unified authority. He also advocated creating "a corps of civil servants prepared by special schooling and drilled, after appointment, into a perfected organization, with appropriate hierarchy and characteristic discipline."[62]

This association of theory and practice was reinforced throughout what is today termed the classical period in the study of American public administration. Before 1940 the discipline was dominated by four doctrines:

—the distinction between politics (as the expression of the public will) and administration (as the execution of the public will);

—the need for a scientific approach to the study of administration;

—the objective of using that approach to discover the principles of administration; and

—the goal of achieving economy and efficiency in government administration through the application of those principles.[63]

Although the wisdom of these doctrines can be questioned, their intellectual impact cannot. The urge to establish firm principles of public administration and the widespread assumption that good administration had bureaucratic characteristics created a close association between paradigm and field.[64]

Building upon the basic precepts in the Wilsonian paradigm, students of public administration gradually articulated several principles of administration. Such concepts as unity of command, span of control, chain of command, departmentalization by major functions, and direction by single heads of authority in subordinate units of administration are assumed to have universal applicability in the perfection of administrative arrangements. Strengthening of the government is viewed as the equivalent of increasing the authority and powers of the chief executive. General-authority agencies are preferred to limited-authority agencies. Large jurisdictions are preferred to small. Centralized solutions are preferred to the disaggregation of authority among diverse decision structures.[65]

Significant challenges to the classical approach to the study of public administration emerged during the 1930s, and by the 1950s a logical-positivist model was well on its way to replacing the scientific search for principles.[66] Nevertheless, the bureaucratic paradigm had been set and has thrived as the conventional wisdom in public administration. "Though scholars stress [the principles'] limitations, no substitute body of normative ideas on how to organize a bureaucracy has taken their place. Consequently, consultants and committees charged with recommending large governmental reorganizations still regularly fall back upon them."[67]

Those who have studied public administration know that it takes more than reasoned criticism, an alternative theory, or a research program demonstrating the need for (or viability of) an alternative to overcome the orthodoxy. All those weapons have been used. The paradigm remains resilient in the face of evidence generated against it by the very science created by those associated with establishing it.[68]

THE RELEVANCE OF BUREAUCRATIC SOLUTIONS. One reason for its strength is that the bureaucratic paradigm continues to be a source of solutions to administrative problems. Academics may point out logical fallacies and contradictions in the model, but government administrators are more interested in what works. "The decisive reason for the advance of bureaucratic organization," observed Max Weber, "has always been its purely *technical* superiority over any other form of organization."[69] That superiority is found in the bureaucratic organization's ability to provide a stable and simplified environment for carrying out administrative tasks. The productive capacities of the organization comes from its ability to reshape or control difficult situations.

Those who challenge the orthodoxy acknowledge some continuing value of the bureaucratic approach but believe that value is severely limited in today's turbulent environment. Osborne and

Gaebler, for example, speak of bureaucracies as creatures of the past that worked superbly

> in crisis, when goals were clear and widely shared, when tasks were relatively straightforward, and when virtually everyone was willing to pitch in for the cause. . . . Bureaucratic institutions still work in some circumstances. If the environment is stable, the task is relatively simple, every customer wants the same service, and the quality of performance is not critical, a traditional public bureaucracy can do the job.[70]

But those preconditions, the authors contend, now exist for only a few public agencies (social security and public libraries, for example); "most government institutions perform increasingly complex tasks, in competitive, rapidly changing environments, with customers who want quality and choice."

These statements reflect a lack of appreciation for the popularity of bureaucratic solutions among public sector managers and the power of bureaucratic organizations to reconfigure their working environments (as well as themselves) in order to achieve the appropriate kind of environmental stability and uniformity. In contrast to the popular antibureaucraticism of the new reformers, Elliot Jaques comments,

> [thirty-five] years of research have convinced me that the managerial hierarchy is the most efficient, the hardiest, and in fact the most natural structure ever devised for large organizations. Properly structured, hierarchy can release energy and creativity, rationalize productivity, and actually improve morale. Moreover, I think most managers know this intuitively and have only lacked a workable structure and a decent intellectual justification for what they have always known could work and work well.[71]

Despite Osborne and Gaebler's statements, the use of bureaucratic methods continues to be widespread and is not limited to stable environments and simple tasks. What is perceived as a movement *away* from bureaucratic forms is more likely a movement *toward* bureaucratic forms that are compatible with the shifting demands of the public sector. Many and varied public sector species have been produced from the bureaucratic genus.[72] As Lau-

rence E. Lynn, Jr. has noted, "while they are unquestionably bureaucracies, government agencies are not the archetypal bureaucracies described by Max Weber."[73] Many of these variations are the
products of institutional contexts, others reflect the politics surrounding their establishment, and still others have been adaptations
in the face of change.[74] Thus what Osborne and Gaebler mistake for
the decline and growing irrelevance of bureaucracy is actually adaptation. The variants differ somewhat from the classical model, but
they retain some of the primary characteristics that made bureaucratic methods such a potent force.[75]

The bureaucratic paradigm continually demonstrates its superiority over alternative approaches by doing more than merely creating
organizations that fit their environs; it transforms itself and its environment to render challenging situations more manageable. As an
organizational methodology, bureaucracies can transform difficult
conditions to more simple, placid states or can adapt their own
organizational forms to environmental features conducive to bureaucratic stability.[76] Consider, for example, redundant bureaucracies, two agencies or programs that perform the same function.
Although contrary to some of the most fundamental principles of
the bureaucratic paradigm, redundancy is widely accepted in practice and theory as a potential bureaucratic solution to some situations. When appropriately designed (or allowed simply to grow)
and applied, redundancy not only provides backup where service
might be interrupted, but also may improve service delivery and
reduce the risks of accidents.[77]

Max Weber understood the power and implications of
bureaucracies' transformational qualities: "Once fully established,
bureaucracy is among those social structures which are the hardest
to destroy."[78] The staying power of bureaucratic solutions is manifest in their ability to adopt widely varying responses to a shifting
environment—from responses that build solutions using current
organizations and programs to those that develop innovative solutions within the confines of the general bureaucratic paradigm.[79]

The success of these adaptations may be the real story behind the
cases cited by Osborne and Gaebler and others because the innovative and entrepreneurial actions taken by practitioners have often
been fostered by the very same bureaucratic context that seemed so
impenetrable and intransigent. Thus while some might regard the
examples Osborne and Gaebler use as demonstrating the possibil-

ity of a nonbureaucratic paradigm, others see in them a reaffirmation of the bureaucratic capacity to adapt.

This more positive assessment marks an important distinction between James Q. Wilson's agenda for deregulating bureaucracy and the reinventing of Osborne and Gaebler and Barzelay. Wilson (and other deregulators) understands the problem-solving potential of government bureaucracies, particularly if they are freed of the constraints that reduce their ability to adapt. "To evaluate the efficiency of a government agency one first must judge the value of the constraints under which it operates; to improve its efficiency one must decide which constraints one is willing to sacrifice."[80]

Yet Wilson also acknowledges a darker side to the paradigm that is fundamental to the hostile opinion many reformers have of bureaucratic methods. The capacities that make bureaucracy adapt so well can also render it incapable of productive long-term adjustments. Described as "self-reinforcing equilibrium" and "dynamic conservatism," it is an affliction manifest in many organizations.[81] The very efforts made to solve problems have consequences that, unless addressed, will threaten those efforts. Rules established to bring about conformity in work force behavior generate resistance that in turn creates the need for more rules or other forms of control that have further adverse consequences, and so on. Although the immediate problem may be resolved, the organization "pays a price for its successful strategies, whose results may prevent the system from making adaptations essential to growth and vitality."[82]

It is this propensity toward dynamic conservatism that most concerns Wilson.

All organizations seek the stability and comfort that comes from relying on standard operating procedures—'SOPs.' When results are unknown or equivocal, bureaus will have no incentive to alter those SOPs so as better to achieve their goals, only an incentive to modify them to conform to externally imposed constraints. The SOPs will represent an internally defined equilibrium that reconciles the situational imperatives, professional norms, bureaucratic ideologies, peer-group expectations, and . . . leadership demands unique to that agency.[83]

If this was to occur, there would be little value in relying on bureaucratic methods—deregulated or regulated. The solution, Wilson contends, is not to seek an alternative form of government operations, but to reduce reliance on government.

Despite the potential drawbacks to relying on bureaucratic methods, bureaucracies remain the primary means for dealing with administrative tasks. Turbulent environments have certainly challenged the capacities of the bureaucratic paradigm, but there is no indication that it has failed as an adaptable way of dealing with most of the challenges facing government administrators.

OPERATIONALITY AND FEASIBILITY OF SOLUTIONS. The impression that the bureaucratic paradigm is relevant to the challenges facing government administration is strengthened by its operationality and feasibility. These awkward terms reflect major criteria most practitioners apply to any suggestions for reform: can they be translated into realistic programs both technically and financially?

In a 1992 meeting of public officials and academics called to discuss the reinventing government agenda, a recurring criticism of Osborne and Gaebler's book was that it did not adequately describe "the process by which change occurs, offering instead such obfuscatory terms as 'paradigm shift' and such seemingly oversimplified notions as 'steering, not rowing.'"[84] It is one thing to talk about change, another to do something about it. Although practitioners might welcome an alternative to the bureaucratic orthodoxy, they are unlikely to accept one that does not provide some practical suggestions.

Feasibility raises different but related concerns. Unless conditions are ripe no reform program—no matter how detailed and well designed—will be taken seriously, and a large number of conditions come into play. One study of common barriers to productivity improvement listed three dozen potential obstacles to public sector innovations.[85] Some are rooted in general conditions and range from legal restrictions and political considerations to the short time horizons of the public and elected officials. Even more barriers—structures and behavioral norms—can block organizational changes from within.[86] And there are personal barriers, reflecting the fact that ultimately change must depend on the people who enact it. Considering all these potential obstructions, it seems a miracle that change occurs at all.

In both operationality and feasibility, the bureaucratic orthodoxy has a considerable advantage over any competing paradigm. The fact that bureaucratic reforms can take place within existing bureau-

274    MELVIN J. DUBNICK

cratized contexts is the principal advantage. Clearly, incremental or complementary innovations are likely to be easier than the radical ones that would be required for a shift to nonbureaucratic methods. For example, Osborne and Gaebler would replace "administrative mechanisms" with a combination of market mechanisms and community empowerment. Markets would bring efficiency and effectiveness, while empowered communities would provide the "warmth and caring" that markets lack.[87] But while offering examples to emulate, Osborne and Gaebler fail to elaborate on the means for achieving them.

Ironically, the reforms that would bring about such innovations would require that government create the right conditions—changing market rules, sharing private sector risks, shifting public investment policies, and so forth.[88] In other words, government would have to engage in a radical transformation to create or improve market mechanisms and community groups while terminating administered programs and probably dislocating people currently served. Implementing changes within existing programs that would sharpen bureaucrats' sensitivity to those they serve would seem more attractive. And there is no shortage of ideas for how to implement such changes. For example, reforms in teaching organizations how to learn have received the attention of theorists and practitioners alike and are even finding a place in the popular media.[89]

A related advantage is historical: existing bureaucratic structures have established relationships that can act as media through which changes can be processed.[90] Organizational cultures and management strategies, if appropriately used, can reorient an agency.[91] And this approach can be inexpensive, especially in contrast with more radical reforms that challenge the very existence of those organizations and the cultural milieu they help define.[92]

One must also add to this advantage the growing knowledge about bureaucratic operations. It is one of the ironies of the bureaucratic paradigm that the author of its greatest critical challenge, Herbert A. Simon, laid the groundwork for administrative sciences, a cross-disciplinary field that continues to generate and test ideas relevant to organizational life. Mining the findings of administrative sciences, analysts have proposed various strategies to increase effectiveness and productivity within the current bureaucratic framework.[93] And other approaches to the study of bureaucracy based on principal-agent models shows promise as an even more fruitful expansion of knowledge about public bureaucracies.[94] As this knowledge grows and is communicated to practitioners, prospects of bureaucratic reform increase and the value of debureaucratized alternatives declines.

It is not surprising, therefore, that there is a growing appreciation of changes that can be accomplished by working within the bureaucratized model of governance. What many public managers have discovered is that it is often easier to reengineer than to reinvent.[95]

CULTURAL AND INSTITUTIONAL IMPERATIVES. The final obstacle to dethroning bureaucracy is more ominous than the rest, for it pits the advocates of debureaucratization against the power of America's cultural institutions. For all its problems, the bureaucratic paradigm remains compatible with America's institutional norms and the cultural values that undergird them.

Administrative reform is more than a political act. It is also an act of cultural change, reflecting and challenging basic social values. The public administration Alexis de Tocqueville observed during his travels in the United States was that in small autonomous communities where democratic culture placed greater emphasis on turnover than on recordkeeping: "After one brief moment of power, officials are lost again amid the everchanging crowd, and as a result, the proceedings of American society often leave fewer traces than do events in a private family.[96] The transition toward a new culture—one based on a national community having to face nationwide challenges—called for a transformation in administration as well. The triumph of the bureaucratic paradigm over the classicism and idealism of the post–Civil War period took several decades.[97] In establishing a new conceptual order, it also created an administrative state and corporate complex hardly imaginable at the turn of the century.[98] The cultural milieu fostering the new paradigm was, like all milieus, a compromise between values of the past and future. Thus while it promoted the adoption of more efficient bureaucratic methods in both public and private sectors, it maintained some biases from an agrarian past deeply suspicious of big business and government.

The result was a cultural dialectic that has both defined and plagued the public sector. The emergence of bureaucracy led to the complementary triumph of values conducive to hierarchical life. This hierarchical culture valued social relationships based on specialized roles for different people—an arrangement that would "enable people to live together more harmoniously than alternative arrangements."[99] But bureaucratization also created a reactionary response, an urge for individualism and life among friends in the small autonomous community of earlier times.[100]

This seemingly self-contradictory setting has encouraged both facilitation and restraint of bureaucratic power. The vehicles for implementing that dualistic imperative have been four complex institutions that act as alternative accountability systems that provide the context of rules and options within which government administrators operate.[101]

—A *political* system that stresses the need for public agencies and administrators to be responsive, particularly to members of the legislature and agency constituents.

—A *legal* system focusing administrators' attention on the fact that theirs is a fiduciary relationship, filled with contractual and other legal obligations.

—A *hierarchical* system in which administrative positions are organized in superordinate-subordinate arrangement, with the top layers having the greatest responsibility and powers.

—A *professional* system through which qualified deference is given to specialists.[102]

The four accountability systems represent four primary values of the administrative state: political responsiveness, the rule of law, efficiency, and deference to expertise.[103] Most have deep roots in U.S. constitutional traditions. Three of the four mirror the Founders' views that there are three forms of legitimate government authority: legislative, requiring political responsiveness; executive, associated with the desire for efficiency; and judicial, reflecting a commitment to the rule of law.[104] The four systems also represent a balance between those who believe bureaucratic institutions can control themselves (through hierarchical and professional mechanisms) and those who contend that external restrictions (political forces and legal requirements) are needed.[105] Furthermore, the systems can be separated into those that tend to specify what bureaucratic agencies can and cannot do (legal and hierarchical) and those that provide for greater discretion (professional and political).

The importance of these accountability systems in day-to-day operations of government agencies varies, but their impact is significant. They shape public administrators' efforts and assist them to manage diverse and often conflicting expectations. One or two will be most important in a given period, but in times of crisis all four can come into play.

These accountability systems have remained stable, reinforced by the relatively unchanging public attitude toward government administrators. To be successful, major reforms of the public bureaucracy will have to contend with the established cultural milieu and institutional setting. This is perhaps the greatest obstacle to the success of the debureaucratization movement.

Among the major advocates of reform, only the deregulators seem aware of the obstacles. James Q. Wilson, for example, accepts the need for a trade-off between the popular desire for effective government and equally popular demand for controls and restraints on bureaucratic power. Because this trade-off is deeply rooted in the American constitutional regime, reforms that require fundamental changes might just be too costly.[106]

CHANGING THE BUREAUCRATIC CULTURE. The debureaucratization movement has yet to get its agenda clear and is still in its incipient stage politically. The people committed to promoting it must spend most of their energies in dealing with those challenges. However, all their efforts will be for naught unless they confront the cultural and institutional power of the bureaucratic paradigm. Convinced of the inherent problems with bureaucracy and bureaucratic solutions, the reformers might ignore the realities that sustain it. Although bureaucratic government has few defenders, it remains an important and pervasive structure of our political, economic, social, and cultural lives. "The way in which a bureaucracy operates cannot be explained simply by knowing its tasks and the economic and political incentives that it confronts," James Q. Wilson has commented. "Culture makes a difference."[107]

Can a powerful cultural force be successfully challenged? Yes, if one takes a sweeping view of history. Is such a powerful cultural force *easily* challenged? Perhaps not. Established cultures are more than value systems; they are ways of life. Once they are as firmly established as the bureaucratic culture is, they perpetuate themselves through adaptation, cooptation, and dozens of other strategies.[108]

To deal with the cultural barriers, the new reformers will need to do two things. First, they will have to develop a strategy for cultural change that complements their political efforts. Cultural change is difficult but possible, particularly in times of turbulence.

That human perception is everywhere culturally biased does not mean that people can make the world come out any way they wish. Surprise—the discrepancy between the expected and the actual—is of central importance in dislodging individuals from their way of life. Change occurs when successive events intervene in such a manner as to prevent a way of life from delivering on the expectations it has generated, thereby prompting individuals to seek more promising alternatives.[109]

Developing a strategy to take advantage of such discrepancies should be high on the movement's list.

Second, the new reformers must develop and continuously promote images to replace those that now support the bureaucratic paradigm. Regardless of their validity, images suggest stories and attitudes extracted from stories that tell people the way things are or the way they ought to be. They establish models for how people act or think they ought to act, and generate expectations that influence behavior and assessment of human actions.[110]

The bureaucratic culture is reflected in four popular images of public administration. The most common is that of the impersonal bureaucrat, an image so deeply ingrained that Americans freely associate *bureaucrat* with all public sector workers. The image comes close to the kafkaesque stereotype of the warders who arrest K in *The Trial*.[111] Another image is that of the agent, the public administrator as someone hired to perform certain tasks in certain ways. Here the stereotype comes from the world of crime and espionage, where public servants (although we rarely think of them as such) commit to completing a mission. A third image is that of the public administrator as the politician, someone whose job is to satisfy his or her constituency by representing their interests and making decisions on their behalf. Finally, there is the public administrator as the expert hired for his or her knowledge and skills who is expected to apply them in a professional manner to the problems of government.

Most discussions of public administration refer to these myths, but it is the image of the bureaucrat that dominates, reflecting the dominance of the bureaucratic paradigm and the public's suspicious view of public servants. Replacing that image, or at least reducing its salience, is an important task for the new reformers. This might prove difficult. The minimalists, for example, have always relied on some variation of the bureaucrat myth in their analysis of what is wrong with government administration. In contrast, Osborne and Gaebler make clear that reinventing government is not another form of bureaucrat-bashing rhetoric: "our intention is to bash *bureaucracies*, not bureaucrats."[112] As for the deregulators, they see their objective as restoring the public's trust in public administration, and thereby "restoring a sense of pride in public service."[113]

## Conclusion

Growing numbers of people are joining the chorus for administrative reform, and a new movement is emerging with considerable political support. Succeeding at reform is not merely a matter of articulating a program and developing the necessary political will and strength to implement it, although those are very important tasks. Displacing the dominant paradigm is crucial, and that will be no easy task.

Perhaps the most foolish thing reformers could do is believe their own rhetoric. The need to rationalize major changes and energize the political forces required to succeed is bound to result in some overstatement. Such overstatement might be expected of the minimalists, who still carry the ideological baggage of their years in power under Reagan and Bush. For the advocates of reinventing government, the power of anecdotes and catchy labels will only take them so far. The more analytical deregulators, in contrast, may find it difficult to sustain their enthusiasm and support for the movement in light of their awareness of the formidable challenges the coalition faces.

Will the new reformers succeed? It is hard to be very optimistic. The cultural hurdle will prove the most difficult, for the distrust of government remains strong despite the growing willingness of Americans to live with greater government involvement in their lives under the Clinton administration. So long as trust is weak, the public will not support reforms that give public administrators more discretion, even with the promise of more innovative, productive, and efficient government.

Nevertheless, if it can find leaders who can mobilize support and sustain political and cultural strategies for change, a new administrative culture might reshape government during the next decade. If it does, it will most likely be a variation of debureaucratization with features strongly influenced by the deregulators. Although the minimalists and reinventors now get greater attention, the deregulators are more strategically positioned to meet the intellectual, political, practical, cultural, and institutional challenges facing administrative reformers.

## Notes

1. Cases like these fill the files of the National Center for Public Productivity at Rutgers University, which collects them as part of its annual awards for exemplary innovations in the public sector. A similar program is run by Harvard University's Kennedy School of Government in conjunction with *Governing* magazine.

2. For example, see Rosabeth Moss Kanter, *When Giants Learn to Dance* (Simon and Schuster, 1989); Peter M. Senge, *The Fifth Discipline: The Art and Practice of the Learning Organization* (Doubleday, 1990); and Tom Peters and Nancy Austin, *A Passion for Excellence: The Leadership Difference* (Random House, 1985).

3. Tom Peters and Robert Waterman, *In Search of Excellence: Lessons from America's Best-Run Companies* (Harper and Row, 1982).

4. On the renewed interest in administrative reform worldwide, see Gerald E. Caiden, *Administrative Reform Comes of Age* (Berlin: Walter de Gruyter, 1991).

5. William A. Niskanen, *Bureaucracy and Representative Government* (Chicago: Aldine Atherton, 1971); Gordon Tullock, *The Politics of Bureaucracy* (Washington: Public Affairs Press, 1965); and James M. Buchanan and Gordon Tullock, *The Calculus of Consent: Logical Foundations of Constitutional Democracy* (University of Michigan Press, 1962). For a critique of this legacy, see Colin Campbell and Donald Naulls, "The Consequences of a Minimalist Paradigm for Governance: A Comparative Analysis," in Patricia W. Ingraham and Donald F. Kettl, eds., *Agenda for Excellence: Public Service in America* (Chatham House, 1992), chap. 4; also Steven Kelman, "'Public Choice' and Public Spirit," *Public Interest*, no. 87 (Spring 1987), pp. 80–94.

On a more prescriptive level, advocates of privatization as a means for limiting government intrusion into daily life were also prominent in developing the theory. See E. S. Savas, *Privatization: The Key to Better Government* (Chatham House, 1987). For an overview of privatization, see John D. Donahue, *The Privatization Decision: Public Ends, Private Means* (Basic Books, 1989).

6. Robert Nozick, *Anarchy, State, and Utopia* (Basic Books, 1974), p. 26.

7. Caiden, *Administrative Reform Comes of Age*, p. 25.

8. James D. Carroll, A. Lee Fritschler, and Bruce L. R. Smith, "Supply-Side Management in the Reagan Administration," *Public Administration Review*, vol. 45 (November–December, 1985), p. 807.

9. Patricia W. Ingraham and David H. Rosenbloom, "Political Foundations of the American Federal Service: Rebuilding a Crumbling Base," *Public Administra-*

*tion Review*, vol. 50 (March–April 1990), p. 214. See also Richard P. Nathan, *The Administrative Presidency* (John Wiley, 1983), especially chap. 6; Chester A. Newland, "A Mid-Term Appraisal—The Reagan Presidency: Limited Government and Political Administration," *Public Administration Review*, vol. 43 (January–February 1983), pp. 1–21; and Peter M. Benda and Charles H. Levine, "Reagan and the Bureaucracy: The Bequest, the Promise, and the Legacy," in Charles O. Jones, ed., *The Reagan Legacy: Promise and Performance* (Chatham House, 1988), pp. 102–42.

10. Also see James Q. Wilson, *Bureaucracy: What Government Agencies Do and Why They Do It* (Basic Books, 1989), p. 369. Wilson attributes the idea of deregulation to Constance Horner, former director of the Office of Personnel Management, and also notes its use in Gary C. Bryner, *Bureaucratic Discretion* (Pergamon Press, 1987), p. 215.

11. National Commission on the Public Service, *Rebuilding the Public Service: The Report of the National Commission on the Public Service* (Washington, 1989), p. 19.

12. See Donald F. Kettl, "Micromanagement: Congressional Control and Bureaucratic Risk," in Ingraham and Kettl, *Agenda for Excellence: Public Service in America*, chap. 5. See also Jeremy Rabkin, *Judicial Compulsions: How Public Law Distorts Public Policy* (Basic Books, 1989).

13. Wilson, *Bureaucracy*, pp. 376–77.

14. E. S. Savas, a major advocate of privatization, as well as James Q. Wilson, who is a principle advocate of deregulating government, are frequently cited in David Osborne and Ted Gaebler, *Reinventing Government: How the Entrepreneurial Spirit Is Transforming the Public Sector* (Addison-Wesley, 1992).

15. More recently, Michael Barzelay's *Breaking Through Bureaucracy: A New Vision For Managing in Government* (University of California Press, 1992), has provided additional articulation for this movement. As do Osborne and Gaebler, Barzelay seeks a postbureaucratic paradigm for government, one stressing values similar to those cited by others in this growing chorus for change.

16. Jonathan Walters, "Reinventing Government: Managing the Politics of Change," *Governing*, vol. 6 (December 1992), p. 29.

17. Tom Shoop, "Goring the Bureaucracy," *Government Executive*, vol. 25 (October 1993), p. 13.

18. William A. Niskanen, "Competition among Government Bureaus," in Carol H. Weiss and Allen H. Barton, eds., *Making Bureaucracies Work* (Beverly Hills: Sage Publications, 1980), p. 167. Niskanen's status is international. His work, for instance, was required reading for top-level officials of the Thatcher government. See Campbell and Naulls, "Consequences of a Minimalist Paradigm for Governance," p. 67.

19. For example, see Lloyd G. Nigro, "Personnel for and Personnel by Public Administrators: Bridging the Gap," in Naomi B. Lynn and Aaron Wildavsky, eds., *Public Administration: The State of the Discipline* (Chatham House, 1990), pp. 185–202.

20. Wilson, *Bureaucracy*, pp. 375–76. See also Theodore J. Lowi, *The End of Liberalism: The Second Republic of the United States*, 2d ed. (Norton, 1979).

21. Osborne and Gaebler, *Reinventing Government*, p. 321.

22. Osborne and Gaebler provide a list of "factors supportive of fundamental change": crisis, leadership, and continuity of leadership, a "healthy civic infrastructure," shared vision and goals, trust, outside resources, and models to follow; Ibid., pp. 326–27.

23. Caiden, *Administrative Reform Comes of Age*, chaps. 4, 5.

24. Christopher Hood and Michael Jackson, *Administrative Argument* (Brookfield, Vt.: Dartmouth, 1991), pp. 178–79; Lennart Gustafsson, "Promoting Flexibility through Pay Policy—Experience from the Swedish National Administration," and Per Laegreid, "Change In Norwegian Public Personnel Policy," in Organization for Economic Cooperation and Development, *Flexible Personnel Management in the Public Service* (Paris, 1990), pp. 27–46; and Roger Cohen, "On Fast Track to (Gasp!) Provinces," *New York Times*, February 13, 1993, p. 4.

25. Bruce L. R. Smith, "Changing Public-Private Sector Relations: A Look at the United States," *Annals of the American Academy of Political and Social Science*, vol. 466 (March 1983), p. 150.

26. See Lester M. Salamon, "The Changing Tools of Government Action: An Overview," in Lester Salamon, ed., *Beyond Privatization: The Tools of Government Action* (Washington: Urban Institute Press, 1989), pp. 3–22; Christopher Hood, *The Tools of Government* (Chatham House, 1983); and Donald F. Kettl, *Government by Proxy: (Mis?)Managing Federal Programs* (Washington: CQ Press, 1988).

27. A major exception was the work of Harvey Sherman; see his "Methodology in the Practice of Public Administration," in James C. Charlesworth, ed., *Theory and Practice of Public Administration: Scope, Objectives, and Methods* (Philadelphia: American Academy of Political and Social Science, 1968), pp. 254–90.

28. Ingraham and Rosenbloom, "Political Foundations of the American Federal Service," p. 213.

29. Corruption has not disappeared as an issue, but it is no longer at the heart of administrative reform efforts. On the role of corruption in American government, see Suzanne Garment, *Scandal: The Culture of Mistrust in American Government* (Anchor Books, 1992); also Peter deLeon, *Thinking about Political Corruption* (Armonk, N.Y.: M. E. Sharpe, 1993).

30. Dieter Grunow considers the public sector as important a force in the rise of modern society as industrialization, urbanization, and democratization. See "Development of the Public Sector: Trends and Issues," in *The Public Sector: Challenge for Coordination and Learning* (Berlin: Walter de Gruyter, 1991), pp. 89–115.

For criticism of the bureaucracy see Henry Jacoby, *The Bureaucratization of the World*, trans. by Eveline Kanes (University of California Press, 1973); Ralph P. Hummel, *The Bureaucratic Experience*, 3d ed. (St. Martin's Press, 1987); and David Nachmias and David H. Rosenbloom, *Bureaucratic Government, USA* (St. Martin's Press, 1980). There are, of course, major exceptions to the criticisms of bureaucracy; for example, see Carl J. Friedrich, *Constitutional Government and Democracy: Theory and Practice in Europe and America*, 4th ed. (Waltham, Mass.: Blaisdell Publishing, 1968), especially chap. 2.

31. The extent to which bureaucratic operatives are victims rather than perpetrators is a controversial issue. Reflecting on the guilt of those who carried out Hitler's orders during the holocaust, for example, Albert Camus considered such actions as crimes of organizational logic rather than crimes of passion. Quoted in Robert Presthus, *The Organizational Society*, rev. ed. (St. Martin's Press, 1978), p. 40.

32. Vincent Ostrom, *The Intellectual Crisis in American Public Administration*, rev. ed. (University of Alabama Press, 1974), p. 19.

33. Barzelay, *Breaking through Bureaucracy*, p. 5.

34. Ibid., chap. 8.

35. This list takes some liberties with Osborne and Gaebler's wording but does capture the essence of the bureaucratic paradigm.

36. Caiden, *Administrative Reform Comes of Age*, p. 124.

37. Wilson, *Bureaucracy*, p. 344.

38. The factors that have led to successes and failures of reform movements are discussed in Neil J. Smelser, *Theory of Collective Behavior* (Free Press, 1962).

39. David Osborne did have an opportunity to provide such advice as a consultant to the NPR task force and in his contribution to the Progressive Policy Institute's *Mandate for Change* [Will Marshall and Martin Schram, eds. (Berkeley Books, 1992), chap. 12], a work filled with suggestions to the new administration. For a critique of Osborne's effort, see John J. DiIulio, Jr., "Thinking in Moderation," *Washington Monthly*, March 1993, pp. 51–53.

40. See the critique of Clinton's NPR efforts offered in Ronald C. Moe, "Let's Rediscover Government, Not Reinvent It," *Government Executive*, vol. 25 (June 1993), pp. 46–48, 60.

41. This is a modification of the approach used by Hood and Jackson, *Administrative Argument*, in their study of administrative doctrines.

42. Dwight Waldo, *The Administrative State: A Study of the Political Theory of American Public Administration*, 2d ed. (Holmes and Meier, 1984), p. 106.

43. Peter Wilenski argues that efficiency stands as the primary theme in all discussions of the purpose of public administration. See *Public Power and Public Administration* (Sydney: Hale and Iremonger, 1986), chap. 8.

44. Michael Barzelay states government's purpose as simply producing "results citizens value." See *Breaking through Bureaucracy*, p. 119.

45. Osborne and Gaebler, *Reinventing Government*, p. 30.

46. Ostrom, *Intellectual Crisis in American Public Administration*, chap. 3.

47. See Osborne and Gaebler, *Reinventing Government*, pp. 159–60; and Barzelay, *Breaking through Bureaucracy*, chap. 7.

48. Wilson, *Bureaucracy*, pt. 3.

49. For relevant discussions on such syntheses, see Robert B. Reich, ed., *The Power of Public Ideas* (Cambridge, Mass.: Ballinger, 1988).

50. Charles Murray, *In Pursuit of Happiness and Good Government* (Simon and Schuster, 1988).

51. For more on entrepreneurial leadership, see Jameson W. Doig and Erwin C. Hargrove, eds., *Leadership and Innovation: Entrepreneurs in Government*,

abridged ed. (Johns Hopkins University Press, 1990), especially pp. 7–8. See note 24 for references on alternative tools.

52. See Robert Maranto and David Schultz, *A Short History of the United States Civil Service* (University Press of America, 1991), chap. 4.

53. David H. Rosenbloom provides an overview of these cultures and argues that a third is emerging. "Thus far, however, [the new culture] has not been accompanied by a coherent political movement. Rather it has been composed of several diverse elements that have evolved somewhat separately. These elements can be joined together, but it may be up to the public administration community to make them cohere." See his "Democratic Constitutionalism and the Evolution of Bureaucratic Government: Freedom and Accountability in the Administrative State," in Peter F. Nardulli, ed., *The Constitution and American Political Development: An Institutional Perspective* (University of Illinois Press, 1992), pp. 132–34.

54. Smelser, *Theory of Collective Behavior*, p. 296.

55. Ibid., p. 297.

56. Tom Shoop, "The Reinvention Rage," *Government Executive*, vol. 25 (March 1993), p. 10.

57. Smelser, *Theory of Collective Behavior*, pp. 298–301.

58. Ibid., p. 302.

59. The release of the National Performance Review report in September 1993 was accompanied by pubic relations efforts that initially drew bipartisan support to the proposed reforms as well as considerable attention from the media. See Shoop, "Goring the Bureaucracy," pp. 12–16. It is too early to judge whether such efforts will generate the needed momentum and support to create a full-fledged movement.

60. Robert T. Golembiewski, *Organizing Men and Power: Patterns of Behavior and Line-Staff Models* (Rand McNally, 1967), p. 2.

61. See Woodrow Wilson, "The Study of Administration," *Political Science Quarterly*, vol. 1 (June 1887), pp. 197–222, reprinted in *Political Science Quarterly*, vol. 56 (December 1941), pp. 481–506. There is, of course, some question of the influence of the essay in the founding of the field; see Paul P. Van Riper, "The American Administrative State: Wilson and the Founders—An Unorthodox View," *Public Administration Review*, vol 43 (November–December 1983), pp. 478–79.

62. Wilson, "Study of Administration," p. 500.

63. Dwight Waldo, *The Study of Public Administration* (Random House, 1955), pp. 40–42.

64. The model of bureaucracy that most intrigued Wilson was that found in the administration of European governments, especially Germany and France. See Daniel W. Martin, "Deja Vu: French Antecedents of American Public Administration," *Public Administration Review*, vol. 47 (July–August 1987), pp. 297–303. Among the emerging middle class, the highly centralized, single-product corporation provided a model that many believed appropriate for government; see Alfred D. Chandler, Jr., *The Visible Hand: The Managerial Revolution in American Business* (Cambridge, Mass.: Belknap Press, 1977). On the movement of American social values toward bureaucratism between 1900 and 1920, see Robert H. Wiebe, *The Search for Order, 1877–1920* (Hill and Wang, 1967), pp. 145–63.

65. Ostrom, *Intellectual Crisis in American Public Administration*, pp. 34–35.

66. Waldo, *Study of Public Administration*, pp. 42ff. For a brief historical overview, see Jonathan B. Bendor, *Parallel Systems: Redundancy in Government* (University of California Press, 1985), pp. 33–39.

67. Alan A. Altshuler, "The Study of American Public Administration," in Alan A. Altshuler and Norman C. Thomas, eds., *The Politics of the Federal Bureaucracy*, 2d ed. (Harper and Row, 1977), p. 6.

68. See Avery Leiserson and Fritz Morstein Marx, "The Study of Public Administration," in Fritz Morstein Marx, ed., *Elements of Public Administration*, 2d ed. (Prentice-Hall, 1959), pp. 27–34, 39–48. Also James W. Fesler, "Public Administration and the Social Sciences: 1946–1960," in Frederick C. Mosher, ed., *American Public Administration: Past, Present, Future* (University of Alabama Press, 1975), pp. 97–141.

69. Max Weber, *Economy and Society: An Outline of Interpretive Sociology*, ed. by Guenther Roth and Claus Wittich (University of California Press, 1978), p. 973.

70. Osborne and Gaebler, *Reinventing Government*, pp. 14–16.

71. Elliott Jaques, "In Praise of Hierarchy," *Harvard Business Review*, vol. 68 (January–February 1990), p. 127.

72. There have been attempts to study the variations or to approach such a study. See Christopher Hood and Andrew Dunsire, *Bureaumetrics: The Quantitative Comparison of British Central Government Agencies* (University of Alabama Press, 1981); also see Hal G. Rainey, *Understanding and Managing Public Organizations* (San Francisco: Jossey-Bass, 1991), especially chap. 5.

73. Laurence E. Lynn, Jr., *Managing Public Policy* (Little, Brown, 1987), p. 79.

74. For institutional contexts, see Rainey, *Understanding and Managing Public Organizations*, pp. 115–17; and Louis C. Gawthrop, *Bureaucratic Behavior in the Executive Branch: An Analysis of Organizational Change* (Free Press, 1969), especially chap. 3. For reflections of politics see Harold Seidman and Robert Gilmour, *Politics, Position, and Power: From The Positive To The Regulatory State*, 4th ed. (Oxford University Press, 1986). For adaptations see Herbert Kaufman, *Time, Chance, and Organizations: Natural Selection in a Perilous Environment*, 2d ed. (Chatham House, 1991). Also see Louis C. Gawthrop, *Administrative Politics and Social Change* (St. Martin's Press, 1971), chaps. 5, 6.

75. See Grunow, "Development of the Public Sector," pp. 101–02.

76. See Victor A. Thompson, *Bureaucracy and the Modern World* (Morristown, N.J.: General Learning Press, 1976).

77. See Bendor, *Parallel Systems: Redundancy in Government*; Donald Chisholm, *Coordination without Hierarchy: Informal Structures in Multiorganizational Systems* (University of California Press, 1989); and Charles Perrow, *Normal Accidents: Living with High-Risk Technologies* (Basic Books, 1984).

78. Weber, *Economy and Society*, p. 987.

79. Louis C. Gawthrop, *Public Sector Management, Systems, and Ethics* (Indiana University Press, 1984), chap. 3.

80. Wilson, *Bureaucracy*, p. 331.

286     MELVIN J. DUBNICK

81. Michel Crozier, *The Bureaucratic Phenomenon* (University of Chicago Press, 1964), p. 195; and Donald A. Schon, *Beyond the Stable State* (Random House, 1971), chap. 2.

82. Ibid., p. 49; also see Victor A. Thompson, *Bureaucracy and Innovation* (University of Alabama Press, 1969), chap. 4.

83. Wilson, *Bureaucracy*, p. 375. Also see Guy Benveniste, *Bureaucracy* (San Francisco: Boyd and Fraser, 1977).

84. Walters, "Reinventing Government," p. 34.

85. David N. Ammons, "Productivity Barriers in the Public Sector," in Marc Holzer, ed., *Public Productivity Handbook* (Marcel Dekker, 1992), pp. 117–36.

86. See Michael Beer, R. A. Eisenstat, and Bert Spector, "Why Change Programs Don't Produce Change," *Harvard Business Review*, vol. 68 (November–December 1990), pp. 158–66.

87. Osborne and Gaebler, *Reinventing Government*, p. 309.

88. Ibid., pp. 290–98.

89. See Chris Argyris and Donald A. Schon, *Organizational Learning: A Theory of Action Perspective* (Addison-Wesley, 1978); Paul W. Waldo, Jr., "A Learning Model of Organization," in Christopher Bellavita, ed., *How Public Organizations Work: Learning From Experience* (Praeger, 1990), chap. 9; and Peter M. Senge, *The Fifth Discipline: The Art and Practice of the Learning Organization* (Doubleday, 1990).

90. See, for example, Philip Selznick, *TVA and the Grass Roots: A Study of Politics and Organization* (University of California Press, 1949).

91. See Richard Beckhard, *Organizational Development: Strategies and Models* (Addison Wesley, 1969); and Edgar Schein, *Process Consultation: Its Role in Organization Development* (Addison Wesley, 1969).

92. The classic expression of this attitude toward change is found in Harvey Sherman, *It All Depends: A Pragmatic Approach to Organization* (University of Alabama Press, 1966).

93. See, for example, Ralph H. Kilmann, *Beyond The Quick Fix: Managing Five Tracks to Organizational Success* (San Francisco: Jossey-Bass, 1984); and Dave Ulrich, Robert E. Quinn, and Kim S. Cameron, "Designing Effective Organizational Systems," in James L. Perry, ed., *Handbook of Public Administration* (San Francisco: Jossey-Bass, 1989), pp. 148–61.

94. See Terry M. Moe, " The New Economics of Organization," *American Journal of Political Science*, vol. 28 (November 1984), pp. 739–77.

95. On the concept of reengineering, see Michael Hammer, "Reengineering Work: Don't Automate, Obliterate," *Harvard Business Review*, vol. 68 (July–August 1990), pp. 104–12. On its use see John Martin, "Reengineering Government," *Governing*, vol. 6 (March 1993), pp. 26–30.

96. Alexis de Tocqueville, *Democracy in America*, translated by George Lawrence (Anchor Books, 1969), p. 207.

97. Wiebe, *Search for Order*, chap. 6.

98. Stephen Skowronek, *Building A New American State: The Expansion of National Administrative Capacities, 1877–1920* (Cambridge University Press, 1982); and Chandler, *Visible Hand.*

99. Michael Thompson, Richard Ellis, and Aaron Wildavsky, *Cultural Theory* (Boulder, Colo.: Westview Press, 1990), p. 6; also Wiebe, *Search for Order*, p. 156.

100. Robert N. Bellah and others, *Habits of the Heart: Individualism and Commitment in American Life* (University of California Press, 1985), chap. 2.

101. There are many ways to conceive of institutions; for example, compare James G. March and Johan P. Olsen, *Rediscovering Institutions: The Organizational Basis of Politics* (Free Press, 1989); and Robert Grafstein, *Institutional Realism: Social and Political Constraints on Rational Actors* (Yale University Press, 1992). I present a vague definition to facilitate the present discussion.

102. See Barbara S. Romzek and Melvin J. Dubnick, "Accountability in the Public Sector: Lessons from the *Challenger* Tragedy," *Public Administration Review*, vol. 47 (May–June 1987), pp. 227–38; also Melvin J. Dubnick and Barbara S. Romzek, *American Public Administration: Politics and the Management of Expectations* (Macmillan, 1991), chap. 3.

103. See Herbert Kaufman, "Administrative Decentralization and Political Power," *Public Administration Review*, vol. 29 (January–February 1969), pp. 3–15.

104. The constitutional doctrine of separation of powers thus fostered at least three organizational approaches to government administration—in David H. Rosenbloom's terms, the managerial (executive), political (legislative), and legal (judicial)—that cannot be synthesized "without violating values deeply ingrained in the United States political culture." See Rosenbloom, "Public Administrative Theory and the Separation of Powers," *Public Administration Review*, vol. 43 (May–June 1983), p. 219. Compare Laurence J. O'Toole, Jr., "Doctrines and Developments: Separation of Powers, the Politics-Administration Dichotomy, and the Rise of the Administrative State," *Public Administration Review*, vol. 47 (January–February 1987), pp. 17–25.

105. This division reflects a long-standing controversy usually traced back to the debate between Carl J. Friedrich, "Public Policy and the Nature of Administrative Responsibility," in C. J. Friedrich and Edward S. Mason, eds., *Public Policy, 1940* (Harvard University Press, 1940), pp. 3–24, and Herman Finer, "Administrative Responsibility in Democratic Government," *Public Administration Review*, vol. 1 (Summer 1941), pp. 335–50.

106. Wilson, *Bureaucracy*, pp. 376–78.

107. Ibid., p. 302.

108. See Thompson, Ellis, and Wildavsky, *Cultural Theory*.

109. Ibid., pp. 4–5.

110. See James Oliver Robertson, *American Myth, American Reality* (Hill and Wang, 1980), p. xv.

111. This is in contrast to the more heroic image of "Bill Bureaucrat" offered by Paul H. Appleby in *Big Democracy* (Knopf, 1945).

112. Osborne and Gaebler, *Reinventing Government*, p. xviii.

113. National Commission on the Public Service, *Rebuilding the Public Service*, p. 13.

# Appendix: Excerpts from Commission Reports

THE National Commission on the Public Service (Volcker commission), the National Commission on the State and Local Public Service (Winter commission), and the National Performance Review, chaired by Vice President Al Gore, have recommended deregulating the public service and otherwise reforming the way government operates.[1] Reprinted here are relevant portions of the reports of these commissions.

## Volcker Commission (1989)

The Commission makes the following recommendations to further enhance (the Federal Office of Personnel Management's, OPM's) agenda for change: First, OPM should continue to deregulate the hiring process by giving departments and agencies broad, but conditional, authority to set their own rules, as well as through aggressive use and expansion of existing authority to experiment and continued use of advisory and clearing-house mechanisms to share information across government . . .

Create a system that gives managers the authority they need to manage. The current system—or, as some maintain, nonsystem—removes important authority from the career managers who are most responsible for the day to day activities of government. Control through multitudes of regulations and procedures, administered by a central agency removed from service delivery, has created mangers with limited power but full responsibility for any problems that occur. Greater congruence between operating responsibility and managerial authority is absolutely necessary. . . .

A manager from the Internal Revenue Service said, "[W]e have a great need for new occupations. The existing classification system just does not serve our needs. For example, engineers for our computer systems—how would you grade and classify such people? How can we hire them? One estimate is that there may be a need for 4,000 to 4,500 new occupations a year [government-wide]. . . ." The OPM should examine the implications of eliminating the Classification Act of 1949 and of allowing all classification activity to occur at the agency level.

The OPM must support small demonstration projects in this and other areas. More flexible and innovative classification schemes should be tested in a variety of agency settings and for a variety of occupations. Managerial discretion should be emphasized.

The Commission recommends the creation of management demonstration projects, under the research and demonstration authority granted the OPM by the Civil Service Reform Act of 1978, whose purpose is to create and monitor experiments in pure managerial flexibility. Managers would be selected for the demonstration from the executive (rather than the scientific or technical) ranks of the Senior Executive Service. The staff assigned, as needed for the duration of the project, would have rank-in-person status. The manager would be given a guaranteed budget for the three-year period, objectives, and the freedom to reach those objectives in whatever way he or she determines most feasible, relying on common sense and the managerial expertise for which he or she was selected. Monitoring would be minimal and would focus on implications of increased flexibility for retention of senior managers and on the transferability of lessons learned to other government settings. The experiments would approximate, to the greatest extent possible, the managerial authority and prerogatives enjoyed by private sector executives.

## Winter Commission (1993)

Creating flat, responsive agencies also involves freeing chief executives, managers, and front-line employees from the thicket of outmoded laws, internal regulations, and controls that has grown up around them over the years. Deregulation is virtually required by de-layering—there will be fewer managers and supervisors available to enforce the rules.

Even without de-layering, however, a reduction in rules is long overdue. Hiring, purchasing, and budgeting systems now often frustrate the goals they were enacted to achieve.

America's civil service was invented 100 years ago to guarantee merit in the hiring process. Sadly, many state and local governments have created such rule-bound and complicated systems that merit is often the last value served. How can merit be served, for example, when supervisors are only allowed three choices from among hundreds of possible candidates for a job? How can merit be served when pay is determined mainly on the basis of time on the job? How is merit served when top performers can be "bumped" from their jobs by poor performers during downsizings?

Over the years, the basic purpose of the civil service system has been forgotten: To recruit the most talented among our citizens into government, not to employ legions of classification experts and personnel administrators who spend their days tracing bumping routes and rewriting job descriptions. State and local governments have a hard enough time as it is recruiting the best and the brightest without actively discouraging them. . . .

The Commission believes that states and localities are best served by a decentralized merit system that helps agencies and departments address issues of hiring and mobility, pay diversity, firing, and the operation of the personnel system. Obviously public sector unions have worked hard in these areas over the years and care deeply about safeguarding workers against management actions they feel are arbitrary. In many jurisdictions it will be pivotal to develop a full partnership with unions to achieve the reforms needed to create a high-performance work force.

### On Hiring and Mobility

Many civil service systems sharply limit freedom to hire in two ways: (1) They rely heavily on written tests that may be biased, out-of-date, poor in predicting performance, and expensive to construct; (2) They sharply limit the number of candidates who are forwarded for interviews, through a "rule of three" or other limiting provision. Under such a rule, only the top three individuals on a list of elegibles are certified for hiring. Placement on the list often depends heavily on performance on a written test, downplaying other important characteristics such as interpersonal skills.

These constraints on managerial discretion were put in place to ensure the primacy of merit, and cannot be dropped without instituting clear protections for those who might face discrimination. Nevertheless, the Commission recommends that states and localities reconsider these requirements in light of today's needs. Many governments are finding that using selection criteria other than written tests is critical to finding and promoting good people. In addition, expanding the list of candidates who can be forwarded for interviews can allow more aggressive recruitment in order to achieve diversity.

The Commission further recommends that effective pipelines for recruiting the best and the brightest into public service be fully exploited. Fortunately, there appears to be a renewed interest in public service as a career. Good intern programs, of which there are many, help make for good government, often serving as fast-track vehicles for outstanding students to enter government service. They should be sustained and expanded.

The Commission also urges that states and localities pay greater attention to seniority and veterans preference rules and recommends that, when they present a problem, limits be placed on their use in determining who gets hired, promoted, and protected during downsizing. Seniority rules, which protect longtime workers, can present a fairness issue, especially for women and minorities. A special advantage in the personnel selection process should only be extended once to any one individual who has served in the military, and then only in order to break a tie between otherwise equally qualified applicants.

The Commission proposes reducing the number of job families into which all employees fit, instead of continuing to wrestle with the hundreds or even thousands of classifications that currently characterize most state and local systems. In states, for example, the number of classifications ranges from as high as 7,300 in New York to as low as 551 in South Dakota. The Commission believes that no more than a few dozen are needed, with some provision for distinctions between positions with job families to reflect different levels of expertise or "bands." Under such a system— which has been recommended by the National Academy of Public Administration for the federal government—the number of job classifications in most jurisdictions would drop significantly. Such a system would allow much greater flexibility in staffing government according to shifting needs and would also permit greater flow of staff among agencies and departments.

The Commission believes that keeping good people once government finds them is equally important. At the same time, employees should not be handcuffed to a lifetime of government service, nor should talented candidates be locked out of lateral entry at midcareer by antiquated, nonportable pension systems. The Commission therefore recommends that states and localities at the least honor the same five-year vesting minimum required of all private firms under federal law. After five years employees could take both their contribution and the government's when they leave and roll the money over into a new pension fund, if they wish. As of 1991, an estimated 40 percent of all state and local employees had to work ten years before becoming vested.

One aim of such mobility reform should be to encourage free movement between the public and private sectors. Many of the skills they require are interchangeable, and it is in the nation's long-term best interest to have its workers understand both worlds.

The Commission advocates a simple pay and promotion structure that would allow much greater flexibility in rewarding good employees and also encourage greater movement of employees across agencies and easier reassignment on an as-needed basis. Such a system uses a small number of broad pay bands, usually three, to replace the complicated grade-and-step system currently in place. Under that system, employee pay is based on a set number of grades—usually 15 or so—and on various steps based on seniority within those grades—usually 10 or so. Not surprisingly, a system with as many as 150 different pay levels can create an enormous amount of conflict within the workplace. Besides being less complex, broad-banding of pay allows managers to reward employees without having to give them a new job title. It allows managers to reassign personnel more easily to meet shifts in demand and priorities.

The Commission proposes that state and local governments reevaluate their pay-for-performance plans. Almost half of all states, and a majority of counties and cities, now have at least some of their employees in pay-for-performance plans. Unfortunately, many of those plans promise far more than they deliver. Some of the systems are unbelievably complicated and paper-intensive. Others are simply poorly administered. Still others are launched without adequate funding. The best available research suggests that pay-for-performance in the public sector has been a disappointment, and that states and localities should be exceedingly cautious about overselling what are likely to be small performance bonuses allocated through a cumbersome and potentially political process. The Commission recommends that such plans be dropped if they are not perceived by employees as fair or if they are underfunded.

The Commission further encourages pay-setting approaches and bonus systems that make it every employee's business to assure the overall success of the organization. For example, team-based pay-for-performance systems—whether the team is several employees, a small unit, or an agency—send the right signal, that employees rise or fall on the basis of outcomes. Gainsharing is a viable step toward such a system. Under a gainsharing formula, workers on a given team split the savings from higher productivity equally with taxpayers, whether through a one-time bonus or an innovation investment fund for the team's future productivity improvements.

## On Diversity

The pattern and the problem are clear. The face of America *outside* government is changing faster than the face of the work force *inside*. Consider the situation in Los Angeles. According to the *Report of the Independent Commission on the Los Angeles Police Department in the Wake of the L.A. Riots*, 37 percent of the city's population is white compared to approximately 69 percent of the city's police officers. In spite of aggressive recruiting of African-American and Latino officers, the city still has a long way to go in assuring that the force both is representative and allows minority officers the opportunity to rise to the highest-level positions.

The disconnection between those whom government serves and those who serve government can only create tensions. There is a very legitimate question as to whether a government can only create tensions. There is a very legitimate question as to whether a government that does not reflect the demographic makeup of the governed can operate effectively over the long haul, or in the face of widespread hostility or resentment on the part of disenfranchised groups.

Remedying this disconnection is going to take more than aggressive recruitment of women and minorities. In some communities government agencies may have to take a leading role in ensuring a diverse work force. The Commission strongly recommends that government not only actively recruit workers to reflect the diversity of the community served, but that it also actively promote investment in all of its young people, encouraging everyone to stay in school and providing them with the opportunity to work in public service.

States and localities have certainly made progress in the area of recruiting women and minorities in the past two decades—the proportion of female, full-time employees increased from 35 percent in 1974 to 42 percent in 1989, while the proportion of minorities rose from 20 percent to 27 percent. But women and minorities still staff the front lines and not the front office. The vast majority of the lowest-paid positions in state and local government are held by women and minorities. Although the imbalance has been substantially redressed since the mid-1970s, states and localities have a long way to go.

The Commission endorses efforts to find innovative ways for women and minorities to break through the ceiling to higher-level jobs. State and local governments should initiate educational opportunities for its current work force that would better prepare underrepresented groups for top management positions. Introducing more flexible hiring and promotional practices can also help these groups move into the middle- and upper-ranks of government.

But money and titles are not the only issues. The Commission believes that part of government's effort to create a work force that mirrors the population it represents also ought to include elimination of traditional barriers to women in mid- and upper-level jobs and in departments that have been traditionally off limits to women. Women are still far more likely to be found in education, health, aging, library, and welfare agencies than in transportation, corrections, agriculture, or law enforcement, yet women have time and again proved themselves to be capable contributors in these and other fields.

## On Firing

Many of the current systems demonstrate the worst of two worlds: The hiring process can be ponderous, frustrating both managers and highly qualified candidates for government jobs, and at the same time the mechanism for releasing poor performers can be even more daunting. Many managers are so stymied by the process that they would rather promote a poor performer into a new, useless job than initiate termination proceedings. Firing should always be a last resort, but once the decision has been made, the Commission recommends that there be mechanisms in place to move it to resolution, preferably through binding arbitration that brings both sides to the table within days.

## On Operating the Personnel System

Most state and local governments rely on highly centralized personnel systems that exert a good deal of control over all personnel decisions government-wide. In California, however, the central board gives the responsibility to the departments under clearly written guidelines, then gets out of the way—thus saving time, money, and frustration. The Commission strongly recommends that states and large local governments consider turning more authority for staffing decisions over to agencies and departments, then acting as a consultant to ensure that such staffing is fair and conforms to all applicable state, local, and federal laws.

The fairness of the civil service hiring and promotional process can best be measured by the quality of the people hired and the work they perform, not by the number of steps in the process, the amount of paperwork involved, or the rigidity of the policies.

### Accelerate the Procurement Process

By far the greatest impediment to fast, sensible government contracting and procurement practices is the multiple layers of approval through which requisitions must pass. The process has become so complex and so expensive that many of our best companies refuse to bid on government contracts because it is simply not worth the time and effort. Government managers and employees, meanwhile, cannot obtain the supplies or equipment they need or cannot get them when they need them. Worst of all, cost, rather than quality, is often the overriding criterion for purchasing and contracting decisions.

In the end, the process really only serves to subvert the goals it was intended to achieve. Competition is reduced, unrealistically low bidding becomes commonplace, and neither the government nor the taxpayers get their money's worth. As a step toward fixing the system, the Commission recommends that any state and local procurement process possess four key characteristics:

—*An emphasis on quality and results over cost,* with clear incentives for high performance and strong penalties for poor work. The low bid cannot be the only or the overriding criterion in selecting a contractor, whether it is a road builder or a foster care provider.

—*A process streamlined enough to keep pace with new technology and procedures.* State and local governments cannot afford to wait two years to procure new computer systems, nor should employees have to wait six months for basic supplies and services. Government must seek devices for speeding up its timetable to provide quick access to supplies and services, perhaps by raising the threshold for noncompetitive bidding, by allowing managers the flexibility to make faster decisions on their own, or by the awarding of multiple open-ended contracts to suppliers who would then have an incentive to provide fast service.

—*A minimum of paperwork.* Multiple reviews and justifications not only slow the process, they add needless costs to the final contract—costs that must ultimately be paid by the taxpayers.

—*A single-signature policy on small purchases.* It makes no sense to force front-line employees to seek multiple signature approval on every small purchase. It makes no sense to require that every piece of equipment or office supply come from the agency or department's central supply department. If an employee needs some relatively inexpensive item and can get it quickly and at competitive cost at a nearby store, management should provide for that sort of quick decision. Adherence to the *trust and lead* strategy implies that our employees have to be trusted to do the right thing.

In sum, governments need to put in place contracting and procurement systems that emphasize quality, efficiency, and accountability for outcomes.

### Eliminate Spend-It-or-Lose-It Budget Systems

Almost all state and local budget systems create enormous incentives toward waste by requiring managers either to spend the money in their budgets by the end of the fiscal year or to send it back to the general fund, and probably suffer a cut in next year's appropriation on top of that. In other words, frugality is punished, not rewarded.

Spend-it-or-lose-it budgets are more onerous still in concert with highly detailed line-item budgets, with specific accounts for virtually every activity imaginable, so that funds cannot be transferred to areas of more serious need. Instead of being able to reprogram funds quickly to meet an emerging problem, managers are locked into strict categories by budget lines. Thus, the Commission believes that every budget system should have four simple features:

—*As few budget lines as possible to give chief executives more flexibility to reprogram funds to meet unforeseen problems and emerging needs.* While the Commission recognizes legitimate legislative responsibilities in both raising and spending funds, chief executives must have considerably more freedom to move funds quickly than they do now. The Commission recommends that states and localities experiment with complete "de-lining" of an agency's budget, guided by clear performance goals set in consultation with the legislature, council, or other legislative body.

—*The ability to carry over unspent funds from fiscal year to fiscal year.* If agencies cannot, managers and employees are being punished for thinking carefully about how to spend money, and rewarded for spending money in an end-of-the-fiscal-year frenzy. Allowing carry-over of a quarter of a given budget line into the next fiscal year is a good first step toward reducing the spend-it-or-lose-it incentives that currently exist.

—*The ability to depreciate capital investments.* Without depreciation, the budget shows long-term maintenance as a luxury, actually encouraging states and localities to wait until our roads, bridges, water systems, and other public works seriously deteriorate before thinking about the future. Such a practice is costly because it discourages the much more sound financial practice of maintaining our infrastructure rather than having to overhaul or replace it—a process, incidentally, that assures that citizens bear the full brunt and aggravation of disrepair. The Commission encourages states and localities to experiment with ways of depreciating physical capital, and, in doing so, to show that the failure to maintain assets is an expensive illusion.

*—A link between spending inputs and program outcomes.* Although performance budgeting is tough to implement, it does get states and local workers thinking about the right thing: *performance.* Instead of asking how many state troopers or city patrolmen have been hired, performance goals ask whether the roads are safer because accident rates are reduced or whether cities are safer because crime rates are down. Instead of asking how many workers there are in our welfare agencies, performance goals ask whether case loads are dropping, family heads are finding jobs, or at-risk children are graduating from high school. The key idea is that program goals should be clear from the start and should then be ratcheted up as a way to motivate workers and give the public a sense of progress and accomplishment.

## National Performance Review

Our federal personnel system has been evolving for more than 100 years—ever since the 1881 assassination of President James A. Garfield by a disappointed job seeker. And during that time, according to a 1988 Office of Personnel Management publication:

> . . . *anecdotal mistakes prompted additional rules. When the rules led to new inequities, even more rules were added. Over time . . . a maze of regulations and requirements was created, hamstringing managers . . . often impeding federal managers and employees from achieving their missions and from giving the public a high quality of service.*

Year after year, layer after layer, the rules have piled up. The U.S. Merit Systems Protection Board reports there are now 850 pages of federal personnel law—augmented by 1,300 pages of OPM regulations on how to implement those laws and another 10,000 pages of guidelines from the Federal Personnel Manual.

On one topic alone—how to complete a standard form for a notice of a personnel action—the Federal Personnel Manual contains 900 pages of instructions. The full stack of personnel laws, regulations, directives, case law and departmental guidance that the Agriculture Department uses weighs 1,088 pounds.

Thousands of pages of personnel rules prompt thousands of pages of personnel forms. In 1991, for example, the Navy's Human Resources Office processed enough forms to create a "monument" 3,100 feet tall—six times the height of the Washington monument.

Costs to the taxpayer for this personnel quagmire are enormous. In total, 54,000 personnel work in federal personnel positions. We spend billions of dollars for these staff to classify each employee within a highly complex system of some 459 job series, 15 grades and 10 steps within each grade. . . .

In 1989, Paul Volcker's National Commission on the Public Service explained, "the complexity of the hiring process often drives all but the most dedicated away." Managers who find it nearly impossible to hire the people they need sometimes flaunt the system by hiring people as consultants at higher rates than those same people would earn as federal employees. The average manager needs a year to fire an incompetent employee, even with solid proof. During layoffs, employees slated to be laid off can "bump" employees with less seniority, regardless of their abilities or performance—putting people in jobs they don't understand and never wanted. . . .

To create an effective federal government, we must reform virtually the entire personnel system: recruitment, hiring, classification, promotion, pay, and reward systems. We must make it easier for federal managers to hire the workers they need, to reward those who do good work, and to fire those who do not. . . .

Action: *OPM will deregulate personnel policy by phasing out the 10,000-page Federal Personnel Manual and all agency implementing directives.* . . .

We will ask Congress to pass legislation decentralizing authority over recruitment, hiring, and promotion. Under the present system, OPM controls the examination system for external candidates and recruits and screens candidates for positions that are common to all agencies, with agencies then hiring from among candidates presented by OPM. Under the new system, OPM could offer to screen candidates for agencies, but agencies need not accept OPM's offer.

Under this decentralized system, agencies will also be allowed to make their own decisions about when to hire candidates directly—without examinations or rankings—under guidelines to be drafted by OPM. Agencies able to do so should also be permitted to conduct their own background investigations of potential candidates. . . .

There is strong evidence that agencies given authority to do these things themselves can do better. Using demonstration authority under the 1978 Civil Service Reform Act, several agencies have experimented with simpler systems. In one experiment, at the Naval Weapons Center in China Lake, California, and the Naval Oceans Systems Center, in San Diego, the system was simplified to a few career paths and only four-to-six broad pay bands within each path. Known as the "China Lake Experiment," it solved many of the problems faced by the two naval facilities. . . .

Action: *Dramatically simplify the current classification system, to give agencies greater flexibility in how they classify and pay their employees.*

We will urge Congress to remove all the 1940s-era grade-level descriptions from the law and adopt an approach that is more modern. In addition, Congress should allow agencies to move from the General Schedule system to a broad-band system. OPM should develop such standard banding patterns, and agencies should be free to adopt one without seeking OPM's approval.

When agency proposals do not fit under a standard pattern, OPM should approve them as five-year demonstration projects that would be converted to permanent "alternative systems" if successful. OPM should establish criteria for broad-banding demonstration projects, and agencies' projects meeting those criteria should receive automatic approval. . . .

Action: *Simplify the procurement process by rewriting federal regulations—shifting from rigid rules to guiding principles.*

The Federal Acquisition Regulation (FAR), the government's principal set of procurement regulations, contains too many rules. Rules are changed too often and are so process-oriented that they minimize discretion and stifle innovation, according to a Merit Systems Protection Board survey. As one frustrated manager noted, the FAR does not even clearly state the main goal of procurement policy: "Is it to avoid waste, fraud, and abuse? Is it to implement a social-economic agenda? Is it to procure the government's requirements at a fair and reasonable cost?"

This administration will rewrite the 1,600-page FAR, the 2,900 pages of agency supplements that accompany it, and Executive Order 12352, which governs federal procurement. The new regulations will:

300 APPENDIX: EXCERPTS FROM COMMISSION REPORTS

—shift from rigid rules to guiding principles;
—promote decision making at the lowest possible level;
—end unnecessary regulatory requirements;
—foster competitiveness and commercial practices;
—shift to a new emphasis on choosing "best value" products;
—facilitate innovative contracting approaches; and
—recommend acquisition methods that reflect information technology's short life cycle.

—develop a more effective process to listen to its customers: line managers, government procurement officers and vendors who do business with the government.

## Notes

1. National Commission on the Public Service, *Leadership for America: Rebuilding the Public Service* (Washington, 1989), p. 29; and National Commission on the Public Service, *Leadership for America: Rebuilding the Public Service—Task Force Reports to the National Commission on the Public Service* (Washington, 1989), pp. 95, 96. National Commission on the State and Local Public Service, *Hard Truths/Tough Choices: An Agenda for State and Local Reform* (Albany, N.Y., 1993), pp. 28–44; and National Performance Review, *From Red Tape to Results: Creating a Government That Works Better and Costs Less* (Washington, 1993), pp. 24, 26–29.

# Index

Lobbies, 64, 72, 73. *See also* Interest groups
Los Angeles Educational Alliance for
  Restructuring Now (LEARN), 48
Los Angeles Unified School District
  (LAUSD), 48
Lynn, Laurence E., Jr., 270–71

McConnell, Grant, 18
MacKay, Buddy, 131, 136, 138. *See also*
  Florida
McLarty, Thomas, 65
Management. *See* Agencies, government;
  Bureaucracy; Civil service;
  Government
Mandates, 168
Manning, Bayless, 75
March, James, 189
Market factors, 45–46, 51, 56, 58–59. *See*
  *also* Contracting out
Mass transit. *See* Transportation
Mayor's Private Sector Task Force on
  Management and Productivity
  (Pennsylvania), 150–51
Meese, Edwin, 68
Merit Systems Protection Board, 89. *See also*
  Equal Employment Opportunity
  Commission
Moe, Terry, 51
Monday Management Group, 178, 185, 191
Moynihan, Daniel Patrick, 243
Murray, Charles, 264

Nannygate scandal, 65
Nathan, Richard P., 8
National Academy of Public Administration,
  46, 89
National Advisory Council for Historic
  Preservation, 178
National Commission on the Public Service
  (Volcker commission), 2, 3, 251,
  252–53, 264, 267
National Commission on the State and
  Local Public Service (Winter
  commission), 2, 3, 160, 251, 264, 267
National Historic Preservation Act, 178
National Performance Review, 10– 11,
  41–42, 47, 52, 86, 96, 97, 167, 253

Natural Gas Policy Act of *1978*, 19
Naval Weapons Center (China Lake,
  California), 53–56, 92–93
Naval Ocean Systems Center (San Diego),
  54, 92
Newark, 143
New Deal, 16, 17–18, 239
Newell, Frederick, 16
News media, 137, 140
New York, 159–60
New York Central Railroad, 240
Niskanen, William A., 254
Nowak, Karen, 144, 150
Nozick, Robert, 251–52

Occupational Safety and Health Act of
  *1970*, 19
Office of Federal Procurement Policy, 125
Office of Government Ethics, 63, 64, 66–68,
  71, 77–78, 79
Office of Management and Budget, 14, 88,
  244
Office of Personnel Management, 14, 41,
  54, 55, 63, 91–92, 94. *See also* Civil
  Service Commission
OGE. *See* Office of Government Ethics
Osborne, David, 133, 175, 188, 253. *See also*
  *Reinventing Government*

Packard Commission on Defense
  Procurement, 118
Page, Logan W., 238
Paquette, Joseph E., Jr., 150
Pendleton Act of *1883*, 14, 23–24, 264
Pennsylvania, 244–47. *See also* Philadelphia
Pennsylvania Intergovernmental
  Cooperation Authority (PICA), 131,
  144, 146, 152
Perot, Ross, 85, 136, 175–76, 181
Personnel. *See* Work force
Philadelphia, 130–31: police, 49; reforms, 8,
  131–32, 143–54
Phoenix, 143
PICA. *See* Pennsylvania Intergovernmental
  Cooperation Authority
Pinchot, Gifford, 16, 238
Pingree, David, 150

Pinkerton, James, 179, 181–82
Pizzi, Charles, 150–51
Police departments: accountability, 198–
200, 201, 202, 208, 215, 227–28,
229–31; communication and *911*
systems, 200–1, 206, 210, 219–21, 225;
community-based policing, 9, 48, 49,
198, 218–26; corruption, 200–1, 204,
208, 215, 230; deregulation, 47–48,
198–99, 202, 229; ethnic bias, 204,
217; Houston, 49; law enforcement,
203–9, 210–11, 215–22, 223, 228; Los
Angeles, 48–49; management, 201–2,
207–11, 224–28, 228–31; New York
City, 49; officials, 200; paperwork,
209; problem solving, 222–26, 228;
professionalism, 226–28; public
administration and, 199–203, 208–9,
228–30; recruitment, 209; reforms,
201–3, 218–31; regulations, 9, 200;
support of, 217, 224, 229, 230;
theories of police administration,
203–11, 212–18. *See also* Bureaucracy
Policymaking, 170, 241, 242–43
Political factors: agencies, 163, 164–65;
bureaucratization, 276; centralization,
50, 268; customer orientation, 167,
179, 180, 181; deregulation, 7, 56,
57–59, 193, 264; government
institutions, 186, 268; police
departments, 208, 229, 231;
privatization, 25; public attitudes, 157,
182; reforms, 135–40, 142, 146,
149–50, 151, 194, 265–67
Patronage: civil service, 160; Philadelphia,
149–50; post–Civil War, 13
Postal Service, 52, 63, 182
Presidential Initiative on Rural America,
178, 184–85, 191
Presidents: agency micromanagement, 40,
42; appointments, 162–63;
decisionmaking, 20. *See also*
*individuals by name*
President's Committee on Administrative
Management, 173
Private sector: compared to public sector,
23–24, 37–38, 172, 180, 214–15, 250;
government and business joint
action, 150; streamlining, 37

Privatization: Philadelphia, 146–48;
railroads, 241; reform and, 25, 28, 52;
theory, 25. *See also* Contracting out;
Procurement
Procurement: bidding, 104–5, 114–15, 119;
change orders, 115; competitive
proposals, 104–8, 114–15, 118–19,
147; contract awards, 113–14, 118–19,
123; corruption, 104, 114–15, 120–23;
costs, 102, 106; current federal
system, 102–15, 126; evaluation
criteria, 106–7, 108–10, 113–14, 116,
117, 118–19, 125; problems, 89–90,
102–3, 107–8, 112–13, 114–15;
privatization, 146–48; proposals, 107,
108, 109–10, 121; quality, 104,
116–17, 117–19, 121, 123, 126;
reforms, 41, 47, 102, 115–26;
regulations, 2, 7, 25, 57–58, 89–90,
102, 106, 108, 121, 244; specifications,
113–15; vendor performance, 102–3,
107–13, 115–16, 117–18, 123–24, 125,
190; weapons systems, 102–3, 105,
119; "wired," 102, 106, 122–23. *See
also* Contracting out
Progressive Era: attitudes toward civil
service, 15–17, 21, growth of
bureaucracy, 13; legislation, 17, 18;
reforms, 5, 12, 13, 14–15, 18–19,
238–39, 265, 266, 268
Public authority, 203. *See also* Agencies,
government; Police departments
Public sector: bureaucratization, 256–59;
business executives, 69–70;
compared to private sector, 23–24,
37–38, 172, 180, 214–15, 250;
deregulation, 1, 3, 7–8, 26–27, 45–47;
Progressive Era, 5; regulation, 1, 2–3,
21, 23–24, 70, 76; strategies, 212–15;
theories of management, 15–19,
212–15, 268. *See also* Civil service;
Ethics; Unions

Quality Vendor Program, 118–19

Railroads, 239–40, 243–44. *See also*
Transportation

Transportation: goals, 237–38, 241–43, 247; legislation, 42–43, 238, 239–41, 242, 244, 245–46; policymaking, 241–43; post–World War II, 239–43; reforms, 238–39, 247; regulation, 9–10, 236–39, 243–47; subsidies, 242, 244–45
Turcotte, William E., 58
21st Century League (Philadelphia), 131

Unified crime reports, 204
Unions: effects, 5, 19, 23; executive order *10988*, 23, 95, 241; opposition to reforms, 26, 56, 86, 94, 95–97, 139, 147–48; Philadelphia, 8, 145–46, 147–48; transportation, 241
Urban Mass Transit Authority, 246
Urban Mass Transportation Acts of *1962, 1964*, 238, 240–41, 245–46
Urban Transportation Administration, 241

Van Riper, Paul, 12, 16
Vendors. *See* Procurement
Voight, Fred, 144
Volcker commission. *See* National Commission on the Public Service

Volcker, Paul A., 2, 3, 230

Waldo, Dwight, 16–17
Walters, Jonathan, 168–69
Watergate scandal, 21, 63, 72
Weber, Max, 199, 269, 271
Whitmire, Kathy, 161–62
Wilkey, Malcolm, 63
Williams, Stephen, 74
Wills, Garry, 194
Wilson, James Q., 2, 3, 78–79, 92–93, 259, 272, 277
Wilson, Woodrow, 12, 13, 16, 268
Winter commission. *See* National Commission on the State and Local Public Service
Winter, William F., 230
Wood, Kimba, 65
Work force: boundary spanners, 191–94; effects of deregulation, 9, 27, 92–93; effects of privatization, 147; effects of regulation, 1–3, 6, 7, 62, 90–91; role, 2–3, 185; supervision, 230. *See also* Bureaucracy; Civil service
Wright, Deil, 171–72